MW01479409

"... of Sea and Sand."
A Drama of Two
Living Deserts

by

Bruce Ferguson Barber

Black Forest Press
San Diego, California
November 2003

First Edition, First Printing

To Harry & Marilyn,
With my
most sincere
Thanks

[signature]

"...of Sea and Sand."

A Drama of Two Living Deserts

by

Bruce Ferguson Barber

PUBLISHED IN TIIE UNITED STATES OF AMERICA
BY
BLACK FOREST PRESS
P.O. BOX 6342
CHULA VISTA, CA 91909-6342
(800) 451-9404

Cover by Aurora Zhivago

Disclaimer

Although the author and publisher have made every effort to ensure the accuracy and completeness of information contained in this book, they assume no responsibility for errors, inaccuracies, omissions or any inconsistency herein. Any slights of people, places or organizations are unintentional.

ATTENTION CORPORATIONS, UNIVERSITIES, COLLEGES and PROFESSIONAL ORGANIZATIONS: Quantity discounts are available on bulk purchases of this book for educational or gift purposes, or as premiums for increasing magazine subscriptions or renewals. Special books or book excerpts can also be created to fit specific needs. For information please contact Lavalands Publishing Company, 317 Heffernan Avenue, #12854, Calexico, CA 92231; ph 619-405-2270; e-mail lavapubs@burntmail.com

Printed in the United States of America
Library of Congress
Cataloging-in-Publication
ISBN: 1-58275-035-1
Copyright November 2003 by Bruce F. Barber
ALL RIGHTS RESERVED

ACKNOWLEDGMENTS

"The whole is equal to the sum of all its parts...and their inter-
action."

— Alfreda Teresa Barber suggested I write this book.
— Jay Price created this books original cover.
— Dahk Knox decided to take a chance on an essentially unknown
author.

I am deeply indebted to each of you who, by your love, devotion
or confidence in me, contributed to the creation of this book.

DEDICATION

This book is dedicated ...

To the memory of Pepe Garcia, who was as devoted to the desert as I. He helped me explore most of the territory described in this book. A frequent desert companion, he was ready to go when I was.

To Glen Conklin, who, in my opinion, was the most knowledgeable of Baja California's many explorers. When I first met Glen, in the offices of his printing company, I was so impressed by the artifacts on display in his waiting room that I asked where they had come from... and we began comparing notes on our individual explorations. At one point I asked if he knew Tajo Canyon. He replied by asking, "Have you walked its Indian trails?" A publisher at the time, I was seeking someone to produce the four-color-separations needed for my magazines' covers. Glen had them made for me at no cost to enable his company to gain experience working with a desktop publisher. I am forever indebted to this remarkable man.

The men and women whose home Baja California really is. You are as loyal, sharing and genuine as the land you live upon.

To every man and woman who finds the Mexican frontier as magnificently beautiful, challenging and rewarding as I do.

And to every man, woman and child of San Felipe: This is Freda's and my way of returning to you the love and kindness you have shown us over the past eighteen years. ¡Reciben un abrazo!

TABLE OF CONTENTS

LIST OF ILLUSTRATIONS

LIST OF APPLICABLE TOPOGRAPHIC MAPS

H11, 3 -   San Felipe
H11, 5-6 -   Lazaro Cardenas
H11, B15 - José Saldaña
H11, B25 - (Sierra Tinaja's) Agua Caliente
H11, B26 - La Ventana
H11, B35 - San Matias
H11, B36 - Llano El Chinero
H11, B46 - Santa Clara
H11, B56 - Algodón
H11, B57 - Punta Estrella
H11, B67 - Bahia Santa Maria
H11, B76 - Matomí
H11, B77 - Puertecitos (Rio Canelo, Rio Blancas, Rio Matomí)

H11, D18 - Isla San Luis (Gonzaga Bay region)
H11, D28 - Jaraguay (Gonzaga Bay region)
H11, D29 - Punta Final (Gonzaga Bay region)

H12, A11 - Pozo Nuevo (Altar Desert region)
H12, A12 - Volcán El Elegante (Altar Desert region)
H12, A22 - Sierra Blanca (Altar Desert region)

Figure 1a – The Mexican Frontier (West)

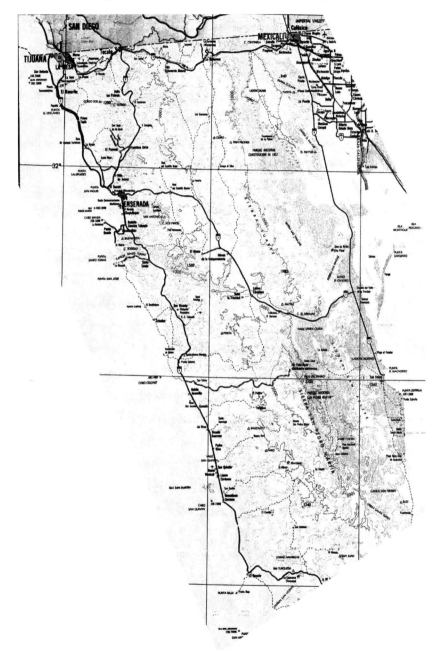

Figure 1b – The Mexican Frontier (East)

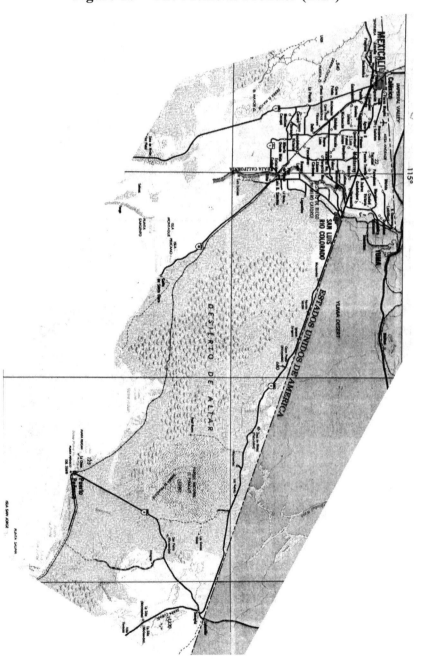

PREFACE

This is a book about people—a few from the sixteenth century and a few more from the twentieth—and the desert exploration I enjoyed with most of the younger of these two groups. I said most because in Part Two I describe two women and a man enjoying other walks of life I think you should know about. This book, then, is the sum and substance of the years I spent exploring the Mexican frontier. *Veni, vidi, vici*: my version, I came, I saw, and I was overwhelmed.

Some desert books begin with the question, "What is a desert?" Owing to my having been so overwhelmed by the deserts described herein, I prefer to begin my book with, "Have you seen a desert with six hundred volcanoes, cubic miles of jet black lava, a dozen craters or half a dozen seas of sand?"

I once read a desert is a waterless place with little or no vegetation. In fact, many of you call deserts barren. Because I don't agree with either description, I prefer to believe a desert is a God-created place intended as an experiment, a land of lost rivers and intolerable temperatures where the scent of mystery breeds legends of lost treasures.

Waterless? Someone decided deserts are places with less than ten inches of rain per year, but I live in the San Felipe Desert where Hurricane Nora dumped twenty-six inches of water in a horrifying eight hours, and she was anything but unique.

Having mentioned water, I hasten to add a note relating to this book's title. In general terms the last major glacial meltdown occurred about nine million years ago, lasted three million years and resulted in a global inundation approximating some six hundred feet. Not only was a high percentage of the landmass covered by this text under water, owing to the geology of this region much of it must be regarded as former sea floor. Therefore, the inevitable effects of sun, wind, rain, erosion and time upon the land described herein were to create a region composed ...*Of Sea and Sand.*

North America is the site of five bona fide deserts including the Chihuahua, the Sonora, the Mojave, the Great Basin and Range, and the Painted Desert with its soaring cliffs, deep canyons and multicolored hills. Within the confines of Mexico's great Sonora Desert—spanning the western half of the Mexican state of Sonora, southern Arizona, southeastern California and most of Baja, California—there is a geopolitically distinct region known as the Mexican Frontier. Within the frontier two unique desert regions bearing their own names are identified as Sonora's El Desierto de Altar (which includes the Gran Desierto de Pinacate Natural Park) and Baja, California's San Felipe Desert. (See Figures 1a & b.) There is, however, a great deal more to each of these regions than the classification "desert" tends to suggest.

Between 200 and 300 hundred million years ago, for example, the plate tectonic processes of subduction, accretion, mountain building and volcanism began manufacturing significant portions of North America. The west-moving continental plate, on which North America resides, and the east-moving pacific plate—with the smaller Caribbean and Cocos plates sandwiched between them— were involved in a collision causing the creation of Central America and southern Mexico. As the eastern edge of the (older and heavier) Pacific plate subducted under the (younger and lighter) western edge of the Cocos Baja, California's mountain ranges were uplifted.

But the collision didn't end there, according to The Geological Society of America's Memoir No. 140. This was such a complex phenomenon—which I'll describe as an immovable object meeting an irresistible force—it caused the Pacific plate to change direction of movement from easterly to northwesterly (in what appears to be a counterclockwise rotation). As the Pacific began that change the Cocos plate—which was by then firmly anchored to it and the Continental plate—buckled and broke into two pieces. That break, that line of fracture, is popularly known as the San Andreas Fault.

Since that day, some five million years ago, the separation caused by the Pacific plate's counterclockwise rotation was measured—with chemical proof from soil samples taken at Mazatlán (in mainland Mexico) and La Paz (in Baja Sur)—as a distance approximating 186 miles. As a result of this unique action, which seems to have happened nowhere else on earth, the Mexican frontier became a place of living drama. Its six hundred volcanoes erupted as did nearby craters. One of those craters, called "Elegante," is a half-kilometer in diameter.

Not to be outdone by geology there is evidence of sustained human habitation in this region spanning at least 39,000 years. This evidence includes giant intaglios, petroglyphs, pictographs, sleeping circles and many of indigenous man's artifacts.

". . .Of Sea And Sand" is divided categorically into five parts described as:

I: My three-year search for the grave of a 16th-century Spaniard.

II: My exploration of Baja, California's backbone mountain ranges.

III: My exploration of Baja's northeastern mountain ranges.

IV: Baja, California's pueblo of San Felipe, and

V: My investigation of equally dramatic but more remote locations including a) an alluvial expanse of western Baja, California,

b) the Sea of Cortés, and c) Sonora's Desierto del Altar (and Sierra Pinacate).

My personal desire to write began during my search for the grave of that 16th-century Spaniard: the first European to set foot on the American state of California. Because I found indications few had been there before me, the places I explored, the geology I happened upon and the natural beauty surrounding me daily literally drove me to share them with those less fortunate.

My search centered in Baja California's Sierra Pinta, one of two adjacent (volcanic) mountain ranges situated about fifty miles south of the international border at Mexicali. Owing to the incomparable beauty of this region, however, I expanded my field of interest to learn what other majestic scenery existed. Later, when I had explored the entirety of this northeastern region, I investigated the Desierto de Altar and the Sierra Pinacate where I drove and walked upon the same moon-like lava several of America's lunar astronauts had experienced during their training,

Originally, there were two Californias: Alta (meaning "upper") and Baja (meaning "lower"), both of them possessions of Mexico. Shortly after Alta California was ceded to the United States, the identifier "alta" was dropped and that state became "California."

Baja California, an 880 miles long peninsula, is now the location of two Mexican states: Baja California and Baja California Sur (meaning "south"). Sometimes referred to as Baja California "Norte" (meaning "north") it is a misnomer for the state of Baja California. Another misnomer, which can be confusing to outsiders, is the term "Baja" which is used in daily conversation to identify both the northern state and the entire peninsula.

Such improper usage is common locally and is as misleading as the single word "Mexico" which is used in Baja to identify both mainland Mexico and Mexico City. My older sister, for example, earned her Master's degree "in Mexico." Anyone who knows her knows she attended the University of the Americas in Mexico City. You will find my use of these colloquialisms throughout the text.

Another difference to be found in this text is the spelling of the name "Cortés." Whereas the English language uses no accent marks on any of its alphabet's letters (consequently the name Cortez), owing to my study of 16th century Spaniards I chose "Cortés," not only because that's the spelling he used, but also as a demonstration of my respect for a man I came to know at least a little better than most.

Baja California is a region almost entirely composed of mountain ranges including: the Sierra de Juarez, Sierra Cucapah, Sierra Mayor, Sierra Las Tinajas, Sierra Pinta, Sierra San Felipe, Sierra San Pedro Martir, Sierra Santa Rosa, Sierra Punta Estrella and Sierra Santa Isabel. Surprisingly, I found its non-mountainous regions—the Mexicali Valley, Laguna Salada and its east and west coastal plains—as dramatic in their own way.

Located in each of these regions are geological features that tugged at my curiosity. Arroyos Grande and Jaquegel, for example, contain one surprise after another. As I motored along the Grande one day, I noticed a narrow passage between adjacent mountain structures. Investigating that passage on foot, I discovered it led to a circular arena (20 feet in diameter) with another narrow passage leading south.

At the end of that southern passage I was stunned to find a man-made dam with "#7" painted on its face. The dam held water which, judging by its height—and surrounding evidence—was fully intended for wildlife. (It was too high for cattle.) Included in that evidence were the remains of a mountain goat—an elderly "gentleman" who had put up a respectable fight before relinquishing his life to a cougar.

Arroyo Grande is about one hundred miles in length. Paralleling its outlet to the barren Laguna Salada, Arroyo Jaquegel carved its bed through eroded materials deposited, over the millennia, from the Sierra de Juarez. With vertical walls 70 feet in height the 100-foot-wide Jaquegel runs straight as an arrow for five miles before turning abruptly to lead, via a number of twists and turns, to its headwaters in the Juarez. (All topographic maps I've seen, including those listed herein and American maps based on those Mexican topos, depict Arroyo Jaquegel improperly. As stated above, it runs straight as an arrow along the eastern base of the Tinaja before emptying into Laguna Salada.)

This is Indian country. There is an old Indian trail here leading from the Juarez (via the Jaquegel) to the Grande and thence to a narrow pass between the Pintas and the Sierra San Felipe. From there the trail leads to the Sea of Cortés where I came upon the largest shell mound of the many adorning Baja's eastern shore. Judging by where they live today, I believe the predecessors of today's Kiliwa Indians created this trail (and the shellmound) at least two thousand years ago.

The remains of other shell mounds can be found a) in the dunes south of San Felipe, b) a quarter-mile south of Campo Villa Marina, c) at Campo Punta Estrella, d) at Pancho's Camp, and e) at Campo Sahuaro (q.v.). Here again, I believe the predecessors of today's Pai Pai Indians created each of these at least two thousand years ago. But because the early Indians lived in separated family groups, I used a system of vectors to learn whether I could determine from where each shell-harvesting family may have come.

I found the mound at Campo Saguaro at the end of a line leading via Crazy Horse Canyon to Parral Canyon. The mound at Pancho's camp is at the east end of a line leading to Arroyo Huatamote, a fact tending to indicate its harvesters could have come from the San Pedro Martir via Agua Caliente Canyon. In support of my belief, there are petroglyphs adorning rocks several miles west of the eastern entrance to that canyon.

The mound at Punta Estrella is in line with the eastern entrance to Arroyo Chanate. By extending that line through the Chanate and across Valle Chico I preferred to believe Punta Estrella's harvesters came via Cajón Canyon (where there are additional Indian drawings). The shell mound south of Villa Marina is more difficult to assign ownership to because it is on the east side of the island-like Sierra Punta Estrella. This mound, however, and the south San Felipe mound can be described as being in line with the place I call

Hidden Valley (and its northeast extension) which tends to place it in line with Teledo Canyon (and still more drawings).

The first European to lay eyes on the Baja California peninsula was a Spanish mutineer in late 1533. My first sighting of it was as a 16-year-old boy who came for clams and oysters. Although I visited the peninsula many times in the interim my second significant sighting occurred on the heels of my retirement by which time I had developed a sense of vision that enabled me to see beyond the horizon.

The beauty of Baja California, to me, is found in every page of its history from its unique creation to the appearance of its birds, insects, animals and, ultimately, mankind. In this book I offer this vision from a vantage point as nondescript as Mexico's Federal Highway #5: the road to San Felipe. You see, almost everything described herein is but a few miles east or west of this road in relative terms, at least.

As a function of man's participation in the frontier's incomparable drama I ask you to think of this road as a project begun in 1492 by Christopher Columbus, extended from Cuba to Mexico in 1519 by Hernán Cortés and delayed in 1536 by the return to civilization of Alvar Núñez Cabeza de Vaca (and his three colleagues). The project was sidetracked in 1539 by Francisco Vázquez de Coronado's expedition to the seven cities of Cíbola but completed in December 1540 by a man named Melchior Díaz.

Not only is this a road with living desert drama along its two sides, had I found Melchior's grave I would have petitioned governmental leaders in Madrid, Mexico City and Washington, D.C. for the funding required to design, manufacture and install a lasting monument to this unsung hero in the most appropriate location: on a pedestal ceremoniously placed on the west side plaza of San Felipe's alabaster Arches—the official gateway to the Sea of Cortés.

Bruce Ferguson Barber

PART ONE

THE MYSTERY OF MELCHIOR DÍAZ

CHAPTER ONE

Introduction to Part One

The Mystery of Melchior Díaz is about a man history placed in the shadows. It touches on slavery, greed, lying and smuggling and suggests the man was murdered. Of common birth, Díaz rose from the ranks of common men to a position of respect as their peer by the nobility of 16th-century New Spain (today's Mexico). A brilliant leader and experienced explorer, he is almost completely unknown beyond the first half of the 16th century.

Melchior Díaz was a man's man who earned the nobility's respect during the years he spent in the wilds of northwestern Mexico (1525 - 1539). A man who spoke at least one Indian language, he had a reputation for succeeding where others had failed. The first mayor and military commander (1531 - 1539) of San Miguel de Culiacán (now the capital city of the Mexican state of Sinaloa) he was also a man in possession of all the social graces.

During the winter of 1539-40 the Viceroy of New Spain ordered Díaz to verify the existence of a remote Indian settlement (in what is now the American state of New Mexico) suspected of being rich in silver and gold. That settlement was the seven-pueblo nation of New Mexico's Zuñi Indians, a nation they called *Chi-ou-na*. (The first of those pueblos encountered by Spaniards was called Háwiku.) Five months later Francisco Vázquez de Coronado, leader of an expedition to that settlement, ordered him to undertake another junket into virgin territory.

This time Díaz became the first European to set foot on land that became the American state of California and the Mexican state of Baja California. (Confusing records show he was the second or third to walk on Arizona soil.) Because these same records provide no explanation for his presence in the Californias, I believe it was exploration: to lift the veil of mystery from yet another New World region and to claim the land in the name of the King of Spain.

In place of honors he might have received for this journey Melchior Díaz met an untimely death. The purpose of this presentation, owing to an incomplete and inaccurate record, is to review the facts, to suggest the possibility of foul play and to describe a curious pile of rocks that may mark the location of this honorable man's grave.

The New World

The discovery of the New World was to unleash upon it a human phenomenon like no other in the history of mankind: the Conquistadors. These men, whose lust for gold was infinite and whose religious fervor was genuine, were the product of some 800 years of fighting and dying to clear its Moorish invaders from Europe's Iberian peninsula.

With no more Moors to fight the men who became *Conquistadores* turned their attention to Christopher Columbus' discovery: The New World. Then, rushing to be a part of it, they became soldiers of fortune, exploring and conquering it for the glory of God... and their own personal profit.

Most notable among them were Hernán Cortés and Juán Pizarro who conquered Mexico and Peru, respectively, in the face of numeric odds of 250:1 against them. Neither of these men, nor any of their true contemporaries, regarded themselves as anything other than a fighting machine. Being conquistadors each knew what was expected of him. Conquering every new challenge, that is, was not only their life's work, it was an integral part of a guiding faith developed during the Moors' occupation of their homeland. It stamped each indelibly, and with that stamp these historically unique men marched into history: an old world was destroyed and a new world begun!

Regarding the Mystery of Melchior Díaz the following paragraphs set the 16th-century stage upon which he rose to fame and from which he disappeared without a trace. This book's readers, men and women of the 20th and 21st centuries, may find it as difficult as I initially did to envision 16th-century Mexico.

To make the task easier we must set aside our knowledge of today's world. Forget modern day wearing apparel, microwave ovens, electric lamps and wristwatches. In their place envision a populace wearing linen and leather; a host of younger men, horses and wagons; an occasional woman; and Indians—bronzed by life under a tropical sun—standing tall and proud.

Surrounding scenery is largely as it was since the beginning without a trace of macadam, concrete or plywood. In fact, much of today's macadam was laid directly on the trails New World Indians carved through the wilderness centuries before the Spaniards (and other Europeans) arrived.

THE PLAYERS ...in order of their appearance:

Hernán Cortés: the Conqueror of Mexico
Panfilo Narváez: Lieutenant Governor of Cuba
Nuño de Guzmán: a power-mad despot
Melchior Díaz: the first mayor and military commander of Culiacán
The Four Survivors of the (1528) Narváez expedition to Florida
Diego de Alcaraz: a slaver (for Guzmán)
Antonio Mendoza: first Viceroy of New Spain

Francisco Vazquez de Coronado: a close personal friend of the Viceroy
Fray Marcos de Niza: a Catholic priest
Hernando de Alarcón: a ship captain
Pedro de Castañeda: an enlisted member of the Coronado expedition

Hernán Cortés (1485 - 1547)

The Spanish base of operations after Columbus was in Cuba. In 1518 the governor of Cuba commissioned Cortés to explore along the east coast of the New World's mainland to learn what he could about Indian village locations. During that voyage Cortés landed several times and, through interpreters, learned of the geographical differences between settled regions. In the general vicinity of today's Vera Cruz, however, he learned of the wealthy Aztec empire at an inland place called Tenochtitlan. With visions of grandeur Cortés moved himself and his men ashore and formulated a plan to conquer the Aztecs.

Owing to the fact his commission contained no authority to march to the interior Cortés burned his ships (to prevent his subordinates' retreat), formed an alliance with local Indians and marched on the Aztec capital. His army included a thousand Indians plus 350 to 400 Spaniards (and their horses) in full battle regalia.

Moctezuma, the Aztec king who believed his visitors could be men from an Aztec myth (that warned of strangers coming from the east) met the newcomers outside the city on November 8, 1519. Welcomed into the city, the Spaniards were provided quarters befitting their rank. Shortly thereafter, however, Cortés tricked Moctezuma into a meeting during which he placed the ruler under house arrest, formed a co-rulership with him and demanded gold. A substantial horde of gold was delivered over the following months, in fear of Moctezuma's life. Cortés' plan was to divide that gold between himself, the King of Spain and his army.

In testimony to his diplomacy, daring and military prowess Cortés maintained his army in the midst of an estimated 100,000 armed Aztecs in an island city with few causeways available as escape routes. The Spaniards, by the way, regarded this city as one of the most beautiful in the world. Owing to its canals and temples, they referred to it as the Venice of the New World.

The following year (1520), the governor of Cuba sent a force to arrest Cortés for overstepping his commission. When Cortés learned of the approaching force, he took part of his army from the city and met it in the high mountain pass to the east. Led by Cuba's Lieutenant Governor Panfilo Narváez, the newcomers were quickly defeated but given a choice to join Cortés or be returned to Cuba with Narváez. Cortés' army was suddenly increased to slightly more than 600 armed soldiers (with horses).

Meanwhile, during the conqueror's absence, the token force remaining in Tenochtitlan massacred many of the Aztec nobility in panicked reaction to festival they conducted involving human sacrifice. Not only did Cortés return to a tense city, on June 30 he led his army in an escape from the city (over the causeways) during which most of the gold was lost. Adding more drama to the scene, at least two of his soldiers were captured and taken to a nearby pyramid where the screaming men were tauntingly sacrificed in full view of their comrades.

In a book written 40 years after the fact, Bernal Díaz described the killing and dismemberment of an Indian woman immediately after this battle for the purpose of rendering fat from her body. The Spaniards used this fat as a poultice they applied to their wounds.

Regrouping his army of Spaniards and Indian allies Cortés built boats and attacked the city in 1521.

The lead man on this boat building project was Juán Cabrillo who later became the first European to set foot on America's west coast when he landed near San Francisco, California.

In the course of fighting their way in, a hand-to-hand battle spanning many days, the Spaniards destroyed building after building to prevent Aztec attacks from those buildings' roofs.

In the months to follow, much to Cortés' sorrow, his army destroyed the entire city, including many of its pyramids upon which hundreds of thousands of men, women and children (including a reported 60,000 in one day) were sacrificed. Adding insult to injury, most of the Aztec literature (referred to by the Latin word "*codex*," meaning "book") was destroyed. The King of Spain never fully forgave Cortés for his destruction of this magnificent city.

As the years passed, Cortés remained active in western Mexico, seeking other wealthy cities. Extending his conquest across Michoacán, his lieutenants reached the Pacific Ocean where they established bases (at Colima and Acapulco) for continued exploration by sea.

Although most of Cortés' ships were lost at sea, one of them safely reached the Moluccas (the first "American" voyage to the Orient) while others sailed north and south to map the coastline. As a result of these voyages, reports of a band of women on an island somewhere to the west frequently reached Cortés' ears. "Native chiefs," he wrote, "affirm that there is an island inhabited only by women…"

Not only did the excitement of exploration continue, living and working conditions aboard Spanish ships were sufficiently harsh as to result in an occasional mutiny. In 1533, for example, a commanding officer was murdered and his ship commandeered by its pilot, Fortún Jiménez, who then sailed west to escape capture and punishment. Several days later, when the mutineers raised a landfall, they sailed north along its rugged coastline until they came upon a bay in which the ship was anchored. We know that site today as Baja California Sur's La Paz Bay.

The shore party discovered pearl oysters and women although one month later the Indian women's men massacred the unwelcome invaders. Those remaining aboard ship watched in terror until they realized they could be next. Only then did they raise anchor, hoist sail and retreat to Acapulco where they gave a full report of the mutiny, the discovery of "Pearl Island" and the massacre.

When news of the discovery reached Cortés, he solicited volunteers to colonize the island and sailed to Spain for a letter of agreement with the king regarding the distribution of profits to be gained from pearls. Upon his return (in 1535) he gathered colonizers, supplies and horses and sailed to Pearl Island. During that crossing Cortés named the body of water they sailed through "*Mar Bermejo*" (Vermillion Sea) as a result of its color (caused by billions of phytoplankton on its unusually warm surface).

Safely ashore on the island, the colonizers soon realized it was remarkably like a place described in a 1509 Spanish novel, *Las Sergas de Esplandian* (which may be likened to *Gulliver's Travels*). In that novel there was an island called "California" populated by a band of Amazon women ruled by Queen Calafia. Pearl Island became California (and subsequently Baja California).

Now, however, with Cortés in California, slavers openly selling Indians to wealthy Spanish landowners, and de Soto causing problems in Cuba, the King of Spain appointed a member of his court as Viceroy of New Spain and sent him west to abolish slavery, protect the Indians and establish a proper level of control over New Spain's citizenry.

Cortés returned to Mexico (in early 1536) to greet Viceroy Antonio de Mendoza. In place of a formal change of command ceremony, the viceroy ordered Cortés into house arrest (in the conqueror's own estate at Cuernavaca) and sent word to California to abandon the colony and return to Mexico.

A few months later, when Cortés heard Cabeza de Vaca's stories (see below) about wealthy Indian villages to the north he sent Francisco de Ulloa to find a water route to them. Sailing from Colima, New Spain's first west coast port, Ulloa had a mapmaker with him who made the first map of the New World's west coast (from Colima to the Colorado River). To their surprise they discovered California was a peninsula (rather than an island) protruding from the mainland.

After circumnavigating the peninsula as far as the 31st parallel, Ulloa returned to Colima, reported his discovery to Cortés and was ordered back to sea to continue his exploration of the newly discovered west coast. Reports of Ulloa's death are confusing. One states he was stabbed by a soldier and died in Mexico. Another claims he never returned from his second voyage of exploration. Whatever happened, his discovery of the California peninsula seems to have gone unrecognized until 1539.

Cortés died in 1547 at age 63. In his will he instructed his son to inquire into a philosophic puzzle that had plagued him since his arrival in the New World: whether Indians were a subhuman species or human beings with souls like Spaniards'.

Panfilo Narváez (14?? -1528)

Sent by the governor of Cuba to arrest Cortés for his unauthorized exploration, Narváez was defeated and forcibly returned to Cuba. Although a favorite of the King of Spain, he was described by a 20th-century historian as a man of little ability, judgment or foresight. Tending to support that description, his 1527-28 expedition to Cael, Florida (a place originally described by Ponce de León) cost the lives of some 400 accompanying Spaniards. A horrifying fact, the expedition is best known for its four survivors.

All but four Narváez expeditioners were either killed by Floridian Indians, drowned at sea during their attempt to return to Mexico or killed by cannibalistic Indians along east Texas or west Louisiana shores. The four, Alvar Nuñez Cabeza de Vaca, Alonso Castillo Maldonado, Andrés Dorantes and his personal body servant, Esteban the Moor, were captured and enslaved by non-cannibalistic (nomadic) Indians. Six years later they were freed during a chance encounter with Spaniards in what is now the Mexican state of Sinaloa. During their enslavement they heard many stories about buffalo and of silver-and-gold-laden communities to the north (Chiou-na). They never saw buffalo (although the did see buffalo robes), nor did they see any of the seven pueblos.

Nuño Beltran de Guzmán (14?? - 1550)

If totalitarian man is one who exercises power over others by making them suffer, Nuño Beltrán de Guzmán, who paid lip service to the Spanish ideal of Christianizing New World Indians, was the 16th century's epitome of such men. "Bloody Guzmán," he was called, sought nothing more or less than riches, power and the destruction of any and all that had more than he had.

The exact date of Guzmán's birth is unknown. He must have been of middle-class birth because in his youth he studied law, a profession normally beyond the reach of peasants' and workers' children. Also unknown is the date of his arrival in the New World although his name first appears in Hispaniola (the island occupied by Haiti and the Dominican Republic). Between 1526 and '28 he served as governor of Mexico's Panuco district (where today's Tampico is located).

From the beginning of his struggle for power the ambitious Guzmán seems to have envied Hernán Cortés so much he was determined to take the conqueror's place. As a demonstration of his totalitarian skills, Guzmán initiated a campaign of defamation against Cortés that included reports to the king's court in Spain claiming Cortés had murdered his wife and was planning to set up an independent kingdom in Mexico. Consequently, when Cortés returned to Mexico (City) from campaigning in Honduras, he was approached by the city's "*Juéz de Residencia*," relieved of his command and placed under house arrest.

The *Juéz de Residencia* was Mexico's premier legal body composed of three men (two of whom were honorable but soon thereafter died of old age). The third member, a court notary named Estrada, was both incompetent and cruel. King Carlos V replaced the *Juéz de Residencia* with a four-man "*Audiencia*" he authorized to rule Mexico. As fate would have it, two of its members died soon after their appointment, leaving it staffed with Bishop Juán de Zumárraga, a kindly man who wished to protect the Indians, and its newly-appointed head, Nuño de Guzmán.

When Cortés was returned to Spain the tyrant Guzman found himself alone at the top of the governmental heap, and terror was not long in coming. He sold Indians into slavery, seized political enemies' estates and did everything in his power to undermine Cortés' supporters. He even confiscated the saddle mule of Pedro de Alvarado who had been Cortés' right-hand man during the conquest.

The chief antagonist to Guzmán's reign of terror was the principled Bishop Zumárraga who, as a man of the cloth, had no military or political weapons but resorted to spiritual ones. Indians mistreated by Guzmán were urged to lodge their complaints with the bishop even though the courageous cleric was the community's political underdog. When he appointed inspectors and judges to hear Indians' complaints, Guzmán invalidated those complaints on the technicality that Zumárraga's consecration as bishop was not official.

When Zumárraga denounced the tyrant from the pulpit, Guzmán, sitting in the cathedral's front pew, did not take kindly to public humiliation. Following one particularly scathing denunciation, Guzmán warned Zumárraga to stick to otherworldly matters in future sermons. When the bishop continued his Sunday morning diatribes, Guzmán ordered thugs to drag him forcibly from his pulpit.

Although Guzmán censored his enemy's mail, Zumárraga outwitted him by persuading a sailor returning to Spain to conceal a letter of complaint to the Crown in a barrel of fat. Zumárraga was highly respected by King Carlos and his advisers. When he read that letter, the king commissioned another *Audiencia* to replace the one led by Guzmán. Though the crown meant well, the plan only succeeded in subjecting another part of Mexico to the tyrant's terror.

Cortés cleared himself of all charges against him and prepared to return to Mexico. When Guzmán heard of the new *Audiencia* and Cortés' impending return, he announced his plan for a new conquest, solicited 500 volunteers (and a large number of Indians), looted the city's treasury and fled Mexico City.

His first conquest along the new trail was King Tangaxoan, ruler of the Tarascan realm in Michoacán, who attempted to placate Guzmán with silver and gold. When Guzmán demanded more and the king couldn't or wouldn't produce it, the tyrant had him dragged behind a horse and burned at the stake falsely explaining he had ordered Tangaxoan's execution because the king had abandoned Christianity and lapsed into paganism.

About the only positive thing that can be said on Guzmán's behalf is that he founded communities that became important Mexican cities. These include Tonalá, the forerunner of today's Guadalajara; Culiacán, capital of the Mexican State of Sinaloa; and Compostela (in the Mexican state of Nayarit) where he established his final estate.

While Guzmán ravaged northwestern Mexico, a region he called New Galicia, the new *Audiencia* issued a warrant for his arrest. Consequently, when Viceroy Mendoza formed his plans for the conquest of the (reported) wealthy Indian villages to the north (see Cabeza de Vaca below), he ordered Francisco Vázquez de Coronado to arrest the tyrant and have him returned to Mexico in chains. Guzmán languished in a Mexico City prison from 1536 to 1538 before being returned to Spain where he remained in prison until his death in 1550.

Melchior Díaz (15?? - 1541)

When Díaz arrived in the New World is unknown. His name first appeared as a volunteer with Guzmán's expedition to New Galicia. Having studied Guzmán, I find it probable he solicited volunteers with promises of huge profits awaiting them in the land from where so many legends originated. Six years later, having found nothing they sought along the trail, Guzmán tired of the sport, created San Miguel de Culiacán, leaving Díaz in charge, and retreated to the south where he founded Tonalá, Tepic and Compostela.

Over the following eight years Díaz developed such a rapport with local Indians, whose language(s) he learned, he was not only respected by them, news of his accomplishments filtered to Mexico where his name became a household word among its nobility.

In the middle 1530s another despot, Diego de Alcaraz, was given permission by Guzmán to found his own settlement of Sinaloa (within a day's march of Culiacán) for processing newly captured slaves. Because Díaz refused to have anything to do with slavery, he became even more popular in Mexico.

One year later, while searching for Indians to enslave, Alcaraz suddenly found himself face to face with a naked, filthy, emaciated, bearded man who looked like anything but an Indian. A startling encounter, that man was Alvar Nuñez Cabeza de Vaca, one of the four surviving Narvaez expeditioners.

Alcaraz (eventually) had the four survivors delivered to Culiacán where Díaz spent two months attending to their every need, restoring them to good health and recording their incredible stories. When he had sufficient information for a comprehensive report, Díaz forwarded that report to the Viceroy in New Spain. When the survivors were well enough to travel, he sent them under armed guard to Mexico via Compostela where Nuño de Guzmán listened to their stories, treated them graciously and loaned them finery befitting their presence before the Viceroy.

Rumors of the survivors' reports spread like wildfire all the way to Cuba. Suddenly, the place they described was no longer a remote Indian village. In its place, a pueblo the survivors had never seen became an empire with a system of weights and measures where men and women marry but once and each family raises its own food in well-tended gardens.

Mendoza's reaction to Díaz's report and to the survivors' personal embellishment of it to his face, was to seek a trustworthy man to find the village they described. Such a man was Fray Marcos de Niza, who gained considerable Indian experience during his years with Pizarro in Peru. Mendoza enlisted Fray Marcos (and Esteban the Moor who brought six Indian friends with him), and the search for the northern cities was begun. Prior to its completion this search would cost Esteban's life as well as the lives of many Indians who accompanied this flamboyant man to Háwiku.

Marcos mispronounced *Chi-ou-na* as "Cíbola." Whereas the name Háwiku is somewhat lost in the historic past Cíbola remains but is often mentioned as "the seven golden cities of Cíbola." Tragically, you will learn, there was no silver or gold in Cíbola.

When Marcos returned from his reconnaissance, Díaz had the padre nursed back to good health as he'd done for the four survivors. Similarly, after hearing the padre's report, he forwarded the information to the Viceroy by special courier. Later, when the padre appeared before the viceroy, he described a city more beautiful than Mexico. Consequently, when news of his report leaked to the populace, earlier rumors were amplified beyond belief.

Owing to the furor caused by these rumors, Díaz became Viceroy Mendoza's most obvious choice to have the padre's discovery verified. Fortunately or unfortunately, depending upon how one views the circumstances, Díaz traveled no farther north than the Sobaipuri Indian settlement at Chichilticale (near Bisbee, Arizona) where he remained snowbound for two months. Because it was from this settlement that a large number of Indians had joined Esteban, Díaz used his snowbound time beneficially by interviewing each that had accompanied Esteban to Háwiku and returned alive.

By the time he departed for Culiacán and Mexico Díaz had checked, double-checked and crosschecked every Indian's story about Esteban and the Zuñi Indian nation, which was well-known by the Sobaipuris. It was from these interviews that he learned there was no gold, no silver and no appreciable metal working of any kind.

While Díaz was snowbound at Chichilticale, the citizenry in Mexico became so emotional over Fray Marcos' report that Mendoza had no choice but to dispatch his expedition, prematurely, under Coronado's leadership. Díaz encountered Coronado at

Chiametla, an Indian camp south of Culiacán, where he described his findings in detail.

Díaz's report to Coronado included, "They cultivate the ground in the same way it is done in New Spain. The men spin cotton and weave cloth, and they have salt from a nearby lake. The country has many fowls and is good for raising corn and beans, but it has no fruit trees and lacks water." In short, there was no reason for anyone to go there except to visit relatives.

Fray Marcos had lied, and the emotions of an entire nation had been falsely aroused. Suddenly Coronado had a problem... or was it twelve hundred problems? Resolving that problem he advanced the expedition to Culiacán where there was ample food and water for all. Placing Tristán Arellano de Luna in charge of the main body, Coronado formed a vanguard of his most experienced men, ordered Díaz (as guide) and Fray Marcos (for his own protection) to accompany him, and departed for Háwiku.

After conquering the pueblo, Coronado asked Díaz to return to the main body, obtain whatever men and supplies he needed and ride to the coast to accomplish what others had been unable to accomplish: to find supply ships sent by Mendoza in support of the expedition.

At this juncture it is important to note Díaz carried a letter from Coronado to Arellano detailing the governor's plans. Therefore, it was not Díaz who selected the men to accompany him but someone with a more intimate knowledge of the character of those men. It is equally important to note that most of the expeditioners' mental and physical states were at low ebb caused by...

. . .a severely limited food supply,

. . .the loss of many horses,

. . .many of these men being subjected to work they had never before known, and

. . .Díaz's report to Coronado having been overheard and leaked among enlisted members of the expedition.

Whereas others had searched for the ships, none had been as well equipped for the task as Díaz who knew of the Indians' commercial and news exchanging systems. Prior to his departure from the place he encountered the main body, a newly created campsite called San Hierónimo de Corazones, Díaz consulted with local Indians to learn whether any of them had heard of the Spanish vessels.

According to a 1937 edition of *The Hispanic American Historical Review*, Díaz did not head for the coast as had all others. Rather, he traveled overland towards present-day Yuma where the captain of those ships, Hernando de Alarcón, was visiting Colorado River Indians.

Near the end of October (1540) Díaz encountered Colorado River Indians who told him Alarcón had departed two weeks earlier but had buried messages in a jar at the base of an emblazoned tree near his anchorage. Riding to that place Díaz found the tree, unearthed the jar and read the messages. With letters in hand he knew his mission was ended. Not only had Alarcón returned to the port of Navidad, Díaz had to decide whether to return to an angry mob of men with insufficient food or explore the previously unknown (Baja California) peninsula.

Díaz and his party of 25 Spaniards and a dozen Ópatas Indians made the first European crossing of the Colorado River. They discovered and reported the Mexicali geothermal site but then, in what was reported as a bizarre accident, Díaz was gored in the groin by his own lance, which he had thrown at a dog chasing sheep. He bled to death and was buried on January 18, 1541. As far as the general public knows, his grave has never been found.

The Four Survivors

After six horrifying years of enslavement to New World Indians, the survivors were freed after a chance meeting between Cabeza de Vaca and Diego de Alcaraz in the wilds of what is now the Mexican state of Sinaloa.

Cabeza de Vaca remained in the New World where he accepted positions of note.

Maldonado and Dorantes returned to Spain and disappeared from notoriety.

Esteban, also known as Esteban the Moor, Esteban the Black and Estevanico, had been captured in Spain and made a servant of Dorantes. The most charismatic of the four, Esteban is described as a kind of "front man" who, all during their trek across Mexico, made initial contact with many Indian villagers.

During Fray Marcos' reconnaissance to Cíbola (see below) he sent Esteban a few days ahead to report the priest's coming and prepare for the holy man's entry into each Indian village along the way. During that trek, his last, Esteban collected a large number of followers from the Sobaipuri Indian camp at Chichilticale who accompanied him to Háwiku.

When he sent word he had sighted the village, Marcos ordered him to stop and await the padre's arrival. Disobeying those orders, the impetuous Esteban, with two greyhounds and his party of (300?) admirers charged ahead, reaching Háwiku nearly a week before Marcos.

Angered by the black's flamboyant behavior and his report of a white holy man's impending arrival, the Zuñis killed and dismembered (or dismembered and killed?) Esteban and as many of his followers as possible as a warning of the their dislike for strangers. An unknown number of escapees returned to Chichilticale.

Diego de Alcaraz (? -1541)

Little is known about this man whom I have taken the liberty of describing as a despot in the image of Bloody Guzmán. It is known he and Díaz, both members of Guzmán's expedition to New Galicia, were enemies. It is also known Díaz prohibited Alcaraz from using Culiacán as a slave-trading base. Consequently, the despot traveled a short distance into the interior and founded a tiny village he named "Sinaloa." He brought the four survivors to Sinaloa, imprisoned and tortured them (for aiding their former captors' escape) and eventually had them delivered to Culiacán.

Alcaraz was removed from the slave trade by Guzmán's arrest by Coronado. His name appears again, however, when Arellano placed him in charge of San Hierónimo de Corazones, which was to become a supply center for the Coronado expedition.

Owing to my years in management-level positions I cannot help wondering whether Arellano rid himself of troublemakers before departing for Háwiku with the expedition's main body. What's more, given the outcome of Díaz's reconnaissance, it is perplexing to think who selected whom. After all, Arellano had a long way to go and Alcaraz hated the ever-popular Díaz.

As what may be envisioned as fitting retribution by a noble man's ghost, Alcaraz was killed during an Indian raid on Corazones shortly after Díaz' survivors returned (from Yuma).

Antonio Mendoza (1490 - 1552)

When Cortés conquered Tenochtitlan, not only did his men destroy the western world's most magnificent city, his actions caused the loss of the gold Moctezuma's subordinates had delivered into his hands. Further, the ongoing problems created by de Soto in Cuba and Guzmán in New Galicia caused King Carlos to appoint a Viceroy as his direct representative in Mexico. As a member of the king's court, Mendoza had proven himself an able administrator with unshakable loyalties to the crown.

Upon his arrival in Mexico (with personal friend Coronado) Mendoza became engaged in a long-term competition with Cortés (in Cuernavaca) and de Soto (who believed there was gold for the taking in Florida). Since Cortés' commission to harvest California's pearls included authorization to explore the continental west coast, he continued to build and send ships to sea for that purpose. When Cabeza de Vaca emerged from the wilderness to relate his stories of unimaginable Indian wealth to the north, both Cortés and de Soto planned to be the first to harvest it.

De Soto's expedition was a tragic failure costing many Spanish and Indian lives. Cortés (unsuccessfully) sent Ulloa to find a water-borne route to the northern pueblos. Consequently, Mendoza solicited Fray Marcos (and Díaz) to find (and verify) the northern community's existence and volunteers to participate in an overland expedition to it.

Mendoza appointed Coronado governor of New Galicia (in 1537) and sent him to Compostela to arrest and return Guzmán to Mexico, quell the Indian riots Guzmán had caused and establish his governmental seat wherever he chose (the previously settled community of Tepic which was about 25 miles north of Compostela). Fray Marcos and Esteban (with his six Indian guides) arrived in Tepic a few months later.

In accordance with Mendoza's orders and when released by Coronado, Marcos proceeded to Háwiku and returned to make his false report. Upon receiving the padre's report (by messenger), Mendoza forbade Cortés from all further exploration and ordered Díaz to verify the padre's findings. Later, owing to pressures from the citizenry of Mexico City (who remembered what had happened when de Guzmán seized control of their city) Mendoza had no choice but to appoint Coronado to lead the expedition.

Mendoza and Coronado invested heavily in the expedition but lost every cent. Beyond that, Mendoza was appointed Viceroy of Peru in 1551. Though in ill health he accepted the post and died in Lima on July 21, 1552.

Francisco Vázquez de Coronado (1510 - 1554)

A long-time friend of Mendoza and a member of the Viceroy's court, Coronado was appointed governor of New Galicia in 1537 and sent there to restore peace to the region. With Guzmán officially removed from the scene, Coronado sent messengers to near-by Indian villages to inform them of Mendoza's imprisonment, his own appointment as governor of the region and his desire to restore peace and prosperity thereto. He then marched to Tepic where he established his governmental offices. While there, Coronado received a messenger from Díaz informing him Culiacán was under siege by renegade Indians.

After insuring his government was properly seated and his post represented by reliable subordinates, Coronado marched the remainder of his army to Culiacán where the combined strength of his and Díaz' soldiers quelled the uprising. The renegade Indian chief was captured and made to stand before a court convened in public by Coronado. As a warning to all such men, the chief's punishment was public disemboweling, quartering and, mercifully, death.

With the region again at peace, Fray Marcos and Esteban were dispatched to find the northern villages, and Coronado returned to Tepic. One year later, following Marcos' return to Mexico and the Viceroy's formation of the Cíbola expedition, Coronado was called to lead that expedition, harvest the Indian wealth and return to Mexico.

As we have already learned, there were no riches in Cíbola, and Coronado returned to Mexico four years later to spend the remainder his life at his hacienda—apparently regarded a failure. In fact, he was subjected to two trials (1544 and '47) to examine the possibility of his mistreatment of Indians during the expedition. He was acquitted on all charges and died at home in 1554.

Fray Marcos de Niza (?-1558?)

Born in Nice, France (hence "de Niza") Fray Marcos served in Central America and Peru before settling in Mexico in 1537. In the autumn of 1538 Viceroy Antonio de Mendoza sought (and Bishop Zumárraga recommended) him as an experienced, reliable, non-self-serving explorer to find the northern Indian communities described by the four survivors.

Departing in the spring of 1538, he reportedly sighted the Zuñi Indian pueblo of Háwiku and returned to Culiacán (and Mexico) to report his find as "bigger than the city of Mexico." Largely on the strength of this description, Viceroy Mendoza launched the most significant of Spain's expeditions to the North American interior.

When Coronado reached Háwiku in July, 1540 he proclaimed Fray Marcos a liar and had him returned to Mexico. Only temporarily disgraced, Marcos may have been assigned as "Provincial," the highest local office in the Franciscan hierarchy. The record was confusing to me because I also read he remained in disgrace on a small pension from Bishop Zumárraga. According to one source Marcos died on March 25, 1558 after having suffered bad health for a decade.

Scholars have been divided since the 16th century as to whether Fray Marcos actually saw Cíbola. Those who charged him with lying offered several explanations. He was accused of turning back to avoid Estévanico's fate and of fabricating his report to avoid displeasing the Viceroy. He was also accused of conspiring with Mendoza to strengthen the Viceroy's case for exploration of the northern frontier. Mexico was so overpopulated with unemployed men that Mendoza's critics leveled a similar charge against him.

Hernando de Alarcón (???? - 15??)

Hernando de Alarcón was Commanding officer of supply-laden ships sent north along Mexico's west coast in support of the Coronado expedition. Aware that supply ships were to be sent by Mendoza, Coronado sent men to the coast to find and signal them, but contact was never made. Consequently, Alarcón continued his northerly heading until arriving at the Colorado River where, it was reported, he sailed to a suitable anchorage about fifty miles upstream.

Continuing in longboats, Alarcón made contact with Colorado River Indians among whom he remained for about two months until, in compliance with his basic orders, he returned to his ships and the port from which he had sailed.

Prior to his departure, as was routine under the circumstances, Alarcón wrote and placed messages in a jar he buried at the base of a prominent tree adjacent to his anchorage. He marked the tree to make it unmistakable and set sail. Those messages described California as a peninsula protruding from the mainland, detailed his two-month relationship with Colorado River Indians, and verified his departure for Navidad.

Pedro de Castañeda (15?? - after 1596)

Pedro de Castañeda was a soldier in Coronado's army who wrote an account of the expedition, largely from hearsay, 20 years after the fact. The account was later rewritten and remains in print today. A note at the end claims copying of the original manuscript was completed in Seville in 1596. Castañeda's account and similar 16th century accounts of adventures in the New World became part of the origins of a novel developed by Cervantes in Spain around 1600.

Figure 2 – Sierra Cucapah – Sierra Mayor

CHAPTER TWO
The Turn-On

I knocked on the door ...and introduced myself to two local residents who, I was told, had material for a story I'd been assigned to write. During that meeting Tim and Robin Navarro provided what I sought plus, following a brief discussion, additional material they thought I might find interesting. I thanked them and, with both hands full, trundled back to my car and home to pour over the magazines, newspapers and photographs I'd been loaned.

What I discovered in that stack was something that took my mind and body away from my home and into some of the most remote desert regions of the Mexican frontier. I discovered Melchior Díaz, a 16th century Spaniard I'd left riding into the sunset 17 years earlier. This time, however, instead of looking down on him from my exalted position as a reader in his favorite chair, I met the 450 year-old ghost of the man face to face. He leaped out at me from the pages of an article by Choral Pepper in a 1980 edition of *Desert* magazine.

Pepper began her article with, "It is my hope that a *Desert* reader will relocate the true grave site of Captain Melchior Díaz." She went on to relate a tale about this beloved man who met his death by accident during a mission to rendezvous with ships carrying supplies in support of Francisco Vázquez de Coronado's expedition to the seven (golden) cities of Cíbola.

As her tale unfolded, she introduced Walter Henderson, a young man living in Southern California who, in the early 1930s, cranked up his Model A roadster and headed south with a friend toward Baja California's San Felipe. Their goal was to find a rare blue fan palm oasis once described to them by a prospector.

According to Pepper, Henderson parked his car at a place called La Ventana and set off on foot. The following day, while returning to their car, they chanced upon a curious pile of rocks they believed to be a grave. Whoever lay beneath it, they reasoned, was obviously revered by his companions who must have numbered more than a few to erect such a monument.

Some years later, while reading Pedro de Castañeda's narrative of the Cíbola expedition, the memory of that desert grave came back to haunt Henderson who suddenly realized that the remote pile of rocks he'd chanced upon in the desert could be the grave of Melchior Díaz. When the Mexican consulate at Los Angeles chose to ignore his suggestions Henderson, who told Pepper he never returned to the site, kept the grave's location secret until the day he revealed it to her.

Although she wrote of Henderson's discovery in books she published prior to the magazine article, it was not until his passing that Pepper revealed the significant elements of his secret in the edition of *Desert* magazine Robin Navarro had loaned me. It was from behind the printed words of that article that the ghost of this Spanish nobleman came forth to suggest I walk the trail Henderson had walked 55 years earlier.

I was fascinated by the story. Somewhere along the road to San Felipe the first European to set foot on California and Baja California (Norte) had been laid to rest. Somewhere out there were the remains of a man overdue for the immortality that justly belonged to him. Somewhere in the nearby desert was the grave of a man lost to his family and their successors. It was a challenge I found impossible to ignore.

In the months that followed I searched for, found and read the only two 16th-century accounts on record of Díaz's reconnaissance to the Sea of Cortés. But when I read interpretations of those accounts by bona fide historians, facts they may have overlooked seemed to suggest Díaz did not die accidentally. Rather, statements interpreted by me as lies suggested he had been murdered.

With these thoughts in mind I began the task of analyzing Pepper's article to learn what hidden messages I might find locked in her wording. Initially, I discovered the bearings she had given for at least one landmark mountain were incorrect. Therefore, anyone following Pepper's directions went in the wrong direction and the grave more than likely remained undiscovered and untouched.

Through further study, I narrowed the field of search to two likely areas covering a maximum of 12 square miles. Before I could conduct my search, however, I had to familiarize myself with the terrain. What's more, to do this job properly, I needed to lay the entire region out in a segmented grid. Then, if the grave was not within my primary and secondary search areas, I could systematically move from segment to segment until it was found.

At one point in my preparations I had the honor to host in my home Sr. Carlos Lazcano Sahagún, one of Mexico's ten Ph.D. spelunkers who argued Díaz was buried in Sonora. Although neither of us agreed on any significant point of the story, Dr. Sahagún reinforced my ambition to find the grave wherever it may be.

During another contact with a professor at the University of New Mexico, I was told scientists don't chase "second fiddlers." How unfortunate, I thought, that such a man would take that position with me when historians, anthropologists and archeologists before me had sought Melchior's grave. His arrogance made me think how exciting it would be to see this second fiddler's story revealed by *National Geographic*, *Archeology* (magazine) and Hollywood as a result of my search.

Díaz arrived in the New World in 1525. Essentially unknown at that time he took his place on the world's stage in 1531 when installed as the leader of a newly created outpost called San Miguel de Culiacán. Four hundred miles north of the nearest European settlement, the site of this fledgling community was so appealing to settlement that the man who created it could not allow it to remain unsettled. That man, the infamous Nuño de Guzmán, traveled south from Culiacán to found and settle Compostela, the site of his retirement estate, Tonalá, the site from which the city of Guadalajara sprang forth, and Tepic, later to become the capital city of the province of New Galicia.

With Guzmán out of the local picture Díaz gained the respect and admiration of Indians residing in the territory surrounding Culiacán and learned at least one of their languages. In addition, during those same years, he became a reliable figurehead in the minds of Mexico City's nobility. In 1536, for example, when the four survivors of the Narváez expedition to Florida surfaced in Culiacán, Díaz nursed them back to health, interviewed them in detail and forwarded reports of their experiences to the Viceroy in Mexico.

Three years later the Viceroy of New Spain ordered Díaz to verify the existence of the survivors' stories (about *Chi-ou-na*) that they reported being as rich in silver and gold as Tenochtitlan had been. Their stories incited an entire nation to fervor over the possibility of unlimited gold to be harvested by the first to find it. Coronado's expedition to Cíbola was an outgrowth of that fervor and Díaz's trek to what is now Yuma, Arizona was directly related.

Whereas historic records establish Díaz's presence at a geothermal site 70 miles southwest of Yuma (20 miles south of Mexicali), the record of his travel beyond that point is confusing. That is, Pedro de Castañeda, a member of the Cíbola expedition, claimed Díaz retreated from the geothermal site while Herbert E. Bolton, a noted California historian, claimed he bypassed the site traveling another five or six days south before his journey ended.

To establish Díaz's line of march from the Colorado River I

needed to know how today's sea level compared with that of the 16th century. Later, with that information in hand, the application of it to my study of Baja's northeastern terrain sent me on a search for topographic maps of the region.

Owing to the level of the Sea of Cortés, to have traveled five or six days south of the geothermal site Díaz had to cross Baja California's (nearby) Sierra Mayor and Laguna Salada. When I made that crossing, via two of the only three passes I found convenient to his route, I satisfied myself the one called Cañada David, more like a highway than a mountain pass, was the one Díaz had used. Whereas Cañada David is closed today, I ruled out the remaining passages due to topography and the fact that the southern passage was not created until the 19th century.

I found a southern pass, opposite the entrance to Campo Mosqueda, too rough to negotiate in a motorized vehicle and, after examining it on foot, came to believe Díaz did not use it. In fact, that attempt reinforced my belief he crossed via Cañada David.

Of interest to me, after examining each passage, was the fact that any crossing of the hourglass-shaped, water-filled portion of Laguna Salada would have to be done at its narrowest point. (See Figure 2, Map Key's 10 & 11.) Although it added nothing to my investigation, I learned the southern passage was/is in a direct line with that narrowest (and shallowest) location. Therefore, no matter which pass Díaz or I ventured through, owing to the shallows our two crossings would have terminated at the same west-side location.

Standing on the west side of the Salada, I was faced with the possibility the grave I sought could be in any one of four adjacent mountain ranges: the Sierra de Juarez, Sierra Tinaja, Sierra Pinta or Sierra San Felipe. Owing to Díaz's recurring need for water, the Juarez would have been the logical place to search and yet, Pepper's article makes no significant mention of the Juarez. In addition, the Sierra San Felipe was too far for Díaz to have reached in six days at the rate I calculated his speed of advance.

If he didn't penetrate the Juarez, and the San Felipe was too far away, the Salada's west shoreline would have led him to Arroyo Jaquegel or Arroyo Grande. At this juncture, therefore, it was easier, and potentially more revealing to attempt to follow Henderson than to commence an arbitrary search involving 200 square miles of lava-strewn hills, mountains, valleys, gullies, riverbeds and sedimentary alluvial fans. Not only did I turn south from this point, I was now heading into the region walked by Henderson and felt it was time to find "La Ventana," a landmark mentioned by Henderson.

In addition, because Henderson and Díaz were now on converging paths, it was time to learn about 16th century Spaniards. I needed to know how much water they carried, what they ate, how and where they obtained their food and the relative importance of sunrise and sunset to them. I also needed to know the ins, outs, ups and downs of the Sierra Pinta and Sierra Tinaja.

Figure 3 – Sierra Pinta – Sierra Tinaja Region

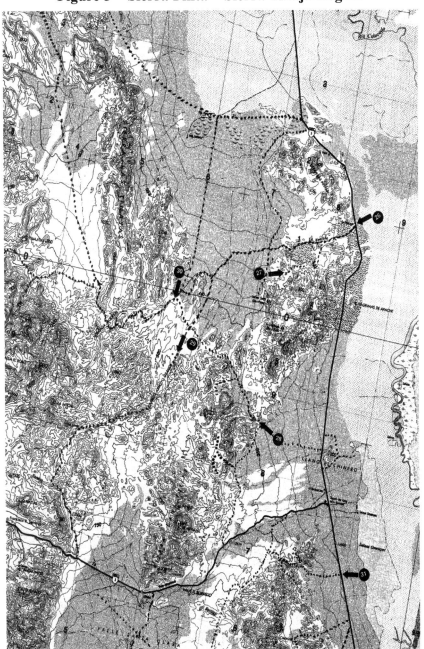

CHAPTER THREE
Familiarization

ONE

Accoording to the historic record Coronado turned to Díaz in Háwiku to ask his friend to return to the main body of the expedition to deliver a letter of instruction to its leader, Tristán Arellano de Luna. Those instructions called for...

... Arellano to hold his position for the purpose of establishing a supply center wherever he was at that moment,

... Díaz' provisioning (men and food) for a trek to the coast to find supply ships sent by the Viceroy, and

... With supplies in hand, Díaz' return to Arellano's campsite from where Coronado could be supplied as needed.

Díaz encountered the expedition at a newly created site the Spaniards named San Hierónimo de Corazones. About 25 miles from the original Corazones (named by Cabeza de Vaca), this site was located along the northern reaches of Mexico's Sonora River. After delivering Coronado's letter and securing the men and guides he needed, Díaz departed San Hierónimo.

One historian described Díaz' passage as southwesterly along the Sonora River to the coast and thence north across the desert to the Colorado River. (Alarcón named it Rio Tizón.) Owing to the absence of potable water between Yuma and the Sonora River outlet to the sea (a vast desert territory), another historian described Díaz' route along an established Indian trail that assured him water, food and updated news. That is, departing the Sonora River from the approximate location of today's Banamichi, his route was described as taking him through today's Cucurpe, Magdalena, Santa Ana and Caborca to the Sierra Pinacate. From the Pinacate (where there was water) it is approximately 80 (straight line) miles across desolate desert terrain to the Colorado River but less than 20 (via a passage subsequently named El Camino del Diablo) to the Gila River, which flows into the Colorado.

Before accepting either historian's opinion, it should be recognized that Díaz was an experienced frontiersman who spoke at least one Indian dialect and knew the Indians had outreaching trade and communications systems enabling them to spread and share news throughout the land. As I studied each route, I remembered the Turquoise Trail—a 1,000-year-old byway used by Indians transporting turquoise from northern mines to the Aztecs of central Mexico—along which pre-Colombian travelers found predictable supplies of food and water. Therefore, in my opinion, Díaz conferred with Indians before departing San Hierónimo, learned of Alarcón's presence on the Colorado and opted for the overland route.

According to Castañeda, Díaz encountered Colorado River Indians (at the intersection of the Gila and Colorado rivers) who told him Spaniards had been there but departed two weeks earlier. They also told him the Spaniards' leader had buried letters at the base of an emblazoned tree near his ships' anchorage.

Díaz rode south, found the tree and recovered the jar with its hidden messages. Now knowing his official mission had ended, and that to return to San Hierónimo without supplies could cause rebellion, Díaz apparently opted to explore the newly discovered peninsula.

After crossing the Colorado, he would have claimed the new land in the name of the King of Spain and headed south to the general locale of Cortés' former pearl-harvesting colony (at La Paz). There he knew he could build a ship and sail to the mainland (Acapulco, Jalisco, Navidad or Colima). Instead, he crossed the river, traveled an estimated ten days south (five or six days from Yuma to the geothermal site and five or six days farther south) and was buried on January 18, 1541.

TWO

I made two preliminary treks into the Sierra Pinta. (See Figure 3, Map Key Numbers 26-La Ventana, 27-Diaz Valley, 28-Pinta Pass, 29-Arroyo Grande & 30-Arroyo Jaquegel.) My first, having entered via a roadway paralleling the La Ventana riverbed, involved noting every detail as I motored along. I came upon a "Y" intersection I recorded and vowed to investigate the right fork later. Moving ahead, I came to another Y and again opted for the left fork. A mile farther along I was surprised to find what appeared to be a one-man mining operation with no one in attendance.

There was a bona fide mine adit, an air compressor (for jack hammering), a sheltered work area complete with kitchen utensils and an outhouse. Because Freda was with me I chose to use the outhouse but broke out laughing when I discovered its seat covered with pure-white rabbit fur. Either the miner enjoyed his wife's company or he was a very fussy man about his personal hygiene.

Scouting around, I found the road (along which we discovered the mine) terminated at a rock-strewn riverbed angling down from a nearby mountain. I also found a second road leading to an adjacent mountain that disappeared around a bend at least 300 feet west of the mine and 50 feet above it. I tried that second road, which was not much wider than my wheel tracks but came to a washout I had not seen from the mine. Backing down that road, the only escape from it, I found myself at a time and place not intended for the timid. Fifty feet is a long way to fall in a four-wheeled vehicle.

Safely on the ground again, we retreated to the first Y and motored along its right fork until the road disappeared into a sandy riverbed where we encountered a third Y. Our options were west or north. The coin I flipped landed on west, and we went as far as we could in that direction. Finding ourselves on a small plateau, we discovered a negotiable ten-foot drop-off into another narrow riverbed leading to Arroyo Grande (which we could see from our elevated vantage point).

Recording the detail, we retreated to the (third) Y and tried its north fork. Up a rocky bank and over another rocky plateau…to nowhere. But, because I could see a way to continue—via a ten foot deep V-shaped arroyo, across a small mesa and along a narrow ridge leading somewhere—I recorded this detail (it wasn't to be tried without another buggy in company) and retreated to the highway.

There is a riverbed on the north side of La Ventana gasoline station. (To avoid confusion, readers should know there is no surface water in any of Baja's eastern mountain ranges other than during and immediately following local rainstorms.) Driving along that bed we motored west about a mile and came upon an incomparable desert scene causing me to name the place "State Park."

In reality, it was nothing more than a wide riverbed with a gentle slope on its south flank and an abundance of palo verde, cholla and flowering brittlebush giving the place an air of tranquility. It was here that I encountered my first mound and, following a thorough inspection of it, realized I would have to check at least a million of them to find the one Díaz' remains were under.

About a half-mile farther along, we entered a bona fide gorge—eight feet wide with 20-foot vertical walls. The west end of this gorge (which was about 100 feet in length) proved to be a natural cul-de-sac above which, I believed, stood the terrain abutting the V we had so recently avoided.

Traveling alone in the desert is problem enough as one negotiates land etched with ditches, gullies, arroyos and a wide variety of comparatively strange desert flora. But traveling in a sandrail adds elements not normally anticipated by the inexperienced. That is, the elements of flat or broken tires, broken axles and engine failure.

During my second trek over considerably worse terrain than the first, I experienced one engine failure and two flat tires… about 75 miles from reliable human contact. Consequently, I explained my project to a man named Frank Albrecht and asked if he and Debbie (see Part Two Chapter Two) would like to accompany Freda and me during our next visit to the Pintas. He leaped at the opportunity with as much enthusiasm for the mystery as I harbored daily.

Debbie, Frank, Freda and I departed early one April morning to arrive at State Park at 8:00 a.m. Mine was a devious plan. I was hoping this area (which included the gorge) would sufficiently heighten their interest in the outing to chance the V.

One hour later, Frank took one look at the ten foot deep waterway and scoffed, "No biggie. We hit it at a 45-degree angle, accelerate carefully on the uphill side and land on top with ease. If not, either of us can pull the other out." His enthusiasm seemed to calm whatever misgivings Debbie and Freda felt… and we hit it with a great exuberance.

Down, over, up and… I made it, with power to spare. Frank was next (the girls half-walked, half-climbed to the opposite side), and we were on our way, our wives surprisingly happy to find we weren't dashed to pieces or whatever else they feared. They didn't realize what was ahead.

The north end of the small rectangular mesa we were now on abutted what appeared to be a sand dune spanning the distance between it and a ridge beyond. That 50 foot long, parabolic-shaped dune fell away sharply on each side, giving it the appearance of a dangerous crossing. One inch left or right, I thought, and…

We made that one, too, and the next thing we knew we were parked on the slope I had seen from the opposite side of the V. Yes, we were lucky, but that's what exploration is about. You take a well thought out chance now and then and see things less motivated men and women never see. (How do you think Columbus felt, or Cortés… or Díaz?)

At this precise moment, to my joyous surprise, when I turned to look at the terrain we had crossed I saw the most magnificent view of a land as beautiful as there is anywhere. We were stopped on a mile-long hill descending some 3000 feet to a pale-green valley floor confined in the west by the red-hued lava of the Sierra Tinaja. Behind the Tinaja the majestic Sierra de Juarez provided a silhouetting background to an already incomparable scene.

That mile-long slope continued another 50 meters above us. We drove to the top, parked, looked around and found ourselves at the top of a crag overlooking the eastern arena. I spotted La Ventana gas station, which reminded me of my quest. Looking west again, I believed the remains of the nobleman I sought rested somewhere within my field of vision. As I stood there, my mind on a 16th-century event, I was suddenly returned to the present when I noticed a pile of coyote dung larger than I'd ever seen.

Like a community bulletin board, this was a mound created by a multiplicity of coyotes. My thoughts turned to the coyotes that made this remote mountain domain their home. How strange they are, the different environments in which we each live. Did the coyote find this, his and her home, as beautiful as we? Did they sit at times to ponder the magnificence of the view of the valley below? Did they marvel at the kaleidoscope of color each changing season brings to these incomparable desert lands? Did the chromatic explosion of desert sunrises and sunsets romantically excite them?

The answers to those questions were not intended for me, but the dung told me there was happiness in this isolated preserve. Readers who are not outdoor enthusiasts may find my mention of animal dung improper. It is mentioned as an item of significant interest to all regarding differences between species. In this case, an animal act similar to urinating for the purpose of saying "I was here" although the absence of such conveniences as bushes, fire hydrants and automobile tires seems to have forced coyotes to a secondary communication mode.

Whereas I found that pile of dung intriguing, I hasten to add I always seek such signs to keep myself informed of who or what may be in the same desert region as me. Information like that can save an otherwise unsuspecting person's life.

Upon completion of our examination of the upper end of the slope we drove a few feet north to learn what we could about the terrain in that direction. Surprisingly, we discovered this ridge formed the south rim of a bowl-shaped watershed emptying into a riverbed. From our elevated vantage point that riverbed represented an escape to the east (the highway and Sea of Cortés).

Satisfied with our accomplishments for the moment, and owing to the time our travel and observations had consumed, we opted for the riverbed and the end of this day's exploration without going into the Grande. Our knowledge of the Pintas was sufficiently increased to enable an expeditious access of the Grande via whichever route we chose during our next visit.

To amplify the beauty of this little-known place, each time I pass through the Pintas I enjoy its flora and fauna to the fullest. The blooming of Baja's palo triste (smoke tree) is one of the most beautiful displays of color in the plant kingdom. An incomparable shade of purple, a fully bloomed palo triste is sufficiently dramatic to make most drivers stop and stare.

Tiny orbs about 5/16 of an inch in diameter appear all at once in May or June, depending on soil temperature. Since most plants depend on soil temperature I suggest the rainbow of Baja's spring colors begins with a carpet of yellow when brittlebush blooms. Lupine provides a second carpeting and desert lily the third, if there's been enough water. I don't know what the volume of one trillion lily blooms amounts to, but I'd be willing to bet our local desert displayed a trillion during the spring of 2001.

Chollas begin blooming in May and, between its many local varieties, offer most colors of the rainbow. Cardón sends out little white trumpets in January but its true flower, from which its seeds are dispersed, appears in May, June or July. And here is an anomaly. In any given stand of cardón less than ten percent throws flowers with seeds and what a bloom it is. A fist-sized bulb suddenly bursts open to display four bright red petals in the center of which is a blackberry jam-like substance with little black seeds 1/16 of an inch in diameter. Can you imagine a 25-ton giant growing from a seed that small?

A wild flower I have never been able to identify blooms in local riverbeds during summer months. It is the size of a person's thumb and the exact shape of an orchid: white petals, purple throat and asexual, it's a treat to present to a lady.

To complete this word picture... with the flora comes the fauna. Over the long term, I have seen at least one cougar per year including an adult that jumped vertically upward directly in front of my sandrail. One of the most beautiful of animals, I can still see that cat with its three-foot tail extended behind and its forelegs parallel to the ground as it disappeared from sight in seconds.

I have seen four bobcats although I see their tracks often. I've seen two kit foxes, six badgers and an animal I cannot identify. This one was black—I've seen two of them—with a white splotch on its chest. Weighing an estimated 50 to 60 pounds, it had a snout and body like a raccoon although its belly was appreciably wider and low to the ground. It walked slowly, as though unconcerned by my sandrail's presence, and waddled as it walked.

I saw my first in the riverbed mentioned above during my second retreat from the Pintas. The second appeared, some 80 miles distant, along a back road to San Felipe's Valley of the Giants. Thank heaven Freda was with me; she saw it, too.

THREE

I sent a letter of invitation to Calvin Blessing of Fallbrook, California. A man I'd known for 40 years, Cal is a well-traveled businessman with an inquiring mind. Two years older than me and equally tall, he speaks fluent Spanish and is a person I knew would challenge my theories to the letter. He is entirely independent, mechanically inclined and, like me, possesses a keen sense of land navigation. Few people, I believed, were more capable of conducting this task than Cal and I.

"What should I bring?" he asked over the telephone.

"Levis, good boots for walking over rough terrain, a hat and a light weight jacket," I replied.

Driving two sandrails we headed for La Ventana and a briefing of all I had done to prepare for this phase of the search. I told him that up to this point I had not been challenged by anyone and that, in my opinion, was not in our best interests. I described my two search areas and the vectors I had established for Area A.

As I knew he would, he questioned me on every point. I made my answers detailed to enable him to understand I had pondered my theories from every conceivable standpoint. When the briefing was concluded and my friend felt confident in what we were to accomplish, we headed for Area A.

As the day wore on I found it difficult to keep my mind on the fact that we were on an expedition in the interest of archaeology, the humanities, at least two foreign counties and the world at large. I cannot imagine scenery more picturesque, more dramatic, more beautiful than that which I encountered on every one of my desert treks where the power of water, wind, sun and rain is displayed by their fantastically incomparable creations.

We spent seven hours that day searching every nook and cranny in the assigned area. Our search continued until Cal's sandrail developed a problem causing a temporary halt to our project. This is precisely the reason I'd invited both Frank and Cal. Having previously experienced breakdowns in the desert, I decided I was risking too much to continue alone. We returned to San Felipe where we made plans for our next trek and the establishment of the boundaries of search area B.

Whereas Cal was a full-time Southern California resident, Frank and Debbie Albrecht are Canadian snowbirds whose presence in San Felipe spanned November through March. Since Cal's availability depended on business demands, he and I could plan and undertake the search whenever his schedule permitted. In fact, owing to his business, there were several occasions when we conducted our planning at his residence rather than ours.

During most of these occasions, I was enabled to continue my research in Southern California's many libraries. That is, over this entire project, I conducted research in a total of 19 libraries spanning the miles between the University of California at Los Angeles and the University of New Mexico.

Cal returned home to acquire equipment we would need. Along the way, he stopped at La Ventana gas station to speak with its employees including an elderly woman I had once questioned. His purpose was to study their answers for information that could assist our cause. Prior to his departure, I gave him copies of Pepper's magazine article and my analyses of it, which he was to study and be prepared to discuss during our next meeting. In addition, he was to obtain copies of the hydrographic chart Pepper had used to prepare her article and contact a publisher he knew in hopes of learning how we might contact Choral Pepper.

Phase Four of our search would commence upon his return. In the interim, I was to complete the essential repairs to his sandrail, lay out area B and obtain a copy of a map I'd learned was made in 1925 by a German prospector. I'm not the only one who thrived on a 450-year old mystery. Now, there were three of us anxious to return.

CHAPTER FOUR
An Analysis

According to Choral Pepper, Walter Henderson had parked his Model A roadster near a window-shaped rock named La Ventana. With no 1930 map of the area and erosion endlessly whittling away at the terrain, La Ventana was not to be found although its location may be reasonably assumed to be in the proximity of a riverbed and a gasoline station bearing the same names. (Separated by a half mile, that riverbed and gas station are about halfway between Mexicali and San Felipe on Federal Highway #5.) Therefore, to avoid wasting time, I needed alternative locations for La Ventana to enable the establishment of more than one starting point from which Henderson could logically have begun his trek to the palm trees. (Any dedicated investigator will also want to know where the nearest blue fan palms are located.)

Whereas his trek was described as involving Arroyos Grande and Tule, the maps I assembled for this search included no such name as "Tule." (A tule, pronounced "TOO-lay" in Spanish, is a type of bulrush normally found in lakes and marshes.) On the contrary, the Grande is shown, and adjacent to it are a relatively short unnamed arroyo and Arroyo Jaquegel. What's more, the unnamed arroyo drains a remote part of the Sierra San Felipe, a fact tending to explain why it was so short: that northern segment of the San Felipe rarely receives water. By comparison, the Jaquegel, carved through sediments deposited from the Sierra Juarez over the millennia, is an impressive waterway that has carried major volumes of water, boulders, rocks, gravel, sand and mud.

Pepper's magazine article described Henderson's trek, in part, as being through the Arroyo Grande watershed. Since all terrain surrounding Arroyo Grande is its watershed, that statement caused confusion but enabled me to know he walked in Arroyo Grande and the Tule. Setting the word "watershed" aside, his presence in Arroyo Grande while seeking blue fan palms meant he had to be crossing the arroyo. And, with a ventana at his back, he had to be in the immediate proximity of the Sierra Pinta rather than the Sierra Mayor or Sierra San Felipe.

The Sierra Pinta is a mountainous conglomeration of ancient volcanoes of varying categories and sizes, lava in many shapes and varieties, and lava flows. Owing to the comparative softness of this material, window-shaped rocks can be found at any given time although each one I found was so soft (until my ultimate discovery), I knew it was but a temporary feature. I also rationalized no one would name such a formation that was bound to disappear in predictable time.

In contrast, the Sierras Mayor and San Felipe are composed of one or more igneous rocks in which I have not seen (nor heard of) a window rock. Add to this fact the absence of bona fide arroyos adjacent to the San Felipe and Mayor and... I believed Pepper's description of Henderson's presence in the Sierra Pinta/Tinaja region.

Next, because Henderson's search for blue fan palms had to lead him towards water, it was time to search for a passage over, through or around the Sierra Tinaja that would allow reasonable proximity to palms before the end of a partial day of walking.

At the place Arroyo Grande empties into Laguna Salada the arroyo's width is ten miles, a dimension tapering to one 150 feet ten miles farther south. Therefore, where Henderson began his walk is of the utmost importance since reducing the distance he walked by as much as one mile makes a significant difference in walking time. Add to this equation the fact that none of the present-day Mexican topographic maps of this region correctly displays the final ten miles of Arroyo Jaquegel. Consequently, anyone following my analysis of Henderson's trek must accept my stated distances, which are:

1) The straight-line distance between Federal Highway #5 and the western base of Sierra Tinaja is 22 miles when measured from the north end of its Laguna Salada crossing.

2) The distance between the western base of the Pintas (at the west end of the La Ventana corridor) and the western base of the Tinaja is 20 miles (via Arroyo Jaquegel).

3) The walking/driving distance between the Sierra Pinta/Sierra San Felipe pass to the western base of the Tinaja via Arroyo Jaquegel is 19 miles.

Having established these distances, there are three routes to the Juarez from the final 12 miles (its northern terminus) of Arroyo Grande:

a. The Indian trail from the eastern base of the Juarez via Arroyo Jaquegel and the Sierra Pinta/Sierra San Felipe pass (to the shellmound south of El Chinero). One version of Pepper's story has Henderson parking near a gold mine in this southern region. Of interest is the fact that this starting location places Henderson near the northernmost of two landmark mountains cited in her magazine article.

b. Via the La Ventana corridor to Arroyos Grande and Jaquegel and over the approximate center of the Tinaja.

c. Via a route departing the northern terminus of the Pintas, crossing the termini of Arroyos Grande and

Jaquegel and the lowest north-end passage over the Tinaja.

The fact that Henderson saw boulders bleached "white as snow" (this is pure writer's drama) reinforced my belief his Tule was my Jaquegel and that he traveled route b or c because the Tinaja has exposed boulders protruding from its sides. The fact that he "walked too far south," corrected his mistake and walked to a campsite within a few hours of his goal caused me to believe his actual route was my Route c.

Baja's prospectors know there is no running water in the Sierras Mayor, Pinta, Tinaja or San Felipe. They also know it is at least 25 miles from Mexico's Federal Highway #5 (at La Ventana gasoline station) to the foot of the Sierra de Juarez and its running water. But, because Highway #5 did not exist in the early 1930s, I needed to know how the original road to San Felipe was routed, and that placed me back in Arroyo Grande. What's more, a former truck driver, a man in his 90s at the time I spoke to him told me there had been a rest stop (La Cocina) along that road near the northern terminus of the Pintas.

While attempting to follow Henderson one must estimate the time of day he arrived in the region (we don't know what time he departed home) and the time he and his friend spent walking. Using information I obtained from the aged truck driver, I assigned three hours to the distance between the international border and La Cocina and three hours and fifteen minutes to La Ventana. Therefore:

Question: How many hours of daylight did Henderson have to do what Pepper's three versions of her story describe him as doing?
Answer: Assumed to be 12 (signifying mid- to late spring).
Question: What time did they arrive at La Ventana from Southern California?
Answer: Unknown, but advice from the prospector

should have suggested a pre-dawn start. I allowed him to arrive at the international border at sunrise and La Ventana at 9:15 a.m. Owing to my discovery of a hard rock ventana nearby, I arbitrarily assigned his parking place at a vent volcano (Cerro Huerfano) near it but in Arroyo Grande.

Question: How far did they walk to (and in) Arroyo Tule?

Answer: I assigned ten miles plus the time consumed by his error and the distance walked to that evening's campsite.

Question: Where did he and his friend camp that night?

Answer: Unknown, but believed to be at a convenient crossing point in the northern Tinaja.

Question: What time did he arise the following morning and what time did he break camp?

Answer: Knowing he had to return to the car before dark and that he had (an estimated) 12 hours of sunlight ahead of him, I have him rising at 6:00 a.m. and ready to depart camp at 7:00 a.m

Regardless of where his camp was, I estimated his speed of advance (in typical desert terrain) ranging between 2.0 and 2.5 miles per hour. I then placed his farthest western position at a distance from the car that would permit him to walk from his campsite to that point and retreat to the car before sunset. Therefore the straight line distance from the car to the campsite is "distance a" and the distance from his campsite to his farthest western point is "distance b." He walked $(a + 2b)$ at an arbitrary rate of two miles per hour (because this allows resting time).

Assuming he broke camp at 7:00 a.m. and returned to the car no later than 6:00 p.m., he would have to have retreated from that farthest western point no later than noon. Therefore, he had an estimated five hours (noon minus 7:00 a.m.) to hunt for the palms and return to his campsite. Five hours equates to a one-way walking distance of ten miles plus adequate time for rest and lunch.

As I have attempted to provide above, the answers to each of my questions will permit reasonable reconstruction of Henderson's route. Proof of that supposition is provided by the proximity of blue fan palms to any point along my route c: they only grow in certain environs.

It is, however, Henderson's return that is most important. Since he didn't find the palms, and it was while returning to the car that he encountered his curious pile of rocks, they must exist somewhere along a line leading to the car. Therefore, a logical starting point should be the car. By positioning the car at the Cerro Huerfano we can create a radius equal to eight and one-half hours of walking (17 miles) between the car and the farthest point west he could have walked and strike an arc over the Sierra Tinaja. Now we find the easiest crossing points through the Tinaja and draw a line from the car via each crossing point to create a vector along which he could have walked. Next, we find the nearest blue fan palms to the western terminus of each vector to establish which of those vectors he did walk.

Somewhere between his overnight campsite and the farthest western point there is the range of hills (which has to be the Tinaja) mentioned in Pepper's article. I made that trek but traversed a slightly different route during my return. Henderson told Pepper, "...the area in which we walked had a western drainage." So did the area in which I walked.

The fact that this trek was undertaken lends itself to my belief that Henderson and his companion were at home in the desert. They had self-confidence, understood land navigation and, although they'd never been in this region, knew where their car was and how to return to it. With these things in mind, I suggest, they sought the path of least resistance... and came upon the grave. I did and didn't so it's back to the drawing board.

According to Pepper's magazine article the two men found a "curious pile of rocks" they examined perfunctorily. They established the presence of desert varnish on the rocks, which is an indication of the amount of time the upper side of a rock was exposed to the elements. Based on desert varnish, then, the two surmised the rocks had been there for many years.

The fact that this pile of rocks is, apparently, in the immediate proximity of the Sierra Tinaja coincides with Díaz' approach and probable campsite after crossing of the Sierra Mayor and Laguna Salada: he was then in the same general vicinity as Henderson.

Having printed and placed two versions of Pepper's story side by side (paragraph by paragraph), I began an analysis of them during which I searched for words demanding interpretation to insure I understood what Henderson or Pepper had said. The results of that analysis appear as a series of statements and unanswered questions on the following pages. With the stage thus set, I now return to Díaz' final adventure at the point he crossed the untamed Colorado River. The reader is asked to envision the 16th century river that, judging from the appearance of the old riverbed from the air, was at least a mile wide.

After crossing the Colorado, Díaz probably traveled south along it to remain clear of the sea of sand (visible from a distance) that locals call "the Yuma Dunes." Riding in that southern direction he would have encountered the west-flowing New River and must have followed it to the Laguna de Los Volcanes, the geothermal site mentioned by Castañeda. In fact, one of Díaz' soldiers recorded, "While traveling in this direction, we came upon some beds of burning lava. No one could cross them for it would be like going into the sea to drown. The ground on which we walked resounded like a kettledrum, as if there were lakes underneath."

The Sierra de Juarez and Coyote mountains are visible from a great distance to the east. Owing to their orientation along a southeast-to-northwest line, I believe Díaz led his men along a line of march that took them the shortest distance to these mountains. Across the Colorado to the New River that is and thence along it to the geothermal site.

The record is vague from this point forward but I had to presume the beds of burning lava were located in the general proximity of Cerro Prieto, a landmark volcano on the northwestern fringe of the geothermal site (at the northwest terminus of the Cerro Prieto fault, a branch of the San Andreas). Whereas Castañeda claims Díaz turned back from this point, Bolton has him continuing in a southerly direction for another five or six days.

Whether they retreated or advanced cannot be proved here except to point out the approximate distance to Yuma from the geothermal site is 75 miles, the distance traveled in five days at Díaz' (assigned) speed of advance. Further, there is no terrain surrounding Yuma that is like the terrain suggested by Pepper's articles. In support of Bolton's findings, I submit Díaz was a man who would not have allowed the geothermal site to deter his goal(s). What's more, because Castañeda wrote this part of his narrative from hearsay, I suggest there were men from whom he heard one or more portions of his story that had something to hide. I further suggest Bolton had access to documents I did not see.

Whatever happened, Bolton said Díaz sustained his fatal injury five or six days after encountering the geothermal site. The reader is now asked to envision the following action as individual frames from a strip of movie film. According to the written record, Díaz became angry when he saw a soldier's dog chasing their sheep. Having warned the soldier on prior occasions, he was now going to make good on an earlier threat.

Frame 1: Spurring his horse to a gallop—with lance in hand—this experienced warrior rode directly toward the dog,

Frame 2: rose up in his saddle,

Frame 3: cocked his arm, and

Frame 4: threw the lance. The lance missed the dog but

Frame 5: stuck in the soil (to stick as reported the "soil" had to be sand because all other surfaces in this immediate region are hard-packed volcanic material) at an angle approximating 45 degrees. Still at a gallop,

Frame 6: Díaz came upon the lance before he could turn or rein his horse to a stop.

Frame 7: The lance penetrated his groin (and may have

penetrated or otherwise torn his femoral artery), lower intestines (bowel) and rear rib cage.

Frame 8: The impact of his body against the lance's blunt end would have driven the lance farther into the desert's (sandy) surface.

Frame 9: His forward momentum, now at the outer end of a pendulum's swing (the lance is the pendulum) would have pried him out of the saddle and slammed him to the ground.

Frame 10: His reflex reaction to the initial pain and his impact with the ground could have added to his injuries although these facts are relatively unimportant.

The day of his burial was listed as 18 January 1541, 113 days after the party's departure from San Hierónimo. To estimate the Díaz expedition's speed of advance I drew upon established facts.

a. Knowing Díaz was aware of a need to expedite his mission, I estimated his speed after reviewing speeds traveled by other New World Spaniards.

b. Traveling with the main body of the Cíbola expedition, a group that included horses, draft animals, hogs, cattle, and sheep, Coronado advanced at an average speed of ten miles per day.

c. He averaged 18 miles per day while traveling with the Vanguard to Háwiku.

d. When Culiacán was under siege, he crossed the jungle between Tepic and Culiacán (a distance of 300 miles) in 13 days. And,

e. Díaz rode 700 miles in 40 days during his verification journey to Chichilticale.

In view of these and similar facts, I assigned a speed of 15 miles per day, and the new question became, "How and where did Díaz spend his final 113 days?"

—The route Díaz traveled from San Hierónimo to Yuma involved about 325 miles requiring at least 35 (travel and rest) days.

—Three days to the emblazoned tree brings that figure to 38.

—I allowed three full days at the tree (38 + 3 = 41) during which he discussed his options and made the decision to continue. (The results of this decision probably weighed heavily on the minds of at least one of his subordinates.)

—Then, according to Bolton, they marched for five or six days north searching for a place to ford the Colorado (totaling 47 days).

Because they were now free to do what they pleased but owing to my suspicion Díaz knew he had malcontents with him, I did not decrease their speed of advance from this point forward. Now, needing rafts for a safe crossing, the Spaniards asked a band of Colorado River Indians to make rafts similar to their own. When the Spaniards realized the Indians were acting suspiciously, they captured one, tortured the truth out of him, killed him and prepared for an attack the following morning. When it came, their guns made it short-lived, and Díaz crossed the river using the Indians' rafts.

I allowed them four days waiting for the rafts, one day to cross the Colorado, five days to reach the geothermal site, one day to bypass it and another five or six days (according to Bolton) to arrive at the accident site (64 days). At this juncture, according to my count, Díaz has 49 days to live although one version of the Díaz tragedy states his men carried him on a litter for 20 days after his accident.

Whereas there could have been additional days spent at Indian campsites along the route, I maximized Díaz' speed of advance to Yuma because of the Coronado expedition's need for food and the drain on Indian food supplies caused by the unexpected arrival of 37 guests. Therefore, although I don't believe he was carried for 20 days, by allowing it and adding two more to attend Díaz on the day of his injury and the day of his death, I arrived at 27 unaccountable days. Whether my count is correct is of no particular consequence because it was the existence of unaccountable time that made me dig as deeply as I did into this historic event surrounding which I discovered discrepancies.

Advancing from the geothermal site, whether five or six days, places the Díaz party in the Sierra Pinta/Sierra Tinaja region. Four hundred thirty–three years later Pepper placed Henderson in the same region. At the beginning of this project I was struck with the question, "If the grave found by Henderson is that of Melchior Díaz why did at least one of his survivors say Díaz lived for 20 days after his accident?" Finding no answers in historic records I was forced to provide my own which included:

a. Pepper erred
b. Castañeda erred…
c. Bolton erred…
d. Díaz' survivors erred…
e. Díaz' survivors lied.

Regarding these thoughts:

a. Without attempting to defend the woman, a friend of Erle Stanley Gardner, I found it difficult to believe she would create and publish a story (three times) that could be proven false through contact with the Mexican Consulate at Los Angeles. Consequently, I accepted the basic element of her story establishing Henderson's discovery in the same region Bolton had placed Díaz at the time of his accident.

b. Proven by historians, Castañeda made several errors. In this case letters from participants in the Cíbola expedition provided corroboration of certain elements of the Díaz expedition. But there is another aspect of this tragedy that is completely unexplained. That is, Cortés ordered Arellano to remain at San Hierónimo. History shows he did not, and that fact must be considered at the moment the men chosen to accompany Díaz were selected. I believe whoever had that responsibility selected the worst of the expedition's malcontents for an easily identifiable variety of reasons.

c. The possibility was not considered.

d. The possibility of errors committed by Díaz's survivors is a matter that may never be proven. Regarding
discrepancies growing out of their report, Castañeda said
the party retreated to the east from the geothermal site.
Had they done so, Díaz' grave would be in Arizona or the
Mexican state of Sonora—places repeatedly searched by
archaeologists, anthropologists and historians who had
access to historic records I never saw. But Bolton places
the party five or six days farther into Baja California.
Accepting Bolton's placement as fact, I assigned the
Spaniards carrying a mortally wounded man on a litter
over difficult desert terrain, a sustained speed of .375
miles per hour during their daylight routine. (I arrived at
that time by the recurring necessity to tend to Díaz'
wounds.) Although I do not believe he was carried, these
calculations place the grave in Baja, California.

e. The possibility of Díaz' survivors' lying remains
strong as a result of discrepancies their story contains.
For example, they reported fighting Indians daily during
their return to San Hierónimo, but none of them had
Indian fighting experience and none of them was wound-
ed. Every other Indian fight described by Bolton in his
Coronado, Knight of Pueblos and Plains mentions casu-
alties among men considered anything but weaklings.
Similarly, reports of Indian-Spaniard skirmishes by
Bernal Díaz (*The Discovery and Conquest of Mexico*),
Cabeza de Vaca (*Adventures in the Unknown Interior of
America*), and Adolph Bandelier (*Southwestern
Archeological Expedition and The Gilded Man*) describe
relatively high percentages of wounded.

Owing to the years I spent professionally analyzing 20th-cen-
tury accidents, I conducted an in-depth analysis of Díaz' reported
accident. In so doing, I first had to determine the speed of a galloping horse. Second, I had to approximate the physical act of rising up in the saddle to throw a lance comparable in length, weight

and balance to the one Díaz carried. Third, I had to guess at his arm strength and, therefore, the force with which he may have hurled his lance. Fourth, I had to approximate the distance an experienced lance thrower may have thrown such a lance from a galloping horse. The formula for this action involves the speed of the horse plus the speed of the thrown lance by a static man. I also had to determine whether an experienced man, as Díaz must have been, would have continued in a straight line after throwing his lance.

Add to these calculations the probability that the most common accident among horse-mounted, lance-throwing men over the past 6000 years (that's about how long man has been riding horses) was the one reported by Díaz' survivors and you have reason to doubt his survivors' report.

Naively perhaps, I rationalized 6000 years of such accidents should have taught lance throwers to turn their horses immediately upon release of the lance. If it didn't, the Greeks, Romans and Carthaginians (and a host of others) must have suffered a terrible toll in preventable accidents, and these were not unintelligent men.

Whereas I do not believe his death accidental, I abandoned my pursuit of foul play when I admitted the answer lies in the grave, and the occurrence of foul play had nothing to do with my search for Henderson's rock pile. (If the grave is found, Díaz' remains must be examined by a competent forensic authority for a cause of death. One or more broken back ribs could corroborate accidental death. A hole in his skull, however, or scratches on ribs protecting the heart, would be an indicator of foul play.)

In The *Journey of Coronado*, historian George Parker Winship presented an "Itinerary of Expeditions" that includes the following entry under the year 1540. "October — Díaz starts from Corazones before the end of September, with 25 men, and explores the country along the Gulf of California, going beyond the Colorado River." In opposition to Winship, I suggest Díaz never reached the country along the Gulf of California until after he passed the geothermal site. Qualifying my claim of unaccountable days, however, Parker's entry could account for them if we allow a slight stretching of imagination.

Working backwards from Henderson's rock pile, a 20-day walk with a mortally wounded man on a litter would place the party in or near San Felipe—a budding resort community 50 miles southeast of the Sierra Pinta. In this case, 50/20 = 2.5, the approximate distance men would walk across sand per day carrying a critically injured man on a litter. Although this is somewhat wildly imaginative, it makes Díaz the first European to set foot on San Felipe soil and thereby justifies the statue I suggested placing as a highlighted international monument at the entrance to this distant desert community.

CHAPTER FIVE
Conclusions

Although I located four others, I spent three and a half years before finding what I believe to be the La Ventana formation mentioned by Pepper in her *Desert* magazine article.

1. Named and used by fishermen (and yesteryear's pirates) as a landmark, there is a three-sided rock structure on the shore east of Highway #5's crossing of the La Ventana riverbed.
2. There are two window-shaped formations in soft lava about a mile west of Highway #5 alongside the La Ventana riverbed. Inexperienced visitors tend to believe one or both of these could be Henderson's Ventana. Owing to the relative density of these formations and the speed of their erosion, I believe Henderson's ventana is "four" below.

3. There is a persistent air stream flowing north over Arroyo Grande from the foot of San Matias grade that many local Mexicans refer to as La Ventana. An east-west corridor through the Sierra Pinta is identified as La Ventana on several maps in my possession. The La Ventana riverbed passes along the eastern three-quarters of this passage.

4. The hard-rock formation I found is located in the first canyon south of the west end of the La Ventana Corridor. On the day I discovered this formation, Cal Blessing discovered half a dozen mounds qualifying as Melchior Díaz' gravesite. I thereupon named the place "Díaz Canyon."

The discovery of Díaz Canyon is an interesting tidbit. We were motoring west via our primary accessway to Arroyo Grande (the La Ventana corridor) when I chanced to notice an odd notch in the mountains a mile to my left. That notch, I told myself, shouldn't have been there. That is, the more I looked at it, the more convinced I became that it was water-carved (indicating a significant watershed existed behind it).

I stopped our procession, pointed to the notch, expressed my thoughts and suggested we check it out. To a man my teammates declined. "We're already late, Bruce. We need to return where we left off yesterday."

Saddened by their lack of curiosity I returned to my sandrail, started its engine and began moving westward, my mind and eyes solidly focused on the notch. Finally, seconds before it disappeared from view I stopped again and told the men, "You go ahead. I'll catch up later. I've got to check that thing out."

Angered by my insistence, they turned and headed for the notch. In fact, because I was on foot at the moment they got there ahead of me. By the time I parked my 'rail Cal had disappeared into the notch, which proved to be a six foot wide, 20 foot long, water-cut channel through hard rock.

I tracked Cal through the notch to a Y where the right leg led a dozen feet westerly to a dead end while the left leg offered unrestricted walking in an easterly direction. I followed his tracks for 100 meters to where they suddenly changed direction. He'd climbed the arroyo's 12-foot bank and… I lost his tracks on the harder floor of this tiny L-shaped canyon surrounded on all sides by mountains.

Looking west, I had a clear view of the canyon's true configuration, a view enabling me to see Cal a mile ahead. Following along behind him I was amazed to find copper ore (in minimal abundance) on the valley's floor. I also came upon a new arroyo deepening from a barely visible summit. To the untrained eye the surface appeared to be level but from that one particular point it was apparent water drained in both directions: east to the notch and west to the canyon's outlet.

Anxiety caused by the mystique of this remote place forced me to hurry along the arroyo to speak with Cal. When the day's ambient temperature came to mind, I uttered an oath, wiped the salt-laden perspiration from my burning eyes and hurried on. By the time I caught up with him Cal had a grin on his face and, pointing to nearby knobs protruding from the sides of the mountains, said, "By God, Bruce, this may be the place."

My anxiety justified, we were so excited we weren't sure what to do next. As we stood there facing each other, I chanced to look above his head and caught site of a hard-rock formation 50 meters away.

"Look," I croaked as I raised an arm to point. Reading the expression on my face, Cal turned, his gaze following my pointing finger and uttered another oath. The date was May 5, 1993. The ambient temperature was 105°F. We had abandoned our sandrails with nothing in hand, were suddenly starved for water (at least a mile and a half away) and frozen in amazement. That hard rock structure had to be Henderson's La Ventana.

I spent three-and-a-half years searching for a grave I believe in. During each of those years and subsequent to them, I paid particular attention to the rate of erosion of the land surrounding my search areas. If the grave is in Baja California and is as described in Pepper's magazine article, it should still exist today. Obviously, that depends upon the number of storms the region was subjected to over the years and the amount of erosion caused by each.

There is nothing about nature that is cast in concrete (except for natural concrete found in certain marine fossil beds). Rainwater will have widened the arroyo alongside the grave but if my understanding of the scene is correct, not to the extent that it would remove the grave or any portion of it. Based on my study of the wording in Pepper's articles, that should not occur for another 200-300 years.

Assuming the basic story is true, we must concentrate on the thoughts of the Spaniards who placed the grave on a knob protruding from a hillside. Similarly, we must abide by Bolton's finding that Díaz marched five or six days beyond the geothermal site, a finding that places him in the Sierra Pinta–Sierra Tinaja complex. And, finding no reason to doubt Henderson/Pepper, our rock pile must be within a nine-hour walk of the original road to San Felipe.

Having considered the erosional forces of sun, rain, wind and earthquake, every possible clue I could glean from Pepper's articles, her hydrographic chart and my topographic maps, and having sacrificed the knees my mother equipped me with for this task, I remain unperturbed: I believe the grave is simply waiting for the next eager investigator.

Born of hope and ignorance, sustained by determination but never consummated, this was an adventure I am proud to have undertaken. The benefits of this adventure are more dramatically demonstrated in the text appearing on succeeding pages. In the final analysis this adventure can be likened to searching for a needle in a haystack (or a man under a milestone). Whether the grave truly exists will remain a mystery until it is found.

On two occasions I asked intermediaries to inform Pepper I wanted to discuss her articles with her. Whereas I heard nothing from the first, the second informed me she recently passed away.

Therefore, for those who have nothing better to do, finding the grave of 16th century Melchior Díaz requires little more than dedicated thought, planning, understanding (of the sciences involved) and, above all, perseverance. As with each of those who preceded me it is my turn to pass the reins, and I do so with a hearty "Bon chance!"

PART TWO

THE BACKBONE
MOUNTAINS

Figure 4 – Sierra de Juarez

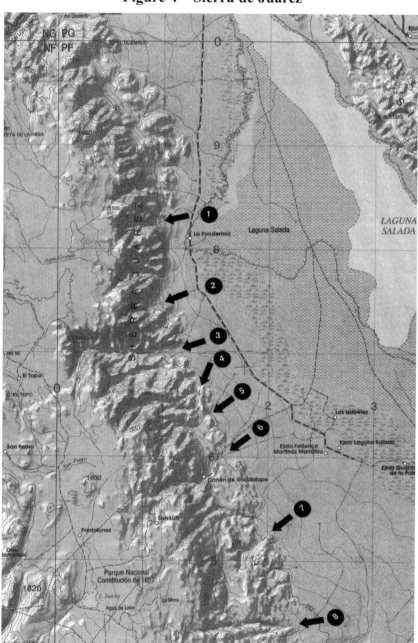

CHAPTER ONE
Introduction to Part Two

ONE

A t this stage of my life I am 73 years of age, weigh 200 pounds, stand five feet eleven inches tall, wear my hair like a two-day growth of beard and still have a grip most men cringe from. Of Scotch and English ancestry I am somewhat stubborn, completely self-sufficient, detest lazy men and have never truly learned how to relax.

Although I made my own way through life, I was lucky on many counts including those experiences that provided me with a well-rounded education. That is, dividing my time on earth by four I spent one-quarter of it (about 18 years) in the mountains, one at sea, one in the desert and the remainder in school where I managed the equivalent of a college education without bona fide degrees.

I grew up in the construction trade, a domain that provided me with early experiences in driving, operating and maintaining heavy equipment. I also had newspaper and magazine delivery routes, worked in restaurants, graduated from high school and joined the U.S. Navy where I found a profession I ultimately spent 33 years enjoying: Maintenance Management Engineering.

Married in 1958 to Alfreda Teresa Danoski, the two of us brought three kids into the world during our working years. I retired in '74 as a commissioned officer of the United States Navy started a second career but retired a dozen years later when an injury sustained during my naval service reared its ugly head.

"Freda," four years my junior, was a straight-A student and working in a bra factory when we met. (Where else should a hard-working man look for the girl of his dreams?) Struck by a car before we were married, she suffered a nasty gash on her head (requiring five or six stitches to close) and a broken collarbone. Not to be outdone by her I was involved in a shipboard accident during which I received second degree burns over fifty percent of my body (with blisters on my back as large as my forearm). A couple of toughies, we were in perfect health by the time the big day (September 13, 1958) rolled around and have remained that way ever since.

Because we spent ten years planning our retirement, when that momentous day dawned we sold our home, bought a recreational vehicle and began the great adventure. We motored across America, spent the fall months of that year in Pennsylvania (visiting her siblings), Connecticut (visiting my older sister), New Orleans and San Antonio (having fun), Nevada City, California (with my mother) and Los Angeles (for Christmas with our daughters). With a World's Fair opening in British Columbia in the spring of '86 we decided to winter-over in Mexico and proceed to Vancouver as soon as the snow was off the highways.

Finding a place to winter over was not as easy as it may sound. You can park a trailer anywhere, but can each of you enjoy anywhere? Consequently, while parked in a military campground near San Diego, we studied maps and campground descriptions until we reduced our options to Baja California's Ensenada and San Felipe and Arizona's Yuma and Gila Bend. Having done our homework, Freda suggested I check out Ensenada while she spent the day cleaning our four-wheeled home—watch me blame it on the kids—which hadn't been cleaned for a week or more.

This chore, my run to Ensenada, became one of the most painful experiences of my life. Driving south, I remembered something our first-born daughter told me about Puerto Nuevo, a lobster fishing community 27 miles south of the international border at Tijuana. I found the place, turned in, parked and went into one of its many restaurants to sample fresh-cooked lobster. (I considered it a late breakfast.)

To demonstrate the pain I suffered that day—while Freda was cleaning house—I stopped again during the return trip, enjoyed my second lobster in four hours and arrived at our trailer appearing as sad as I could possibly manage. I told her Ensenada was cold and dreary and we should check San Felipe, Yuma and Gila Bend but failed to mention Puerto Nuevo and its lobster.

Upon our arrival in San Felipe, about noon the following day, we investigated every nook and cranny, remained overnight and started our return to the trailer the following morning.

San Felipe, a seaside community 125 miles south of the international border between Calexico and Mexicali, is Mexico's official gateway to the Sea of Cortés. It is a shrimping village boasting a growing (American and Canadian) retirement community with a population in excess of 25,000.

I said "started" (our return to the trailer) because my conscience finally got the better of me. I told Freda how I had suffered during my Ensenada run and she told me, "Forget the trailer. Drive to Puerto Nuevo. Drive there NOW! And order me a fresh-cooked lobster… you stinker!"

Shortly after arriving in San Felipe with our trailer, I chanced upon a "Writer Wanted" ad in a local newsletter. Because I did technical writing in uniform that ad offered me an opportunity to learn whether I could write well enough to be published in retirement. Consequently, when I responded to that ad I was interviewed and given an assignment to write an article about San Felipe. I was also given the name of a local couple known to have source material for such an article. That is how and why I went to meet Tim and Robin Navarro (see Chapter One).

By the end of our third week in San Felipe we had fallen in love with the place, bought a property and started construction of our retirement home. Consequently, in place of our proposed run to Vancouver we bought an old Ford Bronco and began exploration.

Whereas the Bronco served us well enough, it was too heavy for the ultimate tasks I had in mind. Consequently, when I had sufficient experience to justify our actions, we sold the Bronco and bought a sandrail. A recreational gem, a sandrail is an open-air, tubular-framed, Volkswagen engine-powered, relatively light weight, 4-wheeled off-road vehicle capable (depending on its tires) of going almost anywhere.

Our sandrail was like Cinderella's slippers to us. That is, compared to the Bronco we could literally "dance all night." In addition to exploring the Pintas we expanded our desert exploration with Pepe and Imogene Garcia, the first Americans we had met in San Felipe.

Imogene went by that name, I-m-o-g-e-n-e, until the first time she held her birth certificate in hand. To her surprise, she learned her name was spelled I-a-m-g-e-n-e: The attending nurse, at the time of her birth, had spelled the name incorrectly. In reaction to that discovery, this fiercely proud woman has gone by the name on her birth certificate to this day and may be the only one in the world with it. Iamgene is pronounced "Imogene" although I found it easier to call her "Em."

Pepe and Em were made for each other. He was born in Peubla, Mexico's city of millionaires, and she in Ohio. He became a professional dancer at an early age but moved to California in the sixties where he became Manager, Mushroom Division, of Castle & Cook's Santa Cruz facility.

A cutie as tall (or short) as Pepe, she was a mushroom division employee who married the boss (also in '58) and was also a terrific dancer. Everything Freda and I ever wanted to know about mushrooms we leaned from these two who became our dearest friends.

Pepe (who passed away in 2001) had a thing for the desert long before he and Em retired to San Felipe. Once they landed here, it wasn't long before they had their own sandrail and spent every available moment in the desert. When we came along, we discovered the four of us had equal desires for desert exploration and the die was cast.

Of the four of us, I'm the one who brought organization to our outings (that's my military mind speaking). By this time I had seen enough of the Pintas to know I had to see as much as I could of the entire region. Therefore, I wanted to start at one end or the other and systematically go through each of the backbone mountain canyons first. When we finished the backbone we would explore each and every passage through the eastern mountain ranges and thereby place Baja California's northeast quadrant in perspective. That is precisely what we did.

TWO

Chapter Two of this Part contains descriptions of other men and women we met and enjoyed locally. Chapter Three contains a basic description of the Sierra San Pedro Martir. Chapter Four describes a mountain climbing trek made by Mexican friends of ours. Chapter Five contains a story resulting from a chance meeting in the San Pedro. Chapters Six and Seven contain descriptions of the San Pedro's many canyons while Chapter Eight contains my conclusions of the content of Part Two.

To set the stage on which these mountains display themselves, they occupy the southern two-thirds of a complexity of mountain ranges ending in the north at Southern California's Morongo Pass (through which America's Interstate Highway #10 passes). Erosion, I presume, began commensurate with the uplift of Baja's backbone mountains so that, by the time uplift ended (90 million years ago), the carving of a series of canyons had begun in their eastern flanks.

As time went on, and rain and snow continued, each canyon was etched in direct proportion to the rain and runoff it experienced. Such activity is a recurring (sometimes deadly) fact of canyon life. Indigenous man came along, discovered the canyons and used them as avenues between his home(s) and his sources of food, household necessities and weaponry. European man arrived, wreaked havoc on indigenous man and melted into the populace. Modern man arrived, found evidence of his predecessors' presence and developed systems for the ongoing study of that evidence (setting the stage for such as me).

Buried deeply within the historic fabric of these mountains are dramatic geologic structures to be discovered, studied and enjoyed. Similarly, there is paleontologic, anthropologic and archeologic evidence in hidden locations at which Mother Nature continues to whittle away. Freda and I, for example, chanced upon two particular treasures a San Diego paleontologist verified as saber-toothed cat fossils.

Also covered in this Part Two are the upper, lower and canyon regions of the Sierra de Juarez and Sierra San Pedro Martir. Further, because the Juarez receives more rain than the San Pedro there is more erosion, more sand and, seemingly, more of everything else these mountains could contain including people.

Casual visitors will find a complexity of full-and part-time residents in each of these mountain ranges but will have no opportunity to evaluate the structure of these mountains. Who, for example, cares about a distant, boulder-strewn cactus and rattlesnake infested canyon? Consequently, who among them has taken the time to evaluate the comparability between these two mountain regions?

Whereas there may be comparability in the upper regions, that's as far as it goes. The canyons cut into each mountain range, the valleys adorning their eastern flanks and the mountain ranges east of each valley are as different from each other as salt is from pepper. There are, for example, uncountable numbers of palm trees growing in the well-watered canyons of the Juarez and next to none in the San Pedro.

What's more, their canyons demonstrate the amounts of water each range received over the millennia. The drama played out by this water—try to envision cubic miles of the stuff zigzagging down any given canyon with its rocky cargo bouncing from wall to wall as it descends. Cargo? I've seen what I estimated to be 200,000-pound boulders at the base of the San Pedro's canyons and others half again that size at or near the base of the Juarez's many canyons.

The evidence for the fury of any given canyon is to be found at its outlet. Diablo and Copal are good examples in the San Pedro while I've chosen Santa Isabel and Los Tanques to represent the Juarez. The dams created along the downhill flank of each canyon's outlet—by boulders, rocks, gravel, mud, sand and vegetable matter—tend to describe that fury. Diablo boasts a half-mile-long dam while Copal's drainage cut a 70 foot wide, 20 foot deep trench into the adjacent desert floor.

Santa Isabel, in contrast, proudly displays an outpouring arroyo varying in width from one-quarter to one-half mile while Los Tanques' dam is twice the vertical, horizontal and longitudinal size of its San Pedro competitor.

As remote as they seem to be, Arroyos Grande and Jaquegel provide additional evidence of the excess of water distributed in this northern region. Granted, the Grande enjoys additional watershed over its 100-mile length but, other than the San Pedro's Matomí, there are no arroyos at the base of the San Pedro's canyons. Adding even more drama to the scene, the canyons penetrating Sierra San Felipe must be ascribed to the drainage of the lake left behind by the most recent ancient sea.

Finally, the 60-miles-long Valle San Felipe cannot hold a candle to the 62 miles of the Laguna Salada, which originally was a deep ocean trench (subsequently filled by the Colorado River system). Measure the accumulated sand in each of these regions, and you'll come away (comparatively) empty handed from the San

Felipe while sand plays such a dramatic role in the Salada that every road there has ever been along the eastern approaches to the Juarez was buried or erased by it many times over.

To drive in the greater Laguna Salada region is a temporary respite from being stuck. This is not only a fact of life, it is the reason you're apt to find but one bona fide road: the unimproved access road from Federal Highway #2 (at the north end of the Salada) to Guadalupe Canyon.

There are, I presume, those who could say, "I've driven the Salada a dozen times and I never got stuck." So have I, but I was lucky as anyone who has driven it repeatedly will tell you. The north, east and west margins of the lake region are paved with deep sand. The southern segment knows sand along its western margin with substantially less throughout its 200 square miles of parched surface. Laguna Salada is not a place to be taken lightly; nor is it a place for anyone to travel alone.

Before describing canyons, it is essential to describe the valleys adjoining each of these two mountain ranges. As indicated above, Laguna Salada is a sedimentary plain filled (reportedly ranging from 800 to 2,000 feet in depth) primarily with sediments from the Colorado River system although each of the Juarez' canyons added their share. One look at the Colorado River system, which now includes the Sea of Cortés, and there can be no wonder where the dust, dirt, sand, gravel, rocks and boulders went that were removed from the Grand Canyon.

In contrast, Valle San Felipe is a landlocked place filled with sediments from the San Pedro's canyons alone. It is a silent place in which the investigator must painstakingly seek each and every answer to his or her questions. The beauty of this place is the fact that the answers are there to be found... without appreciable difficulty!

As far as visible terrain is concerned, the region bordered by San Felipe and Mexicali; San Luís, Somerton and Yuma; Indio, Morongo Pass and Desert Hot Springs is a part of the Colorado River delta. As far as reality is concerned, the Colorado River system created a lake extending from what are now the midriff islands (Tiburón and Angel de la Guarda) to Morongo Pass (west of Palm Springs), and from Mexico's Sierra Madre to Baja's backbone mountains before the Baja California peninsula was ripped from the mainland. Sediments carried by the Colorado were deposited in the bottom of this lake to form the land many of us walk and drive upon today.

When the peninsula was ripped from the mainland and the lake was drained, windblown sand formed a host of dunes throughout the region. The Yuma dunes and Mexico's Altar Desert, virtual seas of sand, are excellent examples but not the only ones. The western half of the Laguna Salada basin is a mixture of dunes and rocky sediments, making passage in any direction difficult.

Try to envision the four-state area of Arizona, Utah, Colorado and New Mexico. Now add direct sun to this four-state surface and watch—as the vacuum caused by rising heated air increases—where cooling air comes from. Following the paths of least resistance, it comes from the Gulf of California although the draw (from this four-state region) is so great it also comes through every coastal mountain pass. As a benefit of this natural phenomenon, electricity-generating windmills were installed along the eastern approaches to Morongo Pass.

Regarding prehistoric Indian activity in the greater San Felipe region, the Cucapah (and their predecessors) occupied the southwestern Mexicali valley region between El Centinela (a landmark mountain west of Mexicali) and La Puerta (a Mexican pueblo south of Mexicali) and fished the nearby Colorado River. The Kumeyaay (and their predecessors) occupied the northern Juarez (Vallecitos, for example) and raided the Cucapah for their seafood. The Kiliwa (and their predecessors) occupied Trinidad Valley and fished the northwestern shore of the Cortés (along the swamp south of the Cerro Chinero salt flats). They also sold salt to other tribal groups mentioned here. The Pai Pai (and their predecessors) occupied the south-central San Pedro Martir and fished the Cortés from San Felipe to the Matomí Wash.

From the estero (swamp) south of El Chinero (an extinct vent volcano 32 miles north of San Felipe) to the mound at Campo El Saguaro (south of San Felipe) I worked Indian shellmounds searching for anything and everything the Indians dropped. In each of these locations I found arrow points, cutting tools and jewelry. I even found a mano (a grinding tool) in one of them.

THREE

The canyons of the Sierra de Juarez (see Figure 4) include, from north to south: Llanos, an unnamed canyon, Palmas Azules (map key #1), Cantú (key#2), Los Tanques (#33), Tajo (#4), Carrizo (#5), Guadalupe (#6), La Mora (#7), Palomar (#8), Santa Isabel, and Agua Caliente. I have not explored Llanos, the unnamed canyon, Palmas Azules or Agua Caliente. As for the others, owing to the extreme paucity of visitors to them, I will forego description beyond what is written below.

My initial exposure to the canyons of the Juarez was due to the courtesy of two Mexican businessmen Freda and I met by chance at Rancho San Francisco in the Sierra San Pedro Martir. This meeting occurred during an unscheduled visit to ranch owners, Aurora and Alberto Dojáquez. As the six of us compared exploratory notes we learned the businessmen were bona fide hikers and amateur mountain climbers, and they learned we were experienced desert explorers.

When they offered to show us the Kumeyaay Indian summer camp at Vallecitos we leaped at the opportunity, made a date and met them two weeks later in Mexicali. Traveling via Federal Highway #2 in two cars, our guides stopped before reaching the top of the remarkable Rumarosa Grade.

The Rumarosa is a treacherous stretch of heavily (truck and bus) traveled twisting, turning, two-lane mountain road extending from the desert floor (20 miles west of Mexicali) to a summit elevation of 4000 feet at the pueblo of Rumarosa. Along most of its 24 miles there is a steep drop-off a few feet east of the pavement. The remains of cars and trucks that didn't make the grade can be seen hundreds of feet below that (frightening?) roadway.

We parked behind them on what may be the only wide spot on that particular road and, while Freda waited in our car, the rest of us walked up a mountainside trail to an ancient Indian lookout station. This site, at the top of a seemingly insignificant ravine, stands about 200 feet above the highway. My guides led the way along a centuries-old trail etched into the hillside and before long we were gazing out over the escarpment.

The view of the Mexicali Valley (and Salton Sea) 4000 feet below was fantastic. At our feet, however, I was delighted to see eight genuine morteros ground into the granite by a succession of Indian women over many years. Above the morteros on adjacent boulders were a dozen petroglyphs and pictographs presumed to be of equal vintage. This site enjoys the protection of isolation afforded by its remote location and the fact that few know of its existence. May it never change.

Arriving in the ancient Indian pueblo of Vallecitos, about five miles west of Rumarosa, we saw numerous (Indian) wall paintings including three in a tiny cave formed by what I presume to have been the chance natural assemblage of three small boulders. Between two of those boulders there is a narrow vertical slit through which the rising winter solstice sun (December 21) shines on one drawing at a time. The color of those drawings, an age-stained white, suggests an age in excess of 1000 years.

We drove to another, more remote location where we parked near the center of the east face of a quarter-mile-long solid granite outcropping. Once again Freda waited in the car while I followed my guides vertically up a granite face across the top of the outcropping to a narrow slit in which we dropped about eight feet down to see two ancient drawings. I tried to photograph those drawings by reflecting light off my undershirt. Afterwards, descending the outcropping, we climbed a little, jumped a little and climbed a little more over narrow ledges weathered into its west-side facing.

This outing was as exciting as it was historic, and strenuous as well. The following day I checked into a San Diego hospital for a previously scheduled total knee arthroscopy. Why? By the time this book was written, I had had five total knee arthroscopies and am positively forbidden to look at another boulder (rock, gravel or sand).

The best way to see a country is to travel it on foot. In my case, having begun the journey in '86, I walked about half of it and motored the other half. Would that I could walk the second half as well for my heart and soul reside in the two living deserts described in this book, each more beautiful than the other.

FOUR

The blue fan palms (*Erythea armata*) at Cantú Canyon are the only canyon palms visible from any appreciable distance east of the canyons. They stand in groves surrounding two oases at the base of the Juarez about 15 miles south of Federal Highway #2. Owing to the availability of natural spring water here, Baja California Governor Esteban Cantú set up a woodcutters' camp in the early 1900's in support of Mexicali's residents' cooking and heating needs. Evidence of this and subsequent camps can still be seen in the rocky ruins only partially hidden by grass. The palm trees stand on each side of a rocky ridge separating the place into two distinct sloughs.

Cañón de Los Tanques involves a difficult walk to find the remnants of many hundreds of palm trees. Because it was so stren-uous, I stopped at this point (about a mile and a half upstream) and retreated. Finding two groups of petroglyphs along the way, I knew there were more to be found upstream but prudence (and my knees) dictated I move on. The entrance is all one needs to understand what happens here.

Tajo Canyon was next and must be the most beautiful of them all. The word "Tajo" means a (structural) cut or opening in a moun-tain and is, I presume, intended to describe this monstrous gorge.

Having investigated as much of this unique canyon as possible and its stands of blue and Washingtonia filifera palms, I prefer to think of it as the Zion National Park of Mexico.

Carrizo Canyon, I was told, was the place in which my former guides honed their mountain climbing skills. There is a hot spring near its entrance in a truly picturesque setting adorned with blue fan palms. Because it was a two-hour walk to the springs, I rested for what seemed like a moment and was startled, an hour later, to learn I had fallen asleep. Regarding growth other than palms, both Tajo and Carrizo canyons are so overgrown with cholla cactus it is difficult to find a pain-free way through their entrances.

Guadalupe Canyon has commercially developed hot springs I bypassed to enable a viewing of the backcountry. Here again, there is a deep gorge-like cavity carved by tumbling water and rocks. How the trees survive is beyond me although every one of these canyons is littered with the remains of those that did not.

I'll withhold comment on La Mora and Palomar except to say Palomar has a hot spring in its backcountry. Santa Isabel, on the other hand, was accessed via fences, gates and padlocks for which my guides had keys. Arrival at the first gate was anticlimactic considering the sandy route we'd followed. There is a road here, but rain and wind frequently dissolve it so I suggest there is no good access route to Isabel. Rather, you adjust your sights to the contour of the mountains surrounding the canyon and head, as best you can, across a rocky, sandy waste of dunes, arroyos and other natural obstacles as memorable as the canyon itself.

Varying from a quarter- to a half-mile in width, the most impressive thing about Isabel is the task it was handed for drainage. Similar to Cañón Los Tanques, this is a monster wash draining a monstrous watershed. The water it enjoys and the debris that water carries, played and continue to play havoc with surrounding terrain, but it does at least one job better than the others. That is, its springtime aromas describe an Edenesque garden paradise. In addition, the broken pottery we came upon tended to describe Indian habitation over at least one sustained period.

Transferring from the floor of these canyons to their upper regions involves a drive via Federal Highway #2 to Rumarosa (or Federal Highway #3 to the eastern boundary of Ojos Negros Valley). From either point there are roads leading to Laguna Hansen. At least two easy-to-find roads lead from the lake to the escarpment where I found this upper region as interesting as the lower.

Since one of Freda's and my original goals was to find every road in the greater San Felipe region and follow it, we were driving along one of Laguna Hansen's roads one day (with Pepe and Em) when I spotted cat tracks and stopped to examine them. As best I could determine they demonstrated a mother cougar with two youngsters she was teaching. It is discoveries like these and the ability to read them that give us so much enjoyment of the desert.

Along the road bordering the south end of the lake we came upon a Mexican man and his son who had trapped a rattlesnake in a bush. As we approached the man came forth with the snake in his hand. Smiling, he introduced himself and described his use of dried rattlesnake meat for medicine.

On a nearby road in the midst of surrounding forest, we came upon an assemblage of boulders that must have been used for one purpose or another by the ancient ones although evidence of their presence has long since disappeared.

There are several Indian sites in this upper region although weather and "lookie-loos" have destroyed most of them. Tragically, to demonstrate this unfortunate side of man's character: when the Vallecitos Indian site was discovered and publicly announced, several of its wall paintings were destroyed by graffiti painters.

About 12 miles south of the lake the east-west road from Ojos Negros Valley to Gongora (at 5,000 feet elevation) leads to a honeymoon lodge and other private properties whose owners rent or lease lots to summering-over enthusiasts. Continue east on this road to intersect another leading to Laguna Hansen and, a little farther east, another road leading south and east to the valley below. (Off-road racers frequently use this last road.)

The road from Ojos Negros to Gongora is steep at first, but we found it in good repair each time we drove it. Winter at this elevation must take its toll, but full-time residents seem to insure it is maintained frequently.

There is an old sawmill (for this upper region's 200-year-old pines and 300-year-old cedars) three miles south of Laguna Hansen. There is also a small community and a host of remote residences scattered throughout the woods in this general locale. In summertime, at least, it is a veritable playland with enjoyable surprises around most every turn. The road from Ojos Negros Valley is well maintained although I cannot say the same about the road from the pueblo of Rumarosa to the lake.

In closing, I must advise any and all who contemplate visiting places described herein to do so with the utmost safety including appropriate maps for each specific region. While there is an abundance of map stores throughout the Pacific Southwest, I have enjoyed the services of one in San Diego and another in Mexicali. Talking about enjoyment, three blocks south of the Mexicali map store there is a fantastic place to eat—Cenaduria Selecta—whether breakfast, lunch or dinner.

The word *cenaduria* identifies a Mexican fast-food establishment. In this case, C. Selecta is anything but fast. It is so popular, that parking is difficult on a good day, and the chances are you'll wait in line for a table. Trust me; I wouldn't mention it if this place weren't worth the wait.

CHAPTER TWO
Friends and Neighbors

You've already met Pepe, Imogene and Calvin. Now it's time to meet others who enriched our lives, whether as San Felipe residents or as desert explorers.

As a reader, I had met Díaz years earlier in the same manner in which I met Sinbad, Captain Ahab, Lord Johnny. But this was different. This was more than a meeting between readers and characters in a book. Díaz wasn't fiction; he had lived and something had happened to him within my sphere of influence. All I had to do was rise up out of my chair, drive a handful of miles, and... because of Robin Navarro I stumbled upon everything this book describes. Wherever you are now, Robin, Thank you! My heart is with you and one day, perhaps, you and I and Melchior will meet again.

Frank and Debbie Albrecht

Canadians who arrived in San Felipe in 1986, they introduced themselves to us while we were building our house, to learn about contractors and house building particulars. They met other North Americans at a local church and began enjoying desert tours with Roger and Sue Egan who knew the local desert better than most.

Shortly thereafter they invited us to accompany them on a sandrail run to Puertecitos (50 miles south of San Felipe). Roger Egan had loaned them a buggy, and they thought we might enjoy the run. Later that morning I was given an opportunity to drive the buggy and my fate was sealed. Like a kid with his first taste of candy I not only wanted more, I ordered a sandrail from Roger.

Six months later Frank and Debbie accompanied Freda and me on our first desert adventure in our new sandrail. We drove to Bahia San Luis Gonzaga, 100 miles south of San Felipe, where we set up camp in the middle of a desert plain within a mile of what proved to be an interesting shoreline. (We found clams by the thousands, almost as many mussels, a variety of oysters, two of scallops and fish in super abundance).

When the ladies said they wanted to collect seashells, and Frank said he wanted to take a nap, I drove the girls to the beach and went to explore the nearby Santa Ynez riverbed. I wanted to know how far upstream I could drive (toward a 17th-century Spanish mission). Whereas the going was rougher than anticipated (very dense brush) I made it to the mountains and at least 200 meters up the riverbed's polished rock floor. When stopped by terrain I could no longer negotiate (boulders), I retreated to our campsite. Along the way I ran into a herd of cattle, zigged when I should have zagged and ran over the largest and freshest cow poop there ever was. Suffice it to say my sandrail and I were both christened.

If champagne can be likened to the sea for christening ships, then cow poop is appropriate for sandrails. You wouldn't believe how thoroughly we were covered. Thank heaven for sand, the medium I used for the 'rail's initial cleaning. As for me, here's my eternal blessing on the makers of Prell shampoo, a smart choice for bathing in salt water!

Prim and proper Debbie was a Registered Nurse, Frank a car salesman. During subsequent desert tours Frank displayed talents Calvin and I sought for our search team. When I invited him to participate he leaped at the opportunity, and we gained a man with mechanical skills superior to our own. After our team's disbanding, they moved to Yuma where Frank participates with a group of banjo players.

Roger and Sue Egan

. . . aretwo are Canadians who've been wintering-over in San Felipe for well over twenty years. Freda and I met them during a 1987 sandrail run to Puertecitos. Among other things Roger was an off-road racer who became a sandrail builder. I ordered my 'rail from him in the spring of '88 and received it when he and Suereturned to San Felipe the following October. Sue is the motherly type who loves and is loved by everyone. Roger showed me the route to Agua Caliente, Valle Chico's hot spring. (See Part three.)

Bill and Donna Curtis

. . . are from Oklahoma. They had a thing for Volkswagen Beetles and owned at least three of them plus their two sandrails (and a pickup truck for towing their trailer). Retired from the U.S. Army, Bill stands at least five-eleven and weighs a fret over 200 pounds. Donna was also tall and handsomely thin with shiny black hair and ficry eyes, making her a strikingly beautiful woman.

They loved the desert and frequently ventured into it by themselves to explore wherever they could. Donna became treasurer for the San Felipe Association of Retired Persons' (SFARP). We lost her to leukemia although she participated in our annual fashion show, as ill as she was, before leaving San Felipe for the last time.

After distributing her ashes on a hillside in our local desert, a place the two of them loved, Bill returned too Oklahoma and is seldom seen—a tragic end to a beautiful love story.

Ken and Sarah Darsch

Residents of San Felipe's south beach community, Ken and Sarah are true desert adventurers ready to go at the slightest suggestion. In fact, this delightful couple usually organizes annual seven to ten-day treks down the peninsula during which they drive none but unimproved roads. In fact, Ken refuses to travel improved roads unless absolutely unavoidable.

Public spirited, they were members of their local Kiwanis Club before arriving in San Felipe. They have supported SFARP since the day it adopted that name and rarely miss one of our desert tours.

He designs and builds Ultralight airplanes including one I wanted to buy before Freda stepped in denied such activity. "Losing you to the desert is bad enough," she told me sternly. "I'm not going to allow you to be dashed to pieces on the side of some remote mountain like those I see on TV!"

He's a true outdoorsman who never learned to slow down. She's his faithful companion, a beautiful woman and a dedicated mom. We're in hopes they'll become a part of SFARP's management team although the distance they have to drive to attend our meetings is a major deterrent.

Dale and Myrna Eubanks

Avid desert explorers from Eureka, California, they, too, were married in '58 (would you believe New Year's Day?). Dale was a high school teacher and Myrna a maternity ward RN. Dale is quite a talker; Myrna is the quiet one but is an excellent director of SFARP's activities. He stands about five-eleven, weighs 195 and has dark blonde hair. She's five-one, 120 pounds with dirty blonde hair and of Finnish heritage.

Dale's on the wagon now (as are most of us), but when he wasn't his glasses gave him away when he had too much to drink. They slid down his nose, and he looked at us over their rims. I often thought if I were ever to write a play, I'd create a character like Dale… staring at the world over the rim of his glasses. Dale is serious; Myrna's fun. She's also a craftsperson who brings homemade table décor to our outings. No matter how far into the desert we go, our lunch table is always covered and decorated with an attractive centerpiece.

Bill and Kay Gabbard

He's retired U.S. Navy, and she's a retired school teacher. They are the most charity-minded couple in town. If it weren't for them, local handicapped kids would not have their school, their school bus and one whale of a lot of other essential stuff. Of equal temperment, they're a lot of fun, although dedicated to the work they've been doing since they arrived San Felipe: charitable fund raising.

They were always on the run; always helping someone else, and may be the most injured couple we know. Bill broke an arm when he fell off a ladder while painting a classroom at the handicappers' school. She also fell (while walking down uneven steps with both arms full), broke a leg, cracked the other ankle and needed a wheelchair for weeks.

They finally retired (from their daily doings) and have joined us on every subsequent desert tour although their summers are still spent finding American schools willing to contribute books for Mexican school children.

Luke and Sandy Hackett

From Montana where Luke had his own mining business, they are comparatively new arrivals that introduced themselves to us at a SFARP meeting. Subsequently, during desert tours in particular,

Luke demonstrated an above-average interest in the desert, its history and my knowledge of it. On the one hand, they are volunteers. On the other they are a public-spirited couple desirous of being involved in SFARP's management.

Luke responded favorably to my request for help with the revision to SFARP's many (would you believe more than 250?) trifold information brochures. Coincidentally, the two of us share many traits. He, for example, loves cooking and computing. When I'm not in the desert (or at the computer), I'm usually in the kitchen.

He and Sandy are both good cooks and have repeatedly contributed to SFARP's filet mignon, babyback ribs, barbecued sausage and barbecued hot wings dinners.

Luke's a big man: somewhere between a football tackle and a line backer. Sandy's indoor, outdoor and creative. They're younger than us, although it really doesn't matter. We sincerely hope to see their names at the top of the SFARP's heap in the not-too-distant future.

Gene and Doris Krause

Retired Air Force, he's from California, she's from Boston. They, too, were married in '58. Gene stands six-one, weighs 170 pounds and wears his gray hair barely long enough to comb. Working on daily chores, including his sandrail's upkeep, defines the muscles of his arms and shoulders. He wears no fat.

Gene is honest, energetic and headstrong. Desert devotees, he and Doris not only participated in every one of my earliest desert tours, she became a permanent fixture in SFARP. Gene insists he'll never accept a position on our Board of Directors but never misses a meeting and is the most reliable of our many volunteers. He is quiet and sincere; Doris is funny. She has a hearing problem, talks real loud, knows something about everything and is as reliable as Gene. God bless military retirees, 58ers and these two.

Art and Margo Madsen

Art was Navy until he received one of those career-ending injuries. He's as tall as me, weighs 190 pounds but at 70+ years of age he still maintains a teenager's physique an is the only man I know with a handshake that'll rattle your cage. Margo is matronly, likes to be in charge, and is good company on a desert run.

When Art retired from a government job in Panama they returned to a ranch they owned in Texas. Later, as did some sixty-six thousand other North Americans, they received a letter from the National Pen Company informing them they'd won a residential lot at San Felipe's newly created El Dorado Ranch. They drove to San Felipe, listened to a salesman's spiel, liked what they heard and saw, accepted the offer and became a part of that rapidly growing community. When they heard of my desert tours they signed on, liked what they heard and saw and became two of my regulars.

We had many enjoyable treks together including one during which Art had a close call and another (described in Part III) involving racers who had a close call. He's fighting Alzheimer's now so we don't see them that often. It makes me wonder why the good guys seldom finish last?

Tom and Robin Navarro

Tom was a solid, serious, good looking seventy-year-old Mexican who'd lived in America at least thrity years. Robin was an American he met and married many years ago. They lived "happily ever after," I suspect, with kids, grandkids, and more. Although I have few dealings with either of them—an occasional meeting during shopping trcks—I owe Robin a heartfelt vote of thanks for her kindness of introducing me to Melchior Díaz.

Hank and Shirley Thompson

Hank is retired Navy. Like me, he's a little meaty, stands 5'10" or 11", and is the only one I know who's done more desert exploration than I have. I think he'd rather be in the desert than anywhere else on earth.

Shirley is, tall, thin, blonde and a dedicated worker, was an accountant and has helped with my accounting since the day I started publishing magazines. This is a lady with a passion for the elderly. As an opportunity to get them out of their houses, she created The Friendship Group, which met the first and third Wednesdays of each month at a local hotel. Two years later, having learned the full scope of my desert activity, she invited me to participate as the group's Director of Activities. I accepted, became president a year later, and changed the group's name to "San Felipe Association of Retired Persons."

Later, while building a house at a beachside Campo, Shirley and Hank included a structure they called "The Lodge" and insisted SFARP use it as their primary meeting site. Consequently, when Hotel Las Misiones closed (we met in their Salon Las Gaviotas for eight years) we accepted Shirley and Hank's offer and have enjoyed it to this day.

Shirley can usually be found at the NET, San Felipe's official Internet Service Provider, and Hank, a reliable friend, continues his desert explorations, but guides or helps to guide SFARP's desert tours on request. The community is a better place for the presence of these two who try to remain silently in the background.

JUNE MARION SNOW

I sat for an hour, recently, listening to one of the most amazing stories I've ever heard. This was a story about a woman who, as a child, was kidnapped, placed in an orphanage, returned to her mother, grew up in show business, married, had children, lost two sisters, a brother, two children, two husbands… and lives each day for its individual beauty.

She was born June Marion Snow in Cleveland, Ohio. Whereas her father was a farmer, her mother was sufficiently talented to open her own restaurant, ultimately, in Los Angeles, California. So it is in Los Angeles, rather than Cleveland, that her story begins. As a three-year-old, she was kidnapped from a neighborhood playground—she remembers the car, some of the scenery and living in Montana. When her abductors could no longer make ends meet, she was clandestinely delivered to an orphanage from where she was returned to her mother.

Because her mother wanted her daughters to become models, June was enrolled in Ethel Merlin's famous studio, Merlin's Kiddies, which produced such notables as Deanna Durbin, Shirley Temple, Judy Garland, Jane Withers, Jackie Cooper, Donald O'Connor, Mickey Rooney and Jackie Cogan. That's right, this lovely lady got her start in the same room, on the same floor, at the same time as these other kids... whom you and I know as stars.

June's childhood was all show business. Because she learned walking with poise, tap dancing, ballet and operatic singing, her career began in vaudeville. In fact, by high school she was a coloratura soprano until fate delivered a show-stopping blow. As though destined to be a singer, a car struck her, one Halloween eve, so forcefully a finger-size piece of wood was lodged in her foot and prevented her from continuing as a dancer. As strange as it may seem, that terrible piece of wood was completely unknown until many years later when her husband inadvertently stepped on the same foot in a manner that forced it to poke its ugly head into the air. She still has the scar from its removal.

A graduate of Los Angeles' John H. Francis Polytechnic High School she became a featured singer in a number of Southern California nightclubs. She was singing in San Pedro, California on the night Tokyo was bombed. In fact, she met her husband-to-be that night, eventually bore him three children and lost him to a heart attack. Before he died, however, and because his initials were the same as those carved into the Black Dahlia's chest, he was arrested, quizzed and cleared as her murderer.

The "Black Dahlia" was the name given to an incomparably gruesome, late 1940s, Hollywood, California murder case.

Because her husband had been a sailor, she donated some 3000 hours, over the course of her singing career, to California U.S.O.s. As a member of the Manhattan Beach Strolling Trio, she reminisced, there was one song (Quizás, Quizás, Quizás) she claims to have sung 100,000 times. Singing in five languages (English, Swedish, French, Spanish and Hawaiian) June eventually teamed with trios and quintets in Palm Springs, Reno, Las Vegas, Guadalajara and Mexico City.

June describes "**HOW I GOT INTO LATIN MUSIC —**" "During an evening in 1954, I went to the (Los Angeles) Wilshire District's Blue Palm night club to enjoy an evening with friends. Because all of us in the music business knew each other the Master of Ceremonies had the spotlight shone on me, introduced me to his audience and asked if I would come to the bandstand and sing a song or two. I sang, but as fate would have it, I happened to sing the only two Latin songs I knew.

"After being escorted back to my table a gentlemen approached, introduced himself and asked if I would consider singing with his (Latin) band at downtown Los Angeles' El Sombrero Ballroom. The following afternoon, I went to the ballroom where I was nearly overwhelmed by the size of the place... where Harry James, Tommy Dorsey, Perez Prado and Tito Puente were among the many popular names routinely playing there.

"As I approached the stage, to render my audition with the ever-popular Frank Delgado band, the drummer called out, "We don't want no dames with this band." Not only was I hired at a time when Latin music was beginning to be accepted by non-Latin Americans, I sang with that band for three delightful years. I became so professionally caught up in the American craze for Latin music my name became a household word in Southern California. And the drummer who didn't want dames on his stage? He remains today as one of my dearest friends.

"Although other languages came more naturally, I learned Spanish when a promoter taught me the words to the songs I was to sing while driving to each performance. 'You don't have to know the language,' he insisted, 'only the words.' By the time I left the Frank Delgado band I had learned 67 Spanish language songs I remember to this day."

A professional dancer, June's sister Bertha traveled to Sweden to discover the family's roots. While there, she met, fell in love and teamed with another professional dancer, Gustav Wally, brother of the internationally famous banker (of the Wallenberg family) who saved many thousands of Jews from Nazi gas chambers. A few years later, Bertha died from a disease she fell victim to on a cruise ship.

June moved to Palm Springs where she worked days at Robinson's Department Store and nights as a singer. It wasn't long until her keen eye caught management's attention, and she was offered a position in Robinson's security department. Although she continued singing (with trios, quartets and quintets), she was promoted, nine years later, to Robinson's Director of Security. An attractive blonde, most the store's clientele never suspected she spent 23 years as a professional detective with as many as 18 bona fide policemen on her staff.

June returned to Manhattan Beach and met a man she resisted at first, but eventually married. Joining him on his sailboat the two spent a dozen years sailing into the sunset until it brought them to the Gulf of California. As it has for many, this incomparable place—with its incomparable sunrises, sunsets, sea life and shores—led them to a decision to make Baja California their home.

Returning to California they sold their boat, collected their belongings and headed south to build the place of their dreams. It was from that wonderful place that her husband drove into the desert one sunny day... and never returned. He was found later, taken to a hospital but never regained consciousness... and another cozy bubble had burst.

Now married to the ever-popular José Castro Castro, "Junio" inaugurated *The Gringo Gazette*, a monthly newsletter, in 1995 when she learned the men and women of her south beach community would be receptive to it. Not only is she a respected publisher, she played a leading role in the establishment of their community center and is respected throughout San Felipe as a pioneer whose heart hangs like a sky full of brilliant stars over an incomparable Baja California and Sea of Cortés.

Her photograph, from those younger years, hangs on a wall in San Felipe's El Nido restaurant. I am honored to know this delightful woman who recently celebrated her 80th birthday. She's no teenager and no longer like her "cheesecake" photos, but you'll have to travel far and wide to find a more beautiful woman.

ARQUITECTA OLIVIA VALDEZ CASTELLANOS

When I asked for this interview I had no idea what I was getting into. I met this charming woman a few years earlier when my wife and I were invited to a luncheon in her home. As a result of that and three subsequent meetings, I developed a nagging feeling I was missing something... it was one of those things I couldn't put my finger on but a feeling demanding I learn more about her. Thank heaven for intuition.

The first of four children born to Carlos and Estella Valdez, Olivia was raised in her family's hometown of Tijuana (Baja California). Owing to the absence of a bona fide high school, she departed home at age 15 to live with an aunt in Alhambra, California where she attended Mark Keppel High School.

Two years later her mother asked her to rejoin the family as they prepared to move to Guadalajara where a superior school system included both a high school and a university. Upon arrival, to her chagrin, she learned the Guadalajara High School would not accept credits earned in Alhambra, and she was required to repeat those two years before advancing to graduation.

Upon registering at the University of Guadalajara she applied for and was accepted in the College of Architecture where, seven demanding years later, she received her doctorate. Try to envision a woman born with a love for the smell of wood and a keen sense of accomplishment through construction. Envision also a woman dedicated to entering a man's world with skills and contributions to match theirs.

During her college years the family returned to Tijuana to enjoy Christmas as it should be: with parents, grandparents, aunts, uncles, brothers, sisters, nieces and nephews. As fate would have it, Olivia spent one Christmas vacation in San Felipe... and fell in love.

First her studies, then her degree and doctorate and, a thousand phone calls later, marriage to Sergio Siqueiros, a local lawyer. They made their home in San Felipe where she hung out her shingle (in 1977). Olivia saw San Felipe, a seaport community, through an architect's eyes, knowing its growth was assured. But, owing to Sergio's contact with men of the shrimping fleet, the newlyweds were to learn all that glittered was not gold.

Not only was there no high school in San Felipe, only those parents who could afford it sent their children to Mexicali schools. So it was that this dedicated couple developed a plan they presented to officials in Mexicali. Sergio and Olivia Sigueiros are the single man and woman responsible for "El Colegio de Bachilleres del Estado de Baja California"—the local high school!

In response to their impassioned pleas the authorizing members of the state government told them "Yes," they could teach in San Felipe so long as each of the other professional men and women living there taught, too. Not only did San Felipe's professionals teach...

a. They began with thirty students in one classroom, at night, in a local grade school where they remained for three years. Subjects taught by each of the "Dedicated

Dozen" were identified according to their degrees. Olivia, for example, who is an architect, taught mathematics and English.

b. They moved to the two-room facility still standing at the east side of El Toro II restaurant where they taught at night for one additional semester.

c. Relocating to the Secondaria (a local grade school), they occupied three classrooms, still teaching at night, during each of the following five years.

d. To put this in perspective, they spent a total of eight years teaching San Felipe's high school kids without pay.

During the last week of September 1985 the State of Baja California opened the doors to the newly constructed high school where Ingeniero Ignacio Rodriguez was seated as its first principal. Seven of the twelve professionals were accepted as teachers and the dream this aspiring couple dared to have so many years before was realized. San Felipe was consolidated into the state's high school fold... and its teachers began receiving pay (although the dedicated dozen never received credit for their eight pioneering years).

Regarding the teachers allowed to continue at the new school, Olivia told me with a twinkle in her eye, the physical stature of these proud men and woman was so slight they became known by their students as Snow White and the Seven Dwarfs.

Arquitecta Valdez Castellanos told me of a dream she had during those early days when she and Sergio strolled along the shore: she envisioned it lined with lights illuminating a pueblo they could be proud of. As I sat there in her office (she became the school's principal in 1998), she identified members of their first class whom I knew as Monica Carrasco (the immediate past Delegada de San Felipe), Jorge Sterling (the present Delegado), Francisco Sosa (a local judge) and his wife (a local architect). And the list goes on, for among her 25 member teaching staff are others including a psychologist, an English teacher and a computer sciences teacher.

During the last week of September 2001, this school celebrated its fifteenth anniversary—La Quinceañera—which, I was warmly told, included every available member of the local Las Amigas club. Las Amigas, I wondered? The school's first graduates were the class of '89. From that and every subsequent graduating class none but a few attended college until 1997. In that year a local women's group called "Las Amigas" came forward with a scholarship program. As a result of those scholarships, peer pressure burst upon the San Felipe scene forcing other qualified students to college.

As the years rolled by, the number of San Felipe's high school graduates attending college increased dramatically. Boarding a bus to Mexicali one day, Director Valdez could not find a seat because they were filled with former students... on their way to UABC (Universidad Autonoma de Baja California).

I asked this visionary woman whose dreams had been fulfilled, what she might wish for the future. She thought for a moment and told me, "I wish my sons would come here and put forth their energies to help this town grow." At the time one of them was studying in Ensenada and the other in Mexicali: one to become an architect, the other a civil engineer.

ANTONIO REYES VACA

This is a story of a man born into abject poverty. It is also a story of a baby boy who rose well above the Shakespearean stage of "mewling and puking in his nurse's arms." Remember Shakespeare? In *As You Like It* he wrote:

All the world's a stage,
And all the men and women merely players:
They have their exits and their entrances;
And one man in his time plays many parts,
His acts being seven ages. At first the infant,
Mewling and puking in the nurse's arms.

And then the whining schoolboy, with his satchel,
And shining morning face, creeping like snail
Unwillingly to school.

"At first the infant... " And second? In this case, between ages
three and four, Tony lost his eyesight to a cause that was never identified. His mother took him to a series of doctors, medical clinics
and specialists where tests were performed to no avail. And yet, six
months later, as quickly as his blindness came upon him it was
gone. To this day there is no answer to the problem nor has there
been any other vision-related problem. One has to wonder if this
Mexico City street urchin wasn't selected by some higher power
to...?

Tony went to school for two or three years but, because poverty knows no such luxury as the inside of a schoolroom, he quit to
join the work force. His first job was carrying groceries for women
shoppers. At his second job he helped a man make toilet seats. He
made bricks at his third job and wax candles during his fourth
although he doesn't remember how long these jobs lasted. The
problem is Tony Reyes is a man whose early life provided no relative importance to dates. He never celebrated a birthday, Christmas,
New Year's or Easter. The only things this growing boy clearly
understood was... if he showed up tomorrow he'd find work and
for it receive a morsel of food or a centavo or two.

During his fifth job, in a sweater factory, this nine or ten-year-
old boy stood on a box to work ...and he still didn't know one day
from the next. Of greater importance to him, as difficult as life was
in the 1920's and '30s', this likeable young man not only managed
to find food and clothing for himself and his mother, he found
honor, integrity and the basic moral principles that have guided him
throughout his life.

He worked in a furniture factory and then for a container man-
ufacturer who he helped with the production of specialized tanks
for soap, propane, sugar cane and gasoline. In fact, because he
never missed a day his employer sent him to job sites in (far off)

Vera Cruz (where he worked on the making of a banana boat), Cuernavaca (more tanks) and Morelos where the work was just as demanding but at least he had clothes, food and lodging. And, he had friends... who surfaced from time to time as though a guardian angel knew precisely when to offer this laborious youngster a helping hand.

As Tony and I sat in his office, he talking and I listening and writing, a smile suddenly brightened his age-wizened face. Out of the darkness of a memory of endless workdays he told me about the first time in his life, this was in Morelos, that he realized a day off. Suddenly, that is, there were Sundays... and he went to a show or a dance although the day he remembers most fondly is January 6, the day of the Three Kings. "This is the real Mexican Christmas," he beamed and went on to describe he and his pals playing together. "Life was really beautiful," he reminisced.

When World War II came to a close he began hearing about the availability of jobs in America. As time went on those same stories changed to reports of men who had gone to America and were making enough money to send some home. Tony was in *Aguas Calientes* when he made up his mind to go. Returning home, for his mother's signature on a paper verifying his age and citizenship he signed the essential contract and headed for America... by train. Now, he was a "Brasero" working on a sugar beet farm in Minnesota, wheat farms in North Dakota and asparagus in Wyoming. He didn't make much money, but he had a job, food and clothing and was sending what he could to his mom.

His eyes sparkled again and I watched him disappear behind a memory of working in the fields with "compadres." What he didn't tell me until later, was how he had suffered in that northern country's cold for it was there that the seeds of arthritis were planted and would appear later in the form of his age-twisted hands.

95

When his contract was fulfilled Tony went to California where he worked with oranges, lemons, lettuce, asparagus and cotton from San José to Bakersfield to San Fernando to Covina. In fact, he was standing on a ladder in an orange grove near Covina when men from the American Immigration Department approached and asked to see his papers.

He grinned again and told me they caught him four times and each time he was taken to Tijuana (where work seemed near-impossible to find). And, because crossing the border was the least of his problems, he returned as fast as he could to find work in the fields... spending a total of five years in the Golden State.

We read about "wet-backs" dying in the desert but who gives these dream-seeking men and women anything more than a passing thought? Tony told me he "jumped the fence" near Yuma and headed for San Diego or Los Angeles. He also told me he ate the food Californians threw away—you and I call that food "garbage."

He hid in caves, slept under bridges and did whatever it took to find work. On one occasion, in Tijuana, he was sleeping behind a pool hall when two policemen awakened him. They wanted to know who he was, where he was from and what he was doing there. They also wanted to know whether he was willing to become a thief under their protection.

If there is a man who has never committed a sin I have to believe it is Tony Reyes. (Speaking of guardian angels...) a friend found him a job in a Tijuana hotel. Shortly thereafter he realized the hotel had clients who arrived, obtained their room key, went into their room for brief periods of time and departed. Time and time again they came and went until their actions aroused his suspicions. Tony described their actions to a friend who suggested he get the key and the two of them would learn what mystery that room held. It was marijuana, and when Tony confronted the men about it, they offered him a job he promptly declined... even with the prospect of "making real money."

Tony met another man in that hotel, a fisherman from San Diego who told him how California's Ray Cannon had discovered the underwater riches of the Sea of Cortés. He suggested Tony go there because it was bound to become a fisherman's boomtown.

During the interview I saw a photo of a school of sardine-feasting totoava churning the water along a San Felipe beach. Standing in their midst was a man who reached into the violent water to grab one of these 150 pound giants by the gills and drag it ashore. The fish were so preoccupied with feasting that they paid no attention to the man's presence.

On another occasion, some 15 years earlier, I spoke to a 90-year-old fisherman who described to me a monstrous school of corvina in a similar circumstance, the surf literally boiling at water's edge. Consequently, because I am a mental time traveler, I can envision the millions (or was it billions?) of fishes the Cortés has known at any given time and their unbelievable feeding frenzies (See Part four, Chapter four) before the mid-20th century.

As a man who has studied the Cortés I will describe the period from 1947 to 1977 as the "period of discovery" before which this incomparable sea was indescribably rich and after which it was tragically depleted.

Tony landed in San Felipe on the leading edge of its first real fishing boom. Although the sea had known commercial fishing for several years that enterprise made no significant change in what was then the world's richest body of salt water.

While spending his first week searching for work he met a man who helped him get a job on a shrimp boat... and Tony discovered seasickness (although he got over it). He went to Ensenada when San Felipe's shrimp season closed but learned most boat captains had long-established crews. Owing to his persistence, however, he landed a job painting a fishing boat. While that job progressed the boat's owner told him he liked the way Tony worked and offered him a job as a deck hand on a sport fishing boat.

For the following three years Tony worked on sport-fishing boats out of San Felipe and Ensenada. And then (another guardian angel?), after buying his first fishing skiff, he rowed a friend (four round-trip miles) to a favored spot off Mt. Machorro's rocky point... for five dollars. That man was so impressed by Tony's sincerity and dedication to work that he found an outboard motor for him (in California), purchased it, brought it to San Felipe, gave it to Tony and allowed him to pay for it in monthly installments.

Now realizing the full measure of the bounty to be reaped in the Cortés, Tony entered into a partnership with San Felipe's Alfredo Ascolani (senior) who owned six fishing skiffs with 10 and 15 horsepower motors. But, owing to an age-old problem, Tony wanted men he could trust to take those boats out and return with all of the day's catch.

When (and only when) he had the men he sought he began a full-fledged sport fishing business. Because this business can make or break a man quickly, he made two startling discoveries: his need for the English language and "the early bird gets the worm." That is, he discovered clients were being lost because most of the fishing boat operators failed to make themselves available when prospective customers wanted to go out. Because there is wantonness to fishing that dictates being where the fish are at the crack of dawn Tony and his crew woke at 3:00 a.m., reported to their boats at 4:00 (for essential preparations), boarded their clients and were heading out to sea by 5:00.

Tony paused for a moment, reflecting on some distant memory, and displayed another incomparable grin as he

described the making of lures out of white-painted fish-
ing weights with double hooks... and his clients reaped
the benefits of a thinking man's enterprise. In fact, Tony's
lures have been sought in San Felipe for many years.

Owing to the fact that Tony conducted a "hands-on" study of the totoava's migratory habits during these early years, he obtained a beachside property opposite the one island in the northern Cortés that they periodically visited. He called the place Campo Miramar although shortly thereafter he changed its name to "Okie Landing" because his clients called anyone who lost a fish an "Okie farmer."

He met a man named David Fink, owner of Davie's Locker in Newport Beach, California, who suggested Tony buy a sports fishing boat and conduct three- and five-day fishing tours. Acting on David's recommendation (as a trial effort), Tony rented a commercial shrimp boat, boarded his clients in San Felipe (and Okie Landing) and gained valuable experience as a sports fishing businessman. In fact, owing to his superior knowledge of the best totoava fishing spots he gained a popularity among sports fishing enthusiasts that resulted in a bevy of clients who have remained with him over the past 25, 30 and 35 years.

Located abreast Isla Lobos (one of Baja, California's Islas Encantadas) Okie Landing is about halfway between Puertecitos and Bahia San Luis Gonzaga. With rented shrimp boats at his disposal his clients boarded his boat at San Felipe or Okie Landing, depending on where the totoava were running.

Whereas Ray Cannon received many accolades for being singularly responsible for awakening Baja, California's fishing industry to the riches of the Sea of Cortés he never met Tony until the day he limped into Okie Landing with an ailing fishing boat motor (which Tony was instrumental in repairing). Prior to that meeting, however, Cannon had written and telephoned Tony many times to inquire about the totoava's migratory habits. Consequently, Cannon wrote about Tony Reyes and his fishing tours in more than one of his many articles for *Western Outdoor News*.

Tony entered into a partnership agreement with the owner of

the San Felipe-based trawler Santa Monica. After outfitting it with 21-foot skiffs and outboard motors he spent the following five years building his fishing tours business. During that period a friend introduced Tony to Tom Ward of Orange, California. Not only did Tom want to become a distant part of the Sea of Cortés fishing boom, he rounded up investors who loaned Tony a large sum of money, recommended a particular fishing boat Tony could buy (in Sonora's Puerto Peñasco) and helped him modify that boat from a fishing trawler to a bona fide sports fisher, which was accomplished in San Felipe.

Tom Ward, who had been a gasoline station owner/operator for many years, opened a business he called "Longfin Fishing Supplies" and became an agent for Tony Reyes Fishing Tours.

When the new boat was ready, Tony had all new 21 foot skiffs with 45-horsepower motors, a reconditioned boat and a list of dedicated clients waiting to join him in San Felipe. On the appointed day and in the traditional fashion, Tony, his investors and privileged clients commissioned the *José Andrés* with a specially selected bottle of champagne and took it to sea for what proved to be another memorable fishing voyage.

Consequently, from that first five dollar bill he collected for rowing a friend to Punta Machorro (and back), to $75.00 fishing cruises, to today's ($800.00 per person) five-day fishing tours to Baja's midriff islands, Tony Reyes literally catapulted himself into the driver's seat by way of a dedication to learning everything he could about sports and commercial (totoava) fishing.

Born June 13, 1923, this diminutive man not only owned his own boat at age thirty-three, he also became one of the most highly respected sports fishermen in San Felipe with a reputation for honesty and integrity that spread from San Felipe to San Diego to Long Beach, Orange County and Los Angeles. His clients number in the thousands, and their catches can be measured in as many tons of grouper, totoava (until it was placed on the Endangered Species list), red snapper, corvina, yellowfin tuna and a dozen other fishes from the world's most prolific sea.

Continuing now with Shakespeare's *As You Like It*, we find:

And then the lover
Sighing like furnace, with a woful ballad
Made to his mistress' eyebrow. Then a soldier,
Full of strange oaths, and bearded like the pard
Jealous in honour, sudden and quick in quarrel,
Seeking the bubble reputation
Even in the cannon's mouth. And then in justice,
In fair round belly with good capon lin'd,
With eyes severe, and beard of formal cut
Full of wise saws and modern instances;
And so he plays his part. The sixth age shifts
Into the lean and slipper'd pantaloon,
With spectacles on nose and pouch on side,
His youthful hose well sav'd a world too wide
For his shrunk shank; and his big manly voice,
Turning again towards childish treble, pipes
And whistles in his sound.

Tony married the girl of his dreams, Dolores Montez of Bahia de Los Angeles, who bore him a son... and the boy went to sea with his dad (and with one of Tony's best friends) to learn the business from the bottom up. Today, while wife and mother looks after the home, 33-year-old Tony Junior is the captain of the *José Andrés* (Tony never held Captain's papers) and the man I interviewed became Director of Public Relations, Tony Reyes Fishing Tours.

Here, then, is a man who never forgot his family ...or his meager beginnings. Regarding family, his mother (who never learned to read or write) passed away (about a dozen years ago) at age 113. He's lost four siblings to date but is close to all remaining brothers and sisters.

Regarding his meager beginnings, many of San Felipe's poor (men, women and children) have benefited from Tony's unending kindness (in the form of food, clothing, money and computers) although he performs his deeds anonymously. Actions I am permitted to describe include the use of his house for the storage of books and equipment solicited by San Felipe's Bill and Kay Gabbard.

Several years ago Bill and Kay started a unique program they called "Book Buddies" under which they roam the American Southwest soliciting American schools to adopt local schools for the purpose of contributing books (in the Spanish language), classroom equipment and materials and funds to permit the creation of libraries, modernized classrooms and newly painted buildings (inside and out).

When a detachment of soldiers came to town, for drug interdiction purposes, they had little more than the typical military outdoor equipage (tents, cots and open cooking fires). Upon learning the detachment was here to stay, it was Tony Reyes who initiated such a substantial movement on their behalf that the federal government authorized the funding and construction of two major multi-storied barracks buildings in which these men could live (sleep, eat and relax) like any other resident.

For the past three years, on behalf of San Felipe's Las Amigas Club, Tony has donated a six-day fishing cruise to the winner of a fund-raising lottery. What's more, he is frequently heard broadcasting the beauty of San Felipe over a popular San Diego radio station. At 79 years of age Tony Reyes is not only San Felipe's elder statesman but, like a star shining in the east; he is this pueblo's patriarch.

Tony has never owned a camera and yet he has more than a thousand photographs of his and his clients' successes. In fact, during the interview, he sorted through several door-sized panels of mounted photographs until, finding the one he sought, he showed me shots that expressed his thoughts rather clearly. Pointing to particular photos he commented, "You know, I think you may be seeing photos no one has ever seen."

Regarding his photos you can see them, too, on San Felipe's web site (www.sanfelipe.com.mx) where Tony Reyes' fishing reports are updated weekly.

Finally, were I to conclude this interview with Shakespeare's final lines from the above quoted excerpt, you would read how he described the seventh stage. Instead, I prefer to ask you to envision this incomparable man as he is today... with a modest grin on his age-wizened face that says, "Life is really beautiful."

Figure 5a – Sierra San Pedro Martir

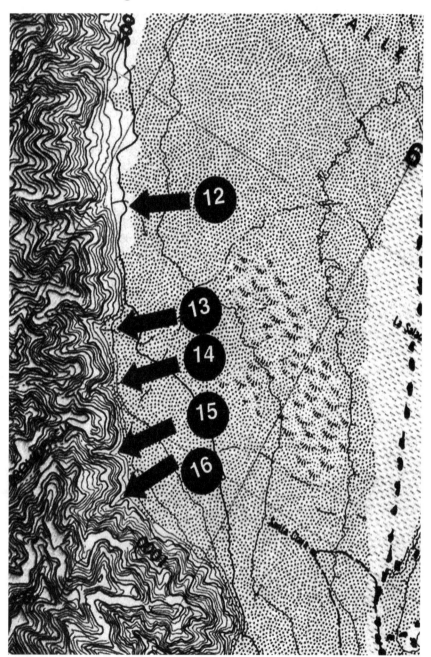

CHAPTER THREE
Sierra San Pedro Martir

FAMILIARIZATION

The beauty of Baja California is dependent upon the eye of the beholder. To me, that beauty begins with the knowledge of its manufacture by the plate tectonic processes of subduction, accretion, mountain building and volcanism. Having begun, my enjoyment of Baja's beauty continues throughout every minute of every day of floral, faunal and weathering activity.

Imagine rainbows of color displayed by thousands of acres of geologic scenery displayed by its Sierra Pinta. Imagine, too, what Freda and I sat and watched while returning from market recently: a bobcat stalking a jackrabbit alongside the roadway. Separated by less than 25 meters, each sat motionless with ears erect and eyes alerted to the least amount of motion until the rabbit suddenly ran to a nearby bush. When the cat followed, each like a bolt of lightning, there was naught to be found. And that, dear friends, that rare opportunity to see nature in action, makes this community as beautiful as any can possibly be.

Geologically speaking, the Baja California peninsula is divided into a continental borderland in the west, a mountainous backbone structure, central plateaus and basins, and desert ranges in the east. Gold, iron, aluminum, copper, silver and sulfur are found in the mountains. Dinosaur fossils, petrified wood and fossilized seashells are scattered along lower regions.

There are three-meters-wide, doughnut-shaped rock formations known as patterned ground. There are agates, onyx, turquoise and geodes. There is jet-black sand, natural glass and a variety of volcanic lavas. There are forests, rivers, waterfalls and cacti. There are 195 plants that grow naturally nowhere else in the world. (As suggested earlier, this is a God-created place for experimentation.)

Whereas western Sonora and parts of southern Arizona boast of their stately saguaro cactus (*Carnegiea gigantea*), Baja, California claims cardón (*Pachycereus pringlei*), the king of all cacti. Towering to 50 feet in the greater San Felipe region, it grows to 70 feet along Baja's Magdalena Plain. (See the cover of the Baja, California Plant Field Guide.)

There are mountain lions, bobcats and mountain sheep; coyotes, foxes and badgers; jack rabbits, bunny rabbits, ground hogs, squirrels and chipmunks. There are snakes (14 varieties of rattlesnakes), scorpions, mate venados (MAH-tay ven-AH-dose or deer killers) and tarantula killers.

There are prickly pear, cholla, ocotillo and ocotillo's granddaddy, cirio (*Idria columnaris*), which is more popularly known in Arizona by its Indian name "boojum." There are farms upon which cotton, corn, garlic and chilies are grown. Other farms produce oranges, lemons, avocados and beans; coconuts, pineapple, potatoes and squash; wheat, grapes, melons and cattle.

There are Tijuana, Ensenada, San Quintín and La Paz; Mexicali, San Felipe, Loreto and Cabo San Lucas. There are fog, rain, snow and heat ...and there is danger. Baja, California is not for everyone. It is mostly desert, mostly remote and sufficiently foreign to be labeled inhospitable although it is paradise to some.

To place this inhospitable land in the context of this book, many of the plants and animals listed above are found within the greater San Felipe Valley region. Freda and I, for example, have picked vine-ripened grapes, watermelons and cantaloupe therein. In addition, there are two cattle ranches and, a few years ago, other prospective ranchers considered a part of a nearby valley for the establishment of an ostrich farm.

DIRECTIONS (in general)

The Sierra San Pedro Martir Mountains are best described in association with their "apron," the San Felipe Valley and, beyond the apron, the Sierra San Felipe. Although these two mountain ranges uplifted during separate geologic eras, like boyfriend and girlfriend they are inseparable: a happy couple sharing the space between them. What's more, the access to each is via a complex network of roads.

The eastern margin of the Sierra San Pedro Martir, for description purposes only, is situated along two north-south lines (a fault, actually) separated by a one-mile offset. This offset is located along a line drawn from the mouth of Diablito Canyon across the valley to School House Point, a local feature named by me for explanatory purposes in this book only. There is a shell of an old school house and there is a point that is the terminus of a particular mountain structure (appearing much like a gigantic comma) rising out of the ground to form a part of the Sierra San Felipe. Of interest is the fact that the San Felipe uplifted along a parallel fault with the same type of offset.

There are twenty true canyons (and several false canyons) carved into the San Pedro's eastern escarpment. (See Figure 5a) From north to south they are identified as Las Abejas, Esperanza (Map Key #12), Copal (#13), Copalito (#14), Diablo (#15) and Diablito (#16). Moving beyond the offset (see Figure 5b), central and southern canyons include Providencia (#17), Tulare (a false canyon), Teledo (#18), En Medio (#19), Oso #20), Cajón (#21), Barroso (#22), Rubí, Verenda, Cardonal, Agua Caliente (see Figure 5c, map key #23), Carrizo, Parral (key #24), and Matomí (#25). I have not investigated (minor canyons) Abejas, Copalito, Rubí, Carrizo or Verenda. Until Hurricane Nora, Agua Caliente had hot springs she buried under at least six feet of eroded overburden.

Whereas geographical features are usually named by cartographers, owing to a multiplicity of cartographers in the greater San Felipe region, there is confusion over the name of the valley separating the Sierra San Pedro Martir and the Sierra San Felipe. One of those cartographers labeled the entire 60-mile valley as "San Felipe." Two others divided this valley into three distinguishable segments and named each separately. The northern segment (between Federal Highway #3 and an east-west line drawn from Diablito Canyon to School House Point) is "Valle Santa Clara." From this line south (less than five miles) to the northern boundary of the central valley vineyard is "Valle San Felipe". The remainder of the valley was called "Valle Chico."

Access to the canyons is as follows: two north-south roads originating at Highway #3 have no names, so I refer to them as West Valley Road and East Valley Road. More properly, perhaps, they may be called the low road (west) and high road (east)— important designations considering the (Santa Clara) valley's dry lakebed and those (annual) occasions when it is a quagmire.

An estimated 65 percent of the Santa Clara's floor is composed of lakebed seasonally softened by rain. Following an imaginary line drawn along the lakebed's longitudinal center West Valley Road is used by farmers, visitors, passersby and racers. This roadway, widened by those preferring not to drive in another vehicle's wheel tracks, is rock-hard in places and dusty in others.

From an Indian's standpoint dust raised by vehicles traversing the lakebed is an easily seen signal. From a sports enthusiast's standpoint (the boy in many of us) it is a place to play: to spin "hookers" (tight circles) and figure eights or speed along a sharply zigzagging path (while wives hold on in utter frustration).

In addition, there are places throughout this northern valley segment where a natural phenomenon called "face powder dust" is encountered. This stuff, when encountered, billows off tires to fill the air with blinding, choking particles that fall on everything within its sphere. Driving through these random sites is one of those occasions when, if you bathed immediately thereafter, and someone saw that bath water, they'd swear you hadn't bathed in a year. Consequently, facemasks are seriously advised.

East Valley Road, the high road, branches into four roads at School House Point: two of them lead (south and west) to the lakebed and two lead east to skirt the lakebed. Of these latter two, beginning as a Y on the east side of School House Point, the left road remains on high ground while the other passes through potentially muddy terrain along the outer fringe of the lakebed.

The high road leads east and south to intersect West Valley Road at the lakebed's southeastern terminus. From this intersection south the roads have but one name each: West Valley Road and East Valley Road (although they remain high and low roads, respectively).

From this point south West Valley Road runs parallel to the base of the San Pedro (although separated from it by at least a mile) via a remote desert community called "Agua Caliente" to its southern terminus at Arroyo Matomí. East Valley Road leads around the east side of a large farm and up the Sierra San Felipe escarpment to intersect Saltito Road (21.5 kilometers west of Federal Highway #5). From that intersection it leads south within one to two miles of the western base of the Sierra San Felipe.

To enjoy valley and canyon features, we usually depart San Felipe via Highway #5 to Saltito Road, turn west and drive to East or West Valley Road depending on our destination.

a) If we're visiting Providencia, Diablito or Diablo canyons, we drive around the farm to its operational headquarters (a large, white Butler building), where we turn west on a new road and proceed to destination.

b) Should our destination be Rancho Chinalito, Copal or Esperanza canyons, Rancho San Pedro Martir or other points north, we proceed north around the farm to the high road and thence to the dry lakebed at any opportune access point.

An interesting landmark visible along this northern route is a granitic avenue descending the east face of the San Pedro between Esperanza and Abejas canyons. This "avenue" is the result of the earthen overburden sliding away to expose an estimated 30 feet wide swath of solid rock spanning the distance from the top of the mountain to the desert floor. I have often wondered whether Indians enjoyed that avenue during periodic rites to prove manhood.

Should our destination be Agua Caliente or Parral Canyon, we generally proceed south from San Felipe via the old Puertecitos Road to Arroyo Huatamote, turn west (into the arroyo) and continue to destination.

Should our destination be Arroyo Matomí, we drive south via Highway #5 but have a choice of proceeding via Crazy Horse Canyon or continuing along the highway to kilometer marker 57 where we turn west onto the Matomí and continue to destination. Each of these locations is described in detail on following pages.

THE NORTHERN CANYONS

The entrance to Esperanza Canyon is hidden but in a picturesque setting with ample parking space under cooling trees where a footpath leads to the canyon's lower and upper pools. Find the canyon on Figure 5a and then find Rancho San Pedro Martir. Head for the ranch but turn on the northeast side of it onto an access road leading past the ranch to the canyon.

Alongside this road you will see random pieces of a six-inch diameter plastic pipe that the ranch's new owners installed in '94. Running between the ranch and Esperanza, its purpose was to provide a continuous supply of water. Imagine the cost of that pipe, its transportation to the ranch, the labor to install it, piece by piece, and the joy realized when it delivered the first drops of water to house and cattle. But, along came Hurricane Nora… Today, the several miles of that broken pipe lay as a sad reminder of the naiveté of uninformed newcomers.

The entrance to Copal Canyon can be impossible to find unless you have the ability to read the desert floor and approach via its drainage waterway. The only other access is via the density of brush on either side of that waterway, a transit most folks don't care for. I call it "cutting trail," and it is the way I prefer to drive. Who, for example, learns anything while following a road created by others?

With Pepe and Em Garcia, and Art and Margo Madsen, I led the way to Copal one day, via the density of local desert brush (from north to south). Because there were times when I could not see appreciably ahead, I hit the brakes on one occasion when I realized I was about to drop some 20 feet into Arroyo Copal. On seeing my brake lights, Art whizzed alongside to ask what had happened. When he saw the Copal he couldn't believe his eyes; it is that impressive. We drove a few hundred meters north, dropped into the arroyo on a 45-degree (down) angle and proceeded to destination.

Copalito is another surprise because it is a shallow, vertically arranged canyon with a small farm located at the entrance to it. This little farm is in a truly beautiful setting with ample trees and an attractive vegetable garden. Surprisingly, as vertical as the canyon is, the surrounding terrain shows no appreciable signs of canyon debris. I suspect whoever owns this truly remote ranchette feels he and she are in their own paradise.

Diablo, on the other hand, is a prominent canyon draining a sizeable watershed. Owing to a monstrous natural dam blocking any direct approach, access to the canyon's mouth is via a quarter-mile-long pathway from the parking area. From this point, the dam gradually tapers to ground level although it is littered with boulders throughout its half-mile length. Suffice it to say the canyon's runoff is in a duly channeled northeasterly direction.

111

From this point of entrance (via the pathway, that is) it is a 100 meter walk over (knee destroying) rocks to a ten-foot water slide. This natural feature is a bona fide polished granite slide emptying into an eight-foot-deep pond. The water in this pond is so clear the algae growing on its rocky bottom gives it an emerald green radiance.

From the slide it is another 500 meters to a picturesque waterfall beyond which none but dedicated mountain climbers pass. This waterfall, and the eroded granite wall it flows against, make good photocopy for anyone interested in unique scenery. That wall is dished with two distinguishable contours indicating at least two speeds (volumes) of flowing water. Here again, the wandering mind will envision a million years (or more) of flow.

Diablo Canyon is the primary access route to Baja's tallest mountain, Picacho del Diablo. Whereas I've been in Diablo at least a dozen times, I learned about this canyon in dramatic detail from one of the two men who guided Freda and me to Vallecitos. That detail is the subject of Chapter Four.

The next canyon south is Diablito. Located precisely at the mountain's 90-degree turn to the east, Diablito is a connecting link to Providencia Canyon. Drainage is not as good here as in other canyons and for that reason there is a swamp in the mouth of the canyon beyond which it is appreciably difficult to pass. Whereas the canyon seems to have many visitors, I sincerely believe most of them came here by mistake, having missed the turnoff to Diablo Canyon.

The entrance to Providencia Canyon is located along the eastern base of Baja's tallest mountain. Access to it is via Diablo/Diablito access road originating at the Butler Building mentioned earlier. Although I lead tour participants to this canyon on a biennial basis parking is limited and somewhat difficult. Beyond the parking area it is an easy walk to the canyon, a small pond (particularly appreciated on warm days) and nearby Indian drawings that serve, for some of us, as a reminder of the men and women who preceded us by a few hundred years.

Another feature worth mentioning is a mile-long ridge extending (eastward) into the valley from the foot of Picacho. This damlike structure stands at least 100 feet tall at the base of the mountain and tapers to valley floor. So abrupt is it, as regards valley floor contour, that the access road from south to north (from the Butler Building to a nearby brahma bull ranch) skirts the eastern tip of the ridge.

CHAPTER FOUR
Assault on the Devil

The room was crowded but quiet (Salvador León and me, his wife and mine, their teenaged daughters and her parents); the lights were low. Salvador pressed a button, and the first slide flashed onto the screen. This was a moment I'd been waiting for: a view of northeastern Baja, California from the top of its tallest mountain. At 41 years of age, Salvador had climbed that mountain with eight other men (both older and younger than he).

They called themselves "Los Rurales" (The Rangers). The best of friends, they were outdoorsmen who frequently took part in Baja's most grueling walking and climbing adventures. Over the previous three years, for example, each had participated in Baja, California's annual "*Caminata*," a 68 mile overland hike from the Pacific Ocean to the Sea of Cortés while one of the eight, Alfonso Cardona, participated in the tortuous 1000 mile "Mission Walk" from Cabo San Lucas to San Diego via Baja, California's 21 Spanish mission sites.

In October of '89 the Rurales were returning from a cross-country hike to Mike's Sky Ranch (in the northern Sierra San Pedro Martir) when, during a rest stop in sight of the 10,154 foot tall Picacho del Diablo, one of them laughed and, pointing to it, said, "That's what I call a real cross-country walk." Eight heads turned as one to stare at the rocky devil. Eroded by more than 90 million years of sun, wind, rain, snow and ice, Picacho stands as a sentinel guarding a land comparatively few are intimately aware of: Baja California, the world's longest oceanic peninsula.

One hundred miles south of the international border at Mexicali, Picacho del Diablo is a part of the eastern boundary of the Sierra San Pedro Martir, the granitic backbone of this five million-year-old peninsula. From its lofty heights, the eye can see nearly 200 miles in any direction.

Salvador began logistics and route planning the day the Rangers returned from the Sierra. They began their physical training with bicycle rides and running up and down a flight of 40 stairs. As their legs and lungs developed, Cardona, who became their leader for this endeavor, led them to four of the most difficult climbing sites in northeastern Baja. They climbed El Centinela twice. Steep, dangerous and painful, they found descending more difficult than the five hours spent climbing this ancient volcano (20 miles west of Mexicali).

They climbed the sandy banks of the Sierra Cucapah three times, seven hours per climb, the sand taking its toll in calf muscles. (Bordered in the east and west by Federal Highway #5 and the L-shaped Laguna Salada, respectively.)

Cerro Prieto, the dormant volcano flanking Mexicali's geothermal site, was another five-hour climb and hard on the lungs. By the end of their second ascent, however, they felt their bodies coming into shape and decided they were ready for the dreaded Carrizo (a backbone mountain canyon) with backpacks! Following their second successful assault on Carrizo, they declared themselves ready for Picacho.

Each man was responsible for his own food and medicine. Each carried 15 freeze-dried meals and a first aid kit (with band-aids, a snakebite kit, aspirin, moleskin, personal medication, lip balm and tweezers). Their toiletries included toilet paper, a comb, a toothbrush and paste, soap, one small towel and "Wet Ones."

Special clothing included hiking boots and two pairs of stockings: men's silk stockings for protection against blisters and heavy cotton stockings for moisture absorption, cushioning and heat radiation. Other garments included thermal underwear, tee and polo shirts, sweaters and bright-colored jackets.

They wore loose-fitting trousers with extra pockets. Gloves, goggles and wool caps completed their attire. Safety gear included sunglasses, whistles, mirrors, ropes and two-way radios. Additional equipment (carried by each man) included a sleeping pad, a sleeping bag, flashlight with extra batteries, a compass, topographic maps, two canteens, a cooking kit, a water filter, waterproof matches, a Swiss survival knife, a lightweight nylon tarpaulin and a space blanket. Several of the men carried a camera and film. Each had trash bags; two of them carried folding aluminum chairs.

On April 27, 1990, splitting into two groups, three of the men drove to the west coast (south of the pueblo of San Telmo) and then east to the National Observatory located at the 9000-foot level ten kilometers north of Picacho. Leaving their car in the safety of the observatory, they donned their heavy packs and hiked several hours down to their first overnight camp. Their goal was Campo Noche where they were to meet their friends at the end of the second day.

Departing Mexicali at the same hour, the remaining six men drove to the foot of Picacho at the southwest corner of Santa Clara Valley. Donning backpacks, they began their assault via Diablo Canyon. Ten hours later they, too, camped for the night.

Arriving at Campo Noche at four the following afternoon, the climbers had experienced a grueling nine-hour hike over boulders and ice-slick walls of granite. Two hours later, when the men of Group A arrived, the team made plans for the following day's climb to Slot Wash at the 7,500 foot level.

Campo Noche is 6300 feet above sea level. A standard safety rule for climbers dictates climbing no more than 2000 feet per day above the six thousand-foot level followed by one day of rest to allow the body the time it needs to adapt to altitude.

High altitude sickness, caused by decreased atmospheric pressure at altitudes where less oxygen is available to the lungs, is a potential problem faced by anyone who ascends to altitudes above 6000 feet. Mountain climbers, however, are exposed to acute mountain sickness (a form of high altitude sickness), high altitude pulmonary edema (an accumulation of fluid in the lungs) and high altitude cerebral edema (swelling of the brain) when they ascend too rapidly to elevations above the prescribed 2000-foot increments.

After a good night's rest the nine-man team began its third day of climbing. They had already come 17 grueling miles and, with 3,854 feet remaining, had several more miles to climb.

Regarding hiking and mountain climbing, a Class II climb is along level ground plus up and down steep hills without the use of the hands. Class III involves steep slopes and boulder hopping. A Class IV climb is a steep ascent involving critical use of the hands while a Class V climb involves ropes, picks, hammers and pitons. The Rangers' assault on Picacho included classes III and IV.

Boulder hopping and scaling shear bluffs the team arrived at Slot Wash campsite (7,500 feet) at 10:00 a.m. and enjoyed a refreshing breakfast while checking in (by radio) with safety centers in San Felipe, Ensenada and San Diego. Ensenada, however, had a grim warning for the climbers: a storm was on the way with 100 mile per hour winds and temperatures cold enough for ice. If it hit the Rangers while aloft, they could be isolated with little or no chance for a rescue party to break through.

Weighing the hazards of exceeding the daily ascent limit, the team elected to continue—with the barest essentials only—believing they could safely make it to the top and back before the storm hit. Two hundred meters from the top, however, one of the men collapsed in the rarified air, his heart racing, blood streaming from his nose.

Now the character of their friendship comes into focus. With success in view—the rim of the earth but 200 meters above—they turned to their fallen brother to lower him to safety on a litter. But that was not to be. The fallen man rallied bravely, suggesting he could descend to Slot Wash alone while his buddies achieved their goal. But Armando Renaum had a different idea. The strongest of the group, he alone guided and assisted his ailing brother to the Wash after racing to the top to enable his claim on the mountain.

Not only had their assault on the Devil been a demanding climb, most of these stalwart men were not mountain climbers in the technical sense. Although outdoorsmen, they were husbands, fathers and businessmen who now stood in the land of the lion and mountain sheep.

Reaching the top and overwhelmed by their success, several of them wept uncontrollably. But the view alone from this monumental mountain could do that to anyone. The achievement of their goal had been difficult but thrilling. In fact, Salvador, whose eyes twinkled with fond memories, told me it was incomparable.

They began their descent after posing for pictures, signing the concealed log at the top, and photographing surrounding scenes. Now, however, because descending involved a different set of hazards, the climbers needed their ropes.

Upon their arrival in Slot Wash at six that afternoon, they found their friend sufficiently recovered to descend to Campo Noche by himself (rather than on a litter). After making that descent with flashlights held in their mouths they reported their position to the three safety centers.

Thirty-six hours later, one and one-half grueling days of rock hopping descent, slipping and sliding on trousers with seats ripped out, Los Rurales stood safely alongside their cars smiling at the devil's peak. There had been nothing easy about Picacho... in either direction.

Staring at the giant they grinned with a thankful self-assurance that said, "Por Diós, we made it." Then, tired and sore, faces swollen, muscles aching as they'd never ached before, the teammates headed home to their families, to soft beds and a few days of well-earned rest. Although one car remained at the observatory, it could wait.

Less than two months later, on June 22nd, the man who didn't make it, forty-two year old Alberto Gruel, stood with Cardona atop Picacho with three others who had never before been there. It was a dream come true for each of these proud men who would eventually tell their grandchildren of the time they made... an Assault on the Devil.

CHAPTER FIVE
The Yucca Department

It was 8:15 on a Sunday morning in spring. I was working at my computer when Pepe Garcia drove up. "Mornin' Pepe," I called when I saw him through a window.

"Mornin', Bruce. Wanna go to the ranch?"

"When?" I inquired, reflecting on Freda's presence in church.

"Now. Em and I are leaving as soon as I get home. We're doing lunch so you won't need anything but your drinks."

"Okay." I acknowledged. "We'll see you there."

The Ranch, I thought. What a super place. Nestled at the 4000-foot level in a small mountain valley, Rancho San Francisco was the property of Alberto and Aurora Dojáquez, a couple about our age who'd bought the land, developed it and moved there from Mexicali when Alberto felt a growing population closing in on him.

They brought nine children into the world, eight daughters and a son. The girls were married and gone now while 21-year-old Gilberto remained at home. Although he'd worked in Indio and Los

Angeles, he returned to the ranch to be his own boss, doing what he enjoyed most. He was as much a part of this ranch as anything or anyone on it.

Father and son had cleared the land, removing trees, bushes, cacti and rocks. They built the house and prepared the soil for what was to become both home and commercial growing plots. They erected fences, horse stalls and a small barn. They even built a second house as an income property.

As the seasons wore on, they prepared additional land and slowly but surely increased the size of their tiny farm until satisfied with the acreage they had under cultivation. Today, these self-styled farmers are reaping a handsome harvest from apples, beans, chilies, corn, peaches, zinnias and roses in addition to their cattle and horses.

Pepe and Em stumbled on the place during one of their camping trips. They introduced themselves, chatted for a while, and the four struck a lasting friendship resulting in visits to the ranch and return visits by Aurora and Alberto to San Felipe. Freda and I were invited a year later.

Thirty miles north, 45 west and a dozen miles south; it was an enjoyable drive through a magnificent part of the desert. In fact, the desert from Cerro Chinero (at the eastern terminus of Mexico's Federal Highway #3) to the foot of the escarpment is as interesting and as varied as one can imagine. I like to think of it as a nursery through which we pass distinctly separate departments.

Along the coastal plain the *ocote* department displays varieties of Ocotillo, their flowers creating a (visual) blanket of orange across the entire desert plain. Climbing Borrego Pass, we come upon the cholla department where a thousand thousand plants are on display in every stage of life. Colors here range from bright yellow to a pleasing shade of rust.

Stopping at the summit we take time for a snack, photographs of Picacho and a (nearby) landmark vent volcano. The view from this place includes a 30-mile panorama of former sea floor (Valle Santa Clara) towered over by the stately mountains.

The maguey department at the north end of the Santa Clara Valley was in brilliant yellow bloom on stalks that had risen 10 to 15 feet above ground. On the ground chipmunks (locally called "Juanchitos") narrowly avoided doom brought on by speeding tires as they darted back and forth across the highway.

Throughout most of the year the desert displays such brilliant shades of green it causes me to ponder the oft-heard expression "a barren desert." I resolve the matter as I did in business when and where I encountered an unfortunate abundance of 20/20 vision incapable of finding beauty. It is an awakening story involving the differences between us all.

San Matias Pass is a 1500-foot ascent to the tiny pueblo of San Matias. It also separates the Sierra San Pedro Martir from the Sierra de Juarez. Approaching San Matias, a tiny Mexican community nestled on a desert plain we pass through the biznaga (barrel cactus) department and later, when we turn off the highway for the final leg of our journey, the yucca department.

At this elevation we happily escape the desert's heat but are not ready to turn our backs on it forever. San Felipe, after all, is our paradise by the sea while this place, high in the ancient mountains, is for trees, mountain lions, bobcats and deer.

The rocks we passed were naturally sculpted and occasionally adorned with piñon pine. An exposure of ancient volcanic ridges completes the scene as we crossed riverbeds whose sediments lay at the bottom of the Cortés some 75 miles east.

Towering clouds silhouetted steep-walled canyons rising above us, occasional sheets of rain discernible in the distance. It was a beautiful morning during which motoring along the lightly wash-boarded road was a pleasure.

Our arrival at the ranch found Pepe and Gilberto chopping wood while Em was at work in the kitchen. Aurora was visiting a daughter in Los Angeles, and Alberto was in the nearby community of Valle Trinidad buying feed for his livestock.

With camera in hand I headed for the four corners of the ranch while Freda went to the kitchen. Along the way I encountered cameramen from Mexicali doing a series for a magazine article they were writing. During a previous visit I had seen samples of their work and envied its quality. We exchanged greetings and stood for an hour comparing notes on the beauty of Baja. What these men didn't know about wall paintings wasn't worth knowing. What's more, humbled by their descriptions of places I hadn't yet experienced, it was during this meeting that I received an invitation for a field trip to Vallecitos.

We returned to the house where I paid my respects to Alberto as the eight of us sat to enjoy carne asada, paella, corn on the cob, baked marinated chicken, a garden-fresh salad, guacamole, piping hot corn tortillas and cool, refreshing beer in the shade of a grape-covered arbor. Our conversation ran the gamut but centered on living where this humble man and his wife had found happiness far from the madding crowd.

At this remote mountain ranch we found friendship, an outpouring of warmth and an appreciation for the mysteries of life. At this refreshing place we discovered the beauty of the yucca department, which goes deeper than the scenes cameras record. At this enviable spa we rediscovered the backbone quality of the Baja California we've learned to love so much. At day's end, hating to leave but knowing we must, Freda and I prepared to return to our own Shangri-La.

"Cuando regresan (When will you return)?" asked Alberto as we turned to walk to our car.

I thought for a moment and, speaking for the two of us, replied, "Mañana, señor. Mañana is soon enough for me."

Regarding this upper region, and another occasion, Freda and I departed San Felipe with Pepe and Em to investigate the mountains above Rancho San Francisco. Finding a road to the east within a half-mile of the ranch, we followed it until we came to a dead end almost directly below (west of) the national observatory, which is perched on a peak at the 9,000-foot level.

Exploring that upper territory, we came upon two magnificent stands of pines and cedars, a fenced cattle ranch, a large brick house, a barn and a herd of cattle. In another direction we drove through a remote stand of burned cedars. How unfortunate it is that Mexico does not provide the funding (or governmental manpower) to fight forest fires in Baja California.

Later, on still another road, we came upon another cattle ranch (called "Cienaguita"), a smaller ranch, an old garnet mine and the north-south road from Trinidad Valley to the east-west road (from the west coast pueblo of San Telmo) to the observatory.

While exploring this area we discovered a hidden one-acre tract of land near Rancho Cienaguita that would be perfect for a temporary campsite. After discussing the matter, we decided to return home, build an outhouse for placement upon it and use this hidden acre as a campsite from which to continue our exploration. Our plan included asking the elderly gentleman we'd seen at the smaller ranch if we could obtain drinking water from his source.

One month later, with Pepe and Em Garcia plus Art and Margo Madsen, we returned with our disassembled outhouse, dug a pit, assembled and installed the thing and began collecting roots for firewood. Set-up chores completed, we drove to the smaller ranch to meet its resident and ask about water. Unscrupulous as we are, we approached our neighbor, introduced ourselves, offered him a beer and chatted for a while.

When we thought it wouldn't appear so obvious, we offered him a five-pound corvina Pepe had taken from the Cortés (this was outright bribery, you know) and asked about the availability of water. Wiser than we, he grinned and pointed to the road, saying, "It's in the trees a quarter-mile beyond the fence. Help yourselves."

The following day we drove to the garnet mine where we found good samples for our travel mementos collection. We then descended a nearby hill to a ranch at the base of the mountain (midway between Cienaguita and the San Telmo Road) and chanced upon a steer's skull that still adorns our house today.

Retreating to the upper region (after exploring an east-west waterway) we headed for Trinidad Valley but were overtaken by an off-road racecar that passed us as though we were standing still.

Fifteen minutes later, as fate would have it, we came upon that race-car again. This time, however, it was perched on the side of a steep hill alongside the road and appeared to be in jeopardy of sliding irretrievably over an embankment.

While the driver remained in his cockpit, his feet frozen to the brake pedal, his co-driver stood at the side of the road where he could stop passersby for help. They'd missed the turn, apparently, lost control and came perilously close to a career-ending accident. We stopped, evaluated the situation and passed a length of rope for the copilot to attach to the stricken racecar. Then, with Art's and my sandrails tied together we used the power of both engines to pull the stricken racer back onto the roadway with Pepe directing the operation.

A short while later, when we arrived at the valley floor, we saw the racers talking to their support crew who'd been waiting with the pilots' wives for their (timed?) arrival. They gave us a hearty wave as we passed, but we couldn't help noticing the animated conversation between the pilot and a woman we presumed to be his wife. We can only guess what that was about.

A point of general information: the place we encountered the racers and their support crew (at the base of the mountain forming Valle Trinidad's southern boundary) was at a "T" intersection where a new road leads (in a westerly direction) through the mountains to San Telmo. Although an unimproved roadway this is a frequently used shortcut to Trans-Peninsular Highway #1 and points south. Should there be doubt or uncertainty about this shortcut, check the relative locations of Valle Trinidad, Ensenada and San Telmo on a Baja California road map. I'm one who does not like driving north to go south when it is not necessary.

Figure 5b – Sierra San Pedro Martir (Center Section)

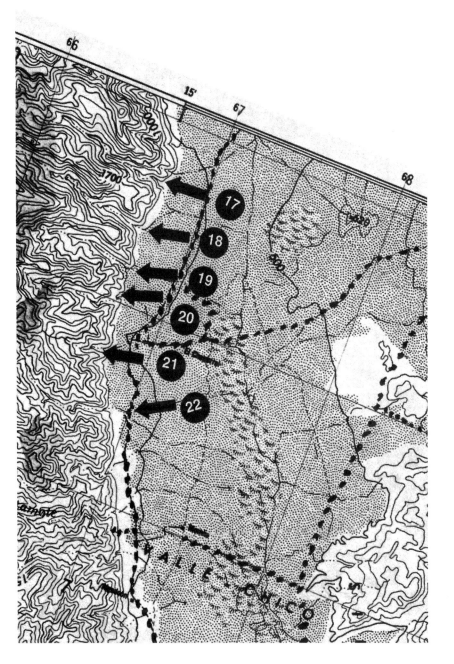

CHAPTER SIX
The Center Canyons

There are two problems, actually, not the least of which is the name. We expect names to be mispronounced, misspelled and misused but seldom misplaced. In this case Cañón Teledo has been misspelled (Toledo on some maps) and misplaced (as described below).

Two thousand years ago the predecessors of today's Pai Pai, Kumeyaay and Kiliwa Indians populated Baja's backbone mountains. While each developed and resided in his own domain, the fact that they intermarried suggests they may have been peaceful people although anthropologists tell us such was not the case.

The Pai Pai were a peaceful farming people living in small family groups spaced far enough apart for privacy and close enough for security. In general, the Pai Pai occupied the southern half of the San Pedro while the Kiliwa, an appreciably smaller group, centered on Valle Trinidad but may have occupied southern portions of the Juarez. The Kumeyaay, more warlike than the others, occupied the northern Juarez centered apparently at Vallecitos.

Each group left a legacy in artifacts including as many as 8,000 rock drawings spread throughout the backbone mountain canyons. Assuming our prior supposition about the coastal shellmounds is correct, Teledo Canyon served as a Pai Pai avenue to the valley floor and thence to the coast. Conversely, it is common to find seashells in the mountains, which must be considered a snacking Indian's debris.

Glen Conklin and I walked a mountainside trail several years ago during which I found seashells in a tiny cave-like structure under a three-foot diameter rock located 100 feet up the side of a comparatively steep hill. In this case, because we were following an old Indian trail, I had to presume the Indian had stopped during his ascent to munch a lunch and toss the shells under the rock.

When I asked Glen why the Indians had created and used this (near-vertical) trail, I was thinking I would have gone around the hill rather than over it. He told me this trail was the shortest distance to their destination and that, in the manner they traveled—which may be likened to the coyote—up, down or sideways made little or no appreciable difference. Shortest distance was their chief concern.

TELEDO CANYON

I belong to a retirees' organization that conducts tours to Teledo (and other locations) to enable participants to see and enjoy some of its Indian drawings. Located on a particular boulder about 400 meters west of the canyon's mouth there are at least 50 drawings to decipher.

Regarding that boulder, estimated to weigh 210,000 pounds, hurricane Nora moved it 22 feet downstream. Assuming the amount of desert varnish on its drawings equates to 800 years, the question becomes, "How many feet has it been moved—including vertically—since Indians last sat upon it for drawing purposes?"

While leading a group of retirees to this "Petroglyph Rock" shortly after hurricane Nora, I came upon a dead deer. Because I found no obvious cause of death, I chose to believe it had drowned (during Nora) when it stepped in the path of a typical wall of descending runoff water. This death reminded me of paleoanthropologist Donald Johanson's discovery of "The First Family."

During his first field trip to Ethiopia's Afar Triangle, Johanson discovered the remains of a 3.2 million year old female australopithecine he named Lucy. During his second season in the same region a member of his team chanced upon bones the team ultimately determined to be the remains of 12 australopithecines that had apparently drowned in a flash flood.

(Although unrelated to my story, this was the first recorded case of man's evolutionary ancestors—males and females with children—being found in company with each other. For clarification, truly ancient man [Australopithecus] was believed to associate with members of the opposite sex during estrus only.)

But we were not in the Afar Triangle, we were in Teledo Canyon where walking among every size rock is dangerous. For this reason I warn tour participants to consider carefully the hazards before deciding to accompany anyone up-canyon, including me. One of my participants (a 72 year-old-man) twisted an ankle about halfway to Petroglyph Rock, fell, scraped both arms and broke his glasses.

Owing to the fact that this is not an uncommon accident, each prospective canyon traveler—regardless of age or gender—must realize walking in such places is not worth the potential hazard. Therefore, in accepting the hazard each participant must concentrate on where he or she is placing his/her feet. That is, stop to view scenery or converse and return concentration to walking when beginning to walk again.

How could I do (or have done) such things and advise others not to do them? I (and those like me) have sufficient experience to insure precisely where we place our feet. We know better than to rush, and we know we must keep our eyes on the trail. A matter of safety, there is no substitute for experience and concentration.

Seasonal visitor Vic Danielson is a bona fide mountain climber and has been farther into our local canyons than anyone I know. On one of his escapades into Teledo, searching for an alternate route to the top of Picacho, he came upon a small place alongside the streambed that must have been an Indian machan's hideaway.

Protected on all sides by sizeable rocks, there was a sleeping hollow under one of them and an estimated 75 petroglyphs etched onto them. One of those petroglyphs was completely free of desert varnish, indicating it had been drawn in modern times. That drawing, two circles with a short vertical dash and a squiggly line below one of the circles, was deciphered by Vic as a statement of remorse over everything modern man has done to his environment. He called that drawing "The River of Tears from the Eyes of God."

Regarding local Indians, they seem to have spent their winters near or on the desert floor and summers at higher elevations. Because there was an abundance of food in the region, they ranged in every direction beyond the canyons to fill their needs. In the mountains, for example, they sought any and all available meat, pine nuts, leaves and seeds from a variety of plants and the bark and branches of carefully selected trees. In the lowlands they harvested cactus, maguey and a wealth of foods from the sea.

Those who do not know how Indians lived may be surprised to learn they harvested rabbits by the gross. That is, almost all Indian babies and grandparents slept under rabbit fur blankets. Thinking of the number of Indians there must have been in pre-Colombian times is it any wonder rabbits have such a reputation for reproduction?

When I think of our local canyons, I think of them as avenues, for it is here in the solitary beauty of each that I escape to the faded days of old and the beauty the Indians enjoyed. Invariably, while traveling these rocky realms, my mind wanders to times ranging between 200 or 300 to a million years ago… where history is written on and by the rocks.

To understand that beauty you need not dwell in bygone millennia or reflect on creation as a thing of the past. Rather, think of erosion and the fact that it not only created these magnificent avenues but continues this endless task with every passing day.

To witness that beauty stand first on the east side of the valley flanking the San Pedro (Valle Chico) and see a north–south mountain range with discernible cleavage suggesting the existence of canyons. Then stand at the mouth of any canyon and see something you would not otherwise believe. In place of the constriction the word "cleavage" tends to suggest you'll find yourself gaping, in Oso and En Medio, at 200-meter-wide openings.

Speaking of these rocky realms there is no difference between the trail you might take and the trail the Pai Pai walked a thousand years before. Yes, unknown storms have shuffled the boulders a bit, even changed their wandering courses, but these water–washed avenues are as interesting today as they were when the use of a trail began with the need for something an Indian didn't have. Maguey, for example, was the source of the fibers indigenous man used for his nets, shoes and skullcaps—the one that protected his forehead from the weight of whatever he and she carried in the net on their backs.

If you or I needed something like maguey, we'd probably go to a supermarket, but because Indians had no supermarkets, they had to know where to find their needs, and that is what makes these trails so interesting.

There is an abundance of maguey growing in Borrego Pass (along Federal Highway #3) in the general vicinity of kilometer marker 173. There is an abundance of fruiting opuntia (*nopale*s in Spanish and prickly pear in English) in San Matias Pass. There is an abundance of straight–branched bushes (the kind used for arrows) growing in Arroyo Huatamote. If you studied the shore, you'd find an abundance of different varieties of shellfish clustered in colonies throughout its length.

While thinking about Indians and how and where they hunted (including their seasonal harvests), it may not be generally known or appreciated that they hid essential tools in each harvesting and hunting area to eliminate the need to carry anything other than basic survival essentials. Consequently, those modern-day men and women who understood this all-important fact searched for and found every "stash" the Indians created over the long term. Glen Conklin, for example, told me he found and delivered more than 100 Indian bowls to regional museums, including San Diego's Museum of Man.

Another feature not to be overlooked is the "apron" we follow from desert floor to each canyon's mouth. That is, the final, ever-widening, usually flat, usually boulderless waterway disappearing in the distance from each canyon.

There are literally millions of boulders to be found strewn along the beginning of each canyon's apron, but the farther one follows any given apron to its downstream terminus, the boulders and rocks diminish in number until they are completely absent. Remember, the volume and speed of any given runoff determined how far its rocky burden was carried. Its ability to carry weighted objects is reduced in direct proportion to its speed, depth and width.

The direction each apron follows to some imaginary terminus is dictated by centuries of erosional forces although any new storm can change that direction in a heartbeat. Diablo Canyon's apron, like most of the Juarez canyons' aprons, is an example of a fixed watercourse. That is a watercourse held in place by a substantially strong dam of its own making.

I drove to Cajón canyon shortly after Hurricane Nora (1995) dropped 26 inches of rain on the greater San Felipe region in eight hours. The apron was formerly in the shape of a gently widening fan measuring 50 feet at the canyon's outlet, 100 feet at first bend and 200 feet a quarter-mile farther east.

Beginning 100 feet beyond its granitic mouth, Nora changed that apron from an initial width of 100 to more than 750 feet while one quarter-mile farther east it was a half-mile wide. In addition, this newly cut waterway was completely denuded. That is, the fury that poured out of Cajón that day carved and denuded a path one-half mile wide by one mile in length. Whereas the place we used to cross that riverbed was unremarkable, we now descend a six-foot bank into and out of it.

With Picacho del Diablo as a key reference point, the canyon cut between its two feet is Providencia. The first canyon south of the mountain's base is Teledo. We park on an old apron at the entrance to Teledo Canyon. Not only is there a minor (20 feet wide) waterway between the parking area and the base of the north-side mountain, a walk to the head of that waterway reveals it is blocked by a rocky dam created by one or more subsequent storms. The bottom of the active waterway, leading to Teledo's apron, is at least 30 feet below our parking area.

In similar fashion En Medio Canyon's apron has undergone uncountable changes. For example, it can be approached from both Teledo's and Oso's aprons. In addition, however, it has a somewhat centrally located 150-foot-wide, completely flat and boulder-free waterway shared with Teledo. The presently active waterway from En Medio leads north while the active waterway from Teledo leads south. The two streams meet in a central location (to form a single apron) and head east to the valley floor.

EN MEDIO CANYON

The first time Vic Danielson and I investigated Teledo Canyon we gathered food and gear and drove into what we believed to be that canyon. Later, upon discovering we were in En Medio Canyon, we realized there was an error on at least one of our maps showing the true Teledo as Tulare. Tulare Canyon is a false canyon about one-half mile (as the crow flies) north of Teledo.

En Medio Canyon is the second canyon south of Picacho and includes a 20-foot waterfall, a *cardonal* (car-doan-AL, a forest of cardón cactus) high above the canyon floor and a 60-foot waterfall beyond which it is impossible to pass. This abrupt structure has subsequently reinforced my findings regarding the early Indians' passage from the upper San Pedro, via Teledo Canyon, to the Campo Villa Marina shell mound.

At the end of that particular trek, Vic and I returned to my sandrail to discover its ignition switch in the ON position, an unfortunate fact resulting in a dead battery. Owing to the amount (and depth) of sand in that parking area, pushing the car was out of the question, so Vic walked to a nearby ranch for help. (My knees dictated I stay out of soft sand, prop my legs up and wait.) He returned about two hours later with an elderly Mexican gentleman and a battery he had carried at least a quarter mile because the oldster refused to drive in the sand.

We started the buggy, thanked the man, offered him recompense and headed home. After dropping Vic at his trailer (in the El Dorado Ranch residential area), I headed for San Felipe but didn't make it. My engine died and refused to start again. Moving to the side of the highway, I stuck out a thumb to solicit help for the obvious need. The only car to stop was a pickup truck loaded with Mexican workers whom I asked to tow me to San Felipe. They agreed and minutes later dropped my ailing buggy and me at home.

It was 6:00 p.m. I should have been home at 3:00 to shower, change clothes and rest a bit before attending a scheduled cocktail hour at a neighbor's house. Tired, dirty and frustrated over my ignition mistake and engine failure, I knew Freda would be there now, so I glanced in that direction, 100 meters distant, and saw her with host and hostess on an upper terrace.

Because there are but a few who know the local desert as well as I did, I had told her never try to find me if I don't return on time from the desert. No matter where I say I'm going, I move around so much I could be anywhere. Besides, when it comes to several of the canyons, I could be on one side, a search party on the other and neither of us aware of the others' presence.

Granted, anything can happen to anyone in such remote regions, and I know that as well as the next person. As demonstrated by Vic when we came out of En Medio, those of us who frequent these remote places know where to find the nearest source of help. Fortunately, I am here at the end of my days of exploration to describe the fun I had (and a few instances that were not as much fun).

I once took two of my grandkids on a ride to a nearby desert racetrack. When we didn't return at the time I'd told Freda we would, my first-born daughter became upset, imagining all sorts of tragedies happening to the three of us. In fact, she demanded that her mother send out a search party.

Freda told her, "Leave them alone and they'll come home wagging their tales behind them." We returned a full two hours late to describe the enjoyment the kids had while driving up and down near-vertical sand dunes in a location far removed from the *autopiste* (race track).

No search party on earth could have found us. (Our daughter cooled down when she saw the smiles on her kids' faces. Even she realized that she's a city slicker while her Ma and Pa are desert rats.

OSO CANYON

The third canyon south of Picacho is a different type of eroded waterway. Rather than the typical east-west crevice cut deep into the San Pedro, Oso is L-shaped with a 200 feet wide mouth and a 90-degree turn to the south about a half-mile farther in. The canyon terminates (originates, actually) in a bowl-like watershed an estimated mile south of that turn.

Accompanied by Frank and Debbie Albrecht, I was taken to Oso by a Mexican friend who wanted to show me its Indian drawings. The key to finding the drawings is a 100-foot long (12-inch wide) quartz fissure in the center of a four-foot-wide granite ledge forming a walkway that passes below the drawings. Once this granitic ledge is encountered it is a simple matter of looking at the west rock wall 10 to 15 feet above it to find the two rock faces upon which the drawings exist.

During my second visit to Oso I led a small group of desert enthusiasts including Frank Albrecht, Pepe and Em Garcia. While others set up a temporary campsite in a shaded location along the north side of the canyon's entrance, the four of us departed to see what I believe to be one of the best Indian drawing sites in the area.

It is not a plentiful drawing site (20 drawings, if memory serves correctly), but one I believed we could understand.

When Em found the going more difficult than she wanted to endure, she turned around and headed back to our parking area. But because she had not paid attention to the route we walked, she walked along a trail at least 100 feet south of the parking area— which was surrounded by noise-dampening trees—without realizing her mistake.

When this experienced desert traveler realized she was lost, instead of panicking, she lay down and took a nap. When she woke, about an hour later, she collected her experienced thoughts, heard voices (owing to a down-canyon wind) and headed towards them. Until she returned to camp none of us knew of her ordeal, which, she readily admitted, had been frightening.

There is a lesson here for individual hikers, campers and guides: "Avenues, avenues," the lesson goes, "which one leads to where?" In this case our parking area was in a clump of trees on the north side of a relatively wide canyon entrance. That clump of trees deadened all sound occurring within it. Her mind on other matters, Imogene walked a path of least resistance along the south side… and each of us had assumed everyone knew the way.

Arriving at the Indian drawing site, which occupies two adjacent rock faces separated by a narrow, vertical cave-like structure, we climbed to attain the best possible vantage point for viewing the drawings. While Frank photographed I crawled into the cave, discovered a 12-foot long, 20-inch wide shelf (upon which Indians may have slept) and examined the loose dirt floor for artifacts.

Of the two rock faces with drawings the northern face contains one I believe to be an Indian statement regarding a viewing of or encounter with a Spaniard. If correct, that event dates the drawing between 1688 and 1701, the only period Spaniards are known to have had a bone fide settlement in the region.

Yes, there were Spaniards here during portions of the following century, but they created no bona fide settlement. In support of the Spaniards' 17th-century presence, shortly after the hurricane of 1968, a local Mexican gentleman, walking along undisclosed terrain within the greater San Felipe region, came upon two silver goblets and a small cache of Spanish doubloons. Although I never met the man, his son showed me one of the goblets and several of the coins.

That drawing includes a Christian cross positioned immediately above an elongated, base-up, triangle significantly different from the Indians' "mother" symbol. Because there are mother symbols (equilateral triangles) on the adjacent rock, the difference between each is immediately obvious. The one I call "the Spaniard's triangle" appears but once; the mother symbol appears more than once and is the same on every occasion I've seen throughout southwestern America.

Judging by the amount of desert varnish in the patina of this one drawing, I believe it is possible to make an intelligent guess of its age and, more importantly, the ages of other drawings (in general). Having compared the different color gradients of each drawing's desert varnish I believe "the Spaniard" is the youngest while adjacent drawings range to (a somewhat arbitrary) 1,200 years before present.

I led Frank and Debbie Albrecht into this canyon on another day to enable them to study these drawings. Because we were alone I parked the car on hard ground alongside West Valley Road, an action that made the round-trip trek a little over three miles.

As we started to leave the drawings, Debbie suffered a physical problem that suggested I bring the car as close to the mouth of the canyon as possible. I hurried out to the car, lowered each tire's air pressure and drove over the hardest sand I could find to reduce the distance she had to walk. When we met, about half way, my friends told me they saw fresh coyote tracks on top of mine.

Although I did not see the coyote, I know I've been tracked before. Such an event is not uncommon for anyone traveling alone in the desert. To this day I have a fondness for these wild dogs that insist they will not attack unless injured, cornered or accompanied by others.

While camped at Vandenberg Air Force Base a few years ago, I took early morning walks with my dog. During one of those walks we came upon a coyote that my dog instantly chased. The coyote, more experienced than my pooch, ran a bit, waited a bit, and ran a bit more. When I realized what was happening I called to demand my dog's immediate return. That coyote was leading my pooch into a trap where a multiplicity of coyotes waited. She would have become breakfast for them and naught but a sad memory for me.

CAJON CANYON

The fourth canyon south of Picacho, Cajón, may be the most-visited of all the San Pedro's canyons. Its popularity stems from a twin waterfall structure about one-quarter mile from a convenient parking area. This popularity is strengthened by the existence of accessible Indian drawings. Unknown by most of Cajón's visitors, there are two additional falls within a half-mile of the lower pair.

There is running water here throughout the snowbird season (October through April). The existence of a bathing pond below the lower falls depends upon seasonal amounts of water. Add to that water the eroded debris it can carry, and the pond does or does not exist. Whereas I've enjoyed this pond at a depth of seven feet, I have seen it filled with gravel on more than one occasion.

The Indian drawings are on the flat underside of a large rock located about 100 meters upstream (north side) from the parking area. This rock rests on two others, forming a cave-like structure. Heavy downpours and their rampaging waters eroded the entrance to that cave so that it may be an uphill walk (from the adjacent riverbed) to view the drawings.

The principal drawing is one employing two colors (red and blue) and may represent mountains and an adjacent waterway. Adjacent to it are two black (charcoal?) drawings believed to have been made by Indians and at least two others somewhat obviously made by non-Indians.

Regarding non-Indian drawings, I will never understand why anyone will deface or destroy objects like these that must be recognized for what they are: national historic relics (no matter whose country they may be in). In addition to two damaged drawings at this location, the worst known damage in the region occurred at Vallecitos (west of Mexicali) where vandals grafittied several ancient paintings archeologists ultimately restored.

As I observed the lower waterfalls, I suddenly realized the enormity of what had occurred here. That is, two huge boulders (300,000 pounds?) and a conglomeration of smaller rocks (and vegetable matter) on each side of them have formed a dam. Runoff water encounters this dam and is diverted (like a sluice at a man-made dam) to a low point over which it falls to the pond below.

The succession of storms that brought the boulders to this site had to be of monstrous size to enable the movement of such behemoths. We know, for example, Hurricane Nora dropped a measured 26 inches of rain on the same region during which it moved Teledo Canyon's petroglyph rock 22 feet.

Although I don't know the complexity of Teledo's watershed Nora demonstrated Cajón's watershed to be far greater than most other San Pedro canyons (with the single exception of the Matomí). Applying that information to Cajón's dam, and by evaluating the canyon above the dam, it appears it could have been created in ancient times.

Owing to the size of these dam-forming boulders, it is suggested the rock on which the above-described drawings are located was placed subsequent to them. Having seen a few thousand local petroglyphs and a handful of white pictographs, the colors used in this one drawing suggest relatively modern times.

How deep is the dam and how much debris is there behind it? The vertical height of this dam is about 15 feet. The sedimentary material deposited behind it shows compaction spanning a distance of about one-quarter mile and a maximum width of 70 feet tapering to 15.

How did it withstand Nora? I cannot be sure but believe this previously compacted surface acted as pavement over which Nora's (and an unknown number of prior storms) runoff passed freely (denuding the dam of plant life as it passed).

Another feature worth mentioning is an exposed granitic "L" forming the south side of the canyon's entrance. Owing to the diversionary effect of the base of that L, which is polished by debris-laden water, the downstream side of it provides protection from all such matter. Not only is this downstream side the present-day site of a Mexican's ranchette, I am convinced early Indians used this same spot as a protected home site. What's more, when I asked that rancher whether he'd found Indian artifacts here he steadfastly denied their presence. Wouldn't you?

BARROSO CANYON

The next (true) canyon south of Cajón is Barroso, which can be difficult to find if wind and rain have dimmed the appearance of its access road. That road intersects West Valley Road a little more than a mile south of Cajón.

My first experience in this canyon was on an outing with Pepe and Em Garcia. There was, at the time, a barbed wire fence across the canyon's mouth. We parked among adjacent trees, set up a temporary camp, and the four of us passed through a man-made opening in the fence not wide enough for cattle.

Walking upstream, we came upon three interesting items within the first 400 meters of the fence. That is, a dead coyote yearling, the feathery remains of a pigeon and a wading pond about ten feet in diameter. The yearling, which had starved to death, appeared to have settled itself in a fetal position and given up its life. The pigeon was a victim of the animal world's survival of the fittest. It had relinquished its life to a hawk.

The wading pond seems to have been made for women since they, and most others we subsequently brought to this place, found no reason to wander farther into the canyon. Rather, off go the shoes and plop goes the butt on seats of polished granite.

Pepe and I were too inquisitive to give up here. We continued upstream which meant we had to find a way through a dense growth of cattails (pampas grass) along the north side of the polished (and quite steep) granite waterway. Once beyond the brush, it was but a short walk to a six-foot waterfall. Four hundred meters farther upstream, we came upon a 15 footer. Beyond that we discovered petroglyphs adorning an adjacent wall.

We guided a group of seniors to this canyon on a desert dining tour shortly after Hurricane Nora. One of them, Annie Glover, told us there was no six-foot waterfall, only the 15 footer.

In addition to the removal of that lower waterfall, the fence we originally walked through had also been removed. Judging by its apron, however, I am inclined to believe Barroso's watershed area is small when comparing its debris with that of other canyons. Whereas its tree-shaded parking area is north of the streambed, this canyon's access road crosses that streambed without difficulty a quarter-mile from its terminus.

For dining tour purposes we assign cars to a dedicated parking area on the outer fringe of the shaded area, set up our cooking facility and suggest tour participants claim adjacent sites for their individual comfort and dining enjoyment. In the norm we feed 50 to 60 diners during most of these tours although that number becomes at least 90 when we offer filet mignon and barbecued babyback ribs. (Would you believe five American dollars for a filet mignon dinner?)

The terrain south of Barroso includes the runoff from two smaller canyons (I have not investigated). Of these, one is found at the end of an east-west line drawn from the valley's drug rehabilitation center while the other, named Cardonal, displays an interesting stand of cardón cactus near its narrow mouth. Between them, there is an impressive waterway I originally thought came from a hidden canyon until I discovered it to be a canyon in the making.

Five miles farther south, five difficult miles of rocky road and face powder dust, we come upon the remains of a small agricultural settlement and a canyon known as Agua Caliente which is the opening subject of Chapter Seven.

Figure 5c – Sierra San Pedro Martir (South)

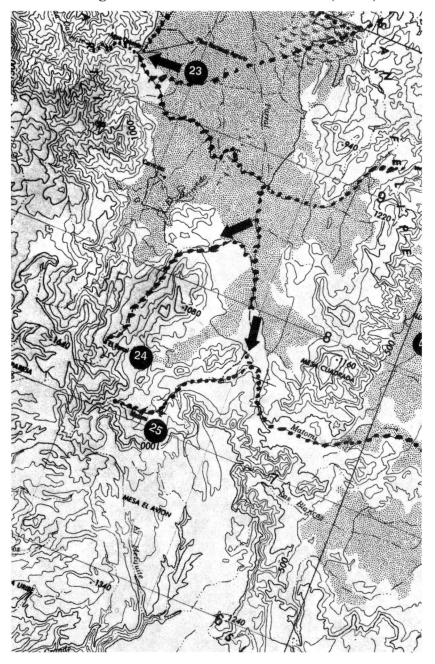

CHAPTER SEVEN
Agua Caliente, Parral and the Matom i

AGUA CALIENTE

The odor of sulfur hung in the air. Crossing the river, we came to a wall of trees marking the end of the road. We had driven forty miles to experience this remote place and now, with our goal but a few feet away, the first to arrive were clambering from their buggies to see the springs.

Thinking back on it, I could hardly believe we had driven through a blinding desert sandstorm to reach this peaceful place where leaves hung in quiet abandon and rays of a late-morning sun bathed us with their warming light. That sudden sandstorm was a thing of the past now as, after six long years, Freda and I once again stood at Valle Chico's hot springs.

We departed San Felipe with eight sandrails, a dune buggy and a pickup truck: twenty men and women on another exciting journey into the San Felipe desert. Originally a typical May morning, halfway across the valley the gentle breeze became a full-fledged sandstorm. Donning what we could for facemasks, we turned on headlights and inched our way along an uncertain roadway until, an hour later, we emerged from the storm like walking from one room to another. In this case, approaching Agua Caliente Canyon, we drove behind the protection of a wind-blocking mountain.

Agua Caliente, the name of a southern Sierra San Pedro Martir canyon with hot and cold water springs, is also the name of a near-by agricultural settlement. From the center of that settlement Hot Springs Road leads two difficult miles along a rocky riverbed to the springs. Rough enough to cause less dedicated visitors to retreat, this is a roadway passing through running water, loose sand, shifting rocks and crowding boulders.

To relieve the tension brought on by the unsuspected sandstorm we stopped a mile into the canyon to photograph a 20-foot century plant in bloom. While relaxing, we saw hummingbirds, hornets, bees and a little Mexican bat extracting nectar from the plant's brilliant yellow flowers as, flying from flower to flower, they pollinated the plant for next year's growth.

Photo session completed and road-weary nerves calmed, we returned to our buggies to continue the journey. Along the way we saw ironwood, elephant trees and bursage; cardón, senita, cholla and prickly pear cactus. Grass was everywhere, but the most dramatic display was a medley of beautiful spring flowers, including the tiny orange trumpets of desert mallow, the nickel-sized light-purple blooms of sand verbena and the delicate white trumpets of evening primrose.

"Water, water everywhere," Mr. Coleridge wrote. "Nor any drop to drink." But the plants were drinking, and what a difference it made on a beautiful spring day. Approaching the hot springs, we forged through a thicket of mesquite, made a final crossing of the river and parked on the beach beyond. We had inched our buggies over boulders, driven through angry water, climbed a difficult riverbank and towed one of our numbers to safety. Arrival was a pleasant relief, and yet it is challenges like these that make our trips so interesting.

Six years earlier Freda and I had walked this same tortuous route with Joe and Marsha Kemp of Lake Tahoe, California. Standing now where we stood then, we noticed a remarkable difference. The ramada was still there, but someone had added living quarters. Not only was the fence repaired, the cattleman's overnight lodging was immaculate.

The hot springs covered an L-shaped area 100 feet long by 20 feet wide. At the southern end of it hot water emanated from a small rounded hillock covered with a dark green grass. Fifty feet away other springs bubbled in a tiny streambed of their making. Black sand lined the bottom of that stream although 30 feet farther along the bottom was a pale yellow where sufficiently cooled water gave up its sulfur.

With at least a dozen in the greater San Felipe region these were the only thermal springs accessible from Valle Chico. There are hot springs at Puertecitos (55 miles south of San Felipe) and a hot water well at Rancho Chinalito (a half-mile north of School House Point). In addition, there are hot springs at Rancho Jamau (vertically above Santa Isabel Canyon), two near an abandoned ranch at Federal Highway #3's kilometer 66 and commercially developed springs at Agua Caliente and Agua Viva farther west along the same road.

Thermal springs originate from sources identified as meteoric and volcanic. Meteoric hot springs involve water that fell to earth as rain or snow, penetrated the earth's crust to depths where it is heated by rocks over which it flows and rises along well-defined fissures to issue forth as springs. Volcanic springs, which can appear as geysers or hot springs, involve subterranean water arriving at the earth's surface for the first time. Whereas Valle Chico's springs and those mentioned above are meteoric, natural volcanic springs can be found at the Mexicali geothermal site.

For clarification purposes only, there are volcanic hot springs at the geothermal site, but most of the steam seen rising from that site originated as surface water pumped into the interior to flash into steam which is harnessed to drive electricity-generating turbines.

Remotely located with a surprisingly sandy beach, the Valle Chico hot springs could be described as a grass-covered spa fringed with a verdant growth of trees. Amid this setting, we enjoyed a relaxing lunch, a brief peek at nature and nearby Indian drawings. Finally, with curiosities satisfied and our clients sufficiently rested, we prepared for our return to San Felipe.

Boil, bubble, toil and trouble: I could wonder how long the springs have been there but sadly must report they are no longer. Hurricane Nora denuded the place and buried the springs…(forever?) Where they once were is now covered by an estimated six feet of earth and another six feet of dense desert shrubbery.

Thinking again of the Kemps, Joe suggested we continue upstream, but the women had been sufficiently frightened by a steer in the nearby thicket that they were anxious to depart. Had we gone upstream, a Mexican friend told me, we would have seen a series of vertical granitic columns. Whether natural or man-made (by local Indians) he couldn't say, but they were located along a ridge directly above the springs.

Adding to the drama of this remote location, Glen Conklin found the remains of a still that he believed had been made and used by Señor Hansen, the man Baja's northern lake was named after. That still would have been used to make the tequila Hansen sold to local Indians.

PARRAL CANYON

Although I have been to Parral Ranch a dozen times or more, I have never been in Parral Canyon. Standing at the corral, I have seen the road leading to the canyon, listened to Art and Margo Madsen describe their experience in it and longed to explore its entirety. But, as fate would have it, those I guided through the area had other places in mind. Consequently, the allocation of what little time we have for desert exploration has never allowed Freda's and my return to the Parral for that purpose. The only way we'll get to see it will be to ask Ken and Sarah Darsch to establish a date and force us to allocate the time.

ARROYO MATOMÍ

Like Arroyo Huatamote, Arroyo Matomí is the other big kid on the block. With a lengthy canyon, a bona fide gorge and a dramatically ornamented riverbed this is one of three most beautiful, most difficult, most demanding waterways of the entire San Pedro Martir region (the third is Rio Canelo in the Sierre Santa Isabel).

Living drama? You haven't lived until you've inched your way down the Matomí's sharp-pointed, boulder-lined upper canyon and gorge carved through an isolated, solid rock mountain from which there is no escape on a bad day. And on good days? The Matomí is a desert explorer's haven… all 45 kilometers of it. And, as remote as it is, it seems to enjoy a number of frequent visitors.

Accessed via Highway #5 or Crazy Horse Canyon (and West Valley Road), we prefer the highway because the total distance is longer than most of other runs, and driving the highway enables an earlier arrival at the Matomí. But, I hasten to add, if this arroyo is worth driving an hour to enter, it is worth making the trek with closest friends, cooking gear, exceptionally good food and a plan to enjoy the place to the fullest. Not only do we usually remain overnight when we plan this run, we invite (or are invited by) friends who love the place as much as Freda and me.

Beginning at highway marker 57 we turn west onto a dirt road etched into the riverbed by frequent visitors. If it is early spring brittlebush will be in bloom displaying its vibrant, daisy-like yellow flowers. A few weeks later and orange is added by desert mallow. Rust and another yellow are added in April by cholla. Similarly, gobernadora adds its tiny white blossoms to create a rainbow of enjoyable colors.

As we approach the mountains, the road bends north briefly to enter a narrow pass I'll call the arroyo's east gate. Beyond this gate we find ourselves surrounded by mountains forming a bowl. The east and south walls of this bowl display deep, colorful layers of geologic history so surprising that either of them is the source of

151

what I call "cover photos." Near the center, protruding through the bowl's sandy floor, are two volcanic formations we call "the boobies" surrounded by an interesting variety of collectible rocks. I have one I removed from here that approximates a red and white checkerboard.

Continuing west, surrounding terrain changes to volcanic mesas along the arroyo's south flank, alluvial deposits on the north and an array of scattered streambeds depositing their runoff onto the Matomí. From the moment we arrive at kilometer 57, our emotions keyed by the prospect of what lies ahead, we have another challenging site in mind, as well. That site, Rio Canelo, is even more dramatic than the Matomí (if that's possible).

Owing to space and time limitations, Rio Canelo is not covered in this text. Because it is one of several adjacent riverbeds draining northeastern Sierra Isabel, to cover it without covering the others would be unacceptable. Whether this coverage becomes a part of another publication remains to be seen. Granting there is more than adequate justification for it, the basic problem involves the time needed to conduct research and exploration.

Nine miles west of the highway, there is a niche in the side of a mesa bordering the arroyo where we spent a night before continuing to Rancho Matomí. It is not an important place—little more than a wide spot in the road— but it was a convenient place with significant protection on three sides for a rest stop during a journey spanning several days. At that point in our journey we were searching for an access to Rio Blancas, found it, explored surrounding terrain and returned to spend the night.

One and a half miles farther west we encounter an intersection where a right turn delivers us eventually to Apache Tears. Although the scenery along Apache Tears Road is beautiful, I don't care for this road because racers and other speeders have shaped it into an unending series of moguls. Up and down, up and down, up and down gets tiresome for those of us who prefer traveling at appreciably slower speeds. But San Felipe's Lou Wells told me the last time he drove it there were no moguls.

Although the ability to find it depends upon the amount of rain this area has recently been subjected to, as well as the number of recent visitors, the access road to the Rio Blancas region is at the intersection of Matomí and Apache Tears roads. In the absence of tire tracks leading south-southwesterly, the true investigator will head in that direction modified only by immediate terrain (see topographic map H11B77). The sudden presence of its (east-west oriented) riverbed and the opening of the surrounding terrain announce arrival in the Rio Blancas region. Not covered in this text, Rio Blancas is a part of the Sierra Santa Isabel region.

The Matomí gorge is next and is a truly difficult, truly exciting passage. All things considered it is easier to drive west to east than east to west although, like the Huatamote, its scenery seems more noticeable when driving east to west. For safety purposes, whichever direction one travels in the gorge the driver's eyes must remain glued to the roadway except when his and her vehicle is stopped. Therefore, stopping frequently enables all visitors to enjoy dramatic scenery to the fullest. In one place, for example, there is a slab of uplifted sandstone protruding at an angle from a northern wall.

That slab and other, equally dramatically sites along the way are but a part of what make this outing one of the region's most memorable. But that's like looking at a bowl of fresh-laid eggs and saying one of them is best when, in a manner of speaking, they're identical. (Or should I say as identical as individuals can be?)

A word of caution here because the gorge can be closed by storm water and driving 20 to 70 one-way miles (depending on point of origin) is a long way to go to learn about closure. Owing to other obligations, Freda and I usually see the Matomí but once every two years (if we're lucky). Since there is no way to know if it is open without knowing who's been through it recently, we usually wait until we've heard it is open.

Should the gorge be closed and a desire to experience Rancho Matomí prevail, an alternate route via West Valley Road terminates within a few feet of the gorge's western portal. Here again, because the southern segment of Valle Chico, beginning at the fence bordering the western terminus of Crazy Horse Canyon Road, drains into the Matomí via the southern branch of Rio Parral and West Valley Road, that descent is as easily eroded as the gorge and can be closed until reworked by heavy equipment.

It is four miles from the west end of the gorge to the western terminus of the drivable Matomí (the arroyo continues another mile west). These last miles can as difficult as any over the entire length of this arroyo. For example, Ken and Sarah Darsch came here with Ray and Rosy Sanders shortly after Hurricane Nora and spent two hours inching over rocks from the West Valley Road intersection to the campsite at road's end.

There are a corral and sleeping quarters at road's end for use by the ranch's cattlemen. In addition to that fenced acre, there is another where we park, set up camp and enjoy good food and chat sessions. The arroyo borders the north side of the ranch although access to it is via a descending rocky walkway adjacent to the cattlemen's sleeping quarters.

Following the waterway upstream, we come upon a 50-tree stand of blue fan palms. An unfortunate fact about these rare beauties is that their dead fans hang to the ground in a profusion of combustible material that is an instant fire when struck by lightning. One sighting of these proud beauties can tell a thousand words of that story.

There is another stand of blues in a nearby stream one-half mile north of the Matomí's corral. Adding interest to that site, there are two Indian graves near the trees and a cave at least a hundred meters above and slightly northeast of them.

Long before this place became a ranch it was an Indian campsite for what I imagine to have been at least a thousand years. Indian relics have been found on the floor of this amazing place (under desert foliage) and in caves adorning adjacent hills. In one of those caves there is a one-inch-thick accumulation of soot on the ceiling while the floor is so loose I have to believe it has been dug for relics in modern times.

There are three broken metates on the floor of another cave. Few collectors of merit will take such pieces, knowing they're of little or no value, but by being allowed to remain where they were used they continue to tell a story of how the ancient ones lived. These were men and women who made a difference in their time: they deserve to be remembered.

Vegetation in this remote region includes the ubiquitous creosote bush (*Larrea farinose* – "*gobernadora*" in Spanish), shadescale (*Atriples* sp.), brittlebush (*Encileia farinosa*) and burrobush (*Franseria dumosa*). Along the broad sandy washes draining the lower elevations of the Matomí I have seen a few ironwoods (*Olneya tesota*) as well as palo verde (*Cercidium floridum*), smoke tree ("*palo triste*" in Spanish) and the desert elephant tree (*Bursera microphylla*).

In addition, although relegated to higher slopes, there are ocotillo (*Fouquieria splendens*), catclaw (*Acacia greggii*), agave (*Agave deserti*) as well as cardón. Above 3000 feet there are forests of piñon (*Pinus monophylla*), yellow pine (*Pinus ponderosa*), juniper (*Juniperus californica*), yucca (*Agave shawii*) and cypress (*Cupressus forbesii*).

Headwaters of the Matomí gather high above the canyon floor where they begin as a trickle, collect somewhat rapidly into a stream, and descend precipitous terrain at the base of which is a narrow plateau 2,200 feet above sea level.

A gentle stream running in an ancient water-cut arroyo along the north side of the plateau, it has seen wilder times as evidenced by the gorge and the density of rocks lining its streambed. Normally peaceful, the Matomí becomes a raging river when its unusually large watershed is inundated with rain.

Adding even more living drama to this magnificent place, several of us have seen cougars searching through our refuse while supposedly we slept. There is an eerie feeling to knowing a wild animal is in your midst. There is an equal and opposite feeling that stems from the knowledge you have been in that animal's presence, it knew you were there, what to do if it had to, but that it came for a significantly different purpose.

During one of our treks to the Matomí we enjoyed the company of a New Zealander who told an evening fireside tale involving Martians landing in a small American community one summer evening. Exiting their spaceship the Martians walked until they encountered two earthlings standing side-by-side offering a military-style right hand salute. One of those earthlings was wearing a nametag identifying himself as "Lead" (the Kiwi pronounced it "leed") while the other's nametag identified it as "No Lead" (no-leed).

The Martians' "earthlings" were gasoline pumps, the military salute was each pump's hose and nozzle assembly properly positioned in their padlocked cradles. Their names were the types of gasoline each dispensed. Need I say we enjoy our desert outings? Especially our overnighters!

During another trek to Rancho Matomí Carl Smith and I walked from the corral to the parallel riverbed to photograph its blue fan palms from above. During that walk Carl suddenly shouted an alarm. Looking over at him (about 20 feet to my left) I saw him jump and point to something on the ground. It was a red rattler absorbing heat from the morning sun. Fortunately for him, Carl saw the rattler a split second before placing a foot directly on it. How he did it I cannot imagine, but he jumped clear of the snake with but one foot on the ground. My photograph shows the snake's tongue testing the morning air, but I firmly believe it never knew either of us was there.

Arroyo Matomí, a self-contained paradise, is the only place we've slept with cougars although it is not the only place we've encountered them. Suffice it to say each of us, they in their way and we in ours, remain a part of the living drama of this incomparable desert place.

CHAPTER EIGHT
Conclusions

The backbone mountains represent more than 90 million years of geologic history. Can you imagine the full measure of geologic, paleontologic, anthropologic and archeologic events that occurred here? A professor who is no longer with us conducted classes in these and related subjects (for local seniors) during retirement years spent in the Southern California community of Anza Borrego. During those studies, which included field trips into the Coyote Mountains, he unearthed fossilized remains of a wooly mammoth. Freda and I chanced upon remains of a saber-toothed cat in the Sierra San Felipe and I found a dead deer in Teledo Canyon.

What is the significance of it all? To me, one who believes history repeats itself, it proves the existence of yesterday. And, because of that belief, I want to know and understand as much as I can about as many of our yesterdays as I have time to examine.

The Sierra de Juarez received more water than the San Pedro. Its canyons are cut deeper and boasts plants essentially unknown in the San Pedro. Whereas there seems to have been more animal activity in these northern mountains, it should follow that there would have been a greater presence of man, but I found no evidence to support that hypothesis.

The Kumeyaay's predecessors created Vallecitos and its outlying watch stations and campsites north and south of Laguna Hansen. But the Kiliwa and Pai Pai left what appears to be far more significant traces of their existence including drawings, shell mounds and artifacts.

The shell mounds account for a high tonnage of harvesting, a fact tending to describe the abundance of the early Cortés. What's more, there seems to have been so much food in the region that early man endured nothing to force him into clothing (the women wore bark skirts) and homes (they slept in shallow hand-dug pits).

Today, with all but a relative handful of indigenous man having passed into history, evidence of their existence remains for the inquisitive to find, study, sort and understand. Freda and I found some of it, but whatever we came across must be considered a drop in the bucket. As far and wide as we traveled we've only skimmed the surface. There were too many of them spread over too much of the country to rate our investigations as anything other than insignificant. Rather, we found beauty we opted to share with others for the single purpose of providing otherwise unavailable opportunities.

Turning our attention to the southern mountains, the Sierra San Pedro Martir and the Sierra San Felipe arose along two parallel faults and are separated from each other by about seven miles. Earlier, we identified the terrain between the mountains as the San Felipe Valley complex (Valle Santa Clara, Valle San Felipe and Valle Chico). The depth of this valley is not known although the depth of nearby locations (the Laguna Salada and the northern Sea of Cortés) is known to vary between 800 and 12,000 feet.

I carried two fossilized discoveries from the Sierra San Felipe to a San Diego paleontologist who told me they originated as bones in a saber-toothed cat. By digging far enough back in time we come to the era in which that cat lived and died, about eight million years.

Because it is entirely possible that cat died in the same manner as the deer I found in Teledo Canyon, it is equally possible a canyon's rampaging waters deposited its carcass somewhere on the valley floor. Other sediments buried the carcass, and four to six million years later it was uplifted and exposed to the endless activity of surface erosion. Two million years after that Freda and I happened along, found the fossils and...

What are our conclusions? The drama played out in the backbone mountain ranges, from uplift to the cutting of their canyons, will continue as long as the sun continues to rise and set. This living drama provides you and me with a place to study and understand, to frequent and enjoy and to preserve for later generations.

We are free, you and I, to look and look again at the incomparable scenery displayed here. Attention to detail will enable those who care enough about what they're seeing to learn even more than I've gleaned from this incomparable land... and to walk the same avenues pre-Colombian man walked.

The number of early man's backbone mountain drawings has never been tabulated although I estimated that number at 8000. Like the drawings many of early man's morteros, metates, manos and many other tools and weapons are still out there to be found in even greater number than Freda and I discovered. Therefore, because we, too, will pass from this scene, newcomers to the region are free to pick up the baton and run with it to provide a successful conclusion to this lengthy and dramatic story.

Because I was forced to quit the canyons there are places like those of the Santa Isabel waiting for the next eager investigator. And with something in excess of 20 intriguing miles in the Canelo there is every reason to go after it, its parallel canyon and the Rio Blancas region. Who knows? You, too, may be able to bed down with cougars...

PART THREE

FIND A ROAD
AND FOLLOW IT

Figure 6a – Sierra San Felipe (Northern Section)

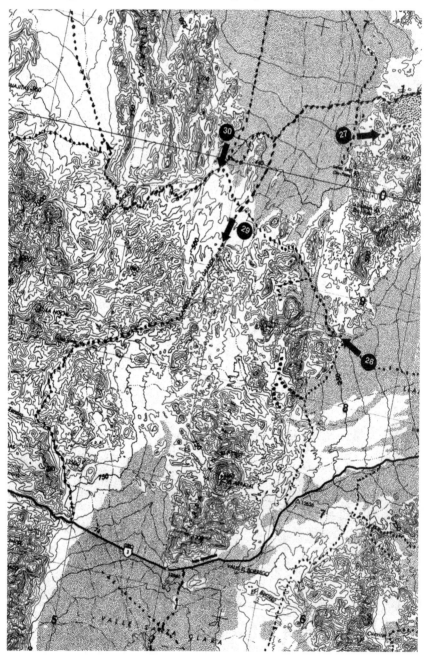

CHAPTER ONE
Introduction to Part Three

Think of the backbone mountains as a foundation upon which to build. Now add Baja's eastern mountain ranges and we find a completely different type of drama. In contrast to backbone mountain canyons, some of which are nearly impossible to negotiate, these eastern ranges are for hands-on enjoyment by anyone willing to venture into them.

Whether you call their highlights canyons, arroyos or passes each of them is an easily visited place offering round trip enjoyment in eight hours or less. In fact, round-trip tours I've conducted to all but the most distant ranges (Sierras Pinta, Tinaja and Mayor-Cucapah) run between four and six hours. For identification purposes, these mountains include seven tertiary ranges (Sierras Cucapah, Tinaja, Pinta, San Felipe, Santa Rosa and Punta Estrella) that I often refer to as "the youngsters" and one oldster, the Pre-Batholithic Sierra Mayor.

Volcanic regions are not generally known as good sources of ore. That is, the best ore deposits are usually found in metamorphic areas and places with hydrothermal waters where chemical composition enrichment can occur. But within this group, encompassing a large volcanic region, there are two pure sulfur sites, at least one surprisingly rich gold mine and an occasional suggestion of other ores.

In this chapter we present information on Sierras Mayor, Cucapah, Tinaja and Pinta and an introductory description of the Sierra San Felipe. Chapters Two, Three and Four contain descriptions of the Sierra San Felipe: that is, its northern, central and southern attractions.

Chapter Five contains descriptions of the Sierra Punta Estrella and its main attraction the Valley of the Giants. Finally, as with each concluding chapter in this book's five main parts, Chapter Six presents our conclusions regarding the impact of this part's content.

SIERRAS MAYOR AND CUCAPAH

The Sierra Mayor is mostly granitic with metamorphosed diorite adorning its flanks and highest peaks. The Sierra Cucapah, as well as the other eastern mountains, is highly distorted schist and recently faulted quartzite over what appears to be a granitic core. Interspersed with these formations are the two volcanically placed sulfur deposits.

a) In the Cucapah the sulfur is located in a west side deposit accessed via a dirt road intersecting Federal Highway #5 at kilometer marker #49.

b) In the Sierra San Felipe, it is located in a volcanically uplifted grouping of (unnamed) hills 20 miles south of the pueblo of San Felipe.

Although its name appears on no map I know of, the Cucapah's southern pass is locally known as "Paseo Azufre" (Sulfur Pass.) In addition, Cañada David, a major division separating the Cucapah into two segments, provided a freeway-like passage to Laguna Salada. Not only did Melchior Díaz pass through these mountains, I believe he crossed via Cañada David although access now appears to have been eliminated by erosion over the years subsequent to my investigation.

Whether Díaz crossed here is pure conjecture based on the fact Paseo Azufre was not created until the late nineteenth century. The chief difference between his and my first confrontation with Laguna Salada (via Cañada David) was our separate modes of transportation. Deep sand would have made no appreciable difference to him (and his horses) while it was a problem to me traveling alone in my sandrail.

Knowing the sulfur mine route existed, I drove Cañada David first, as far as the first deep sand (and a clear view of both the Salada and the Juarez), returned and drove Paseo Azufre where I was surprised to find a small farm (at the western base of the mountains), a dense mixture of brittlebush and gobernadora, and a passage to the west over the hourglass-like Laguna Salada.

Crossing the Salada (via Paseo Azufre) was no problem until I arrived on its west shore. Although my buggy was equipped with extra wide tires (I was using 12.5-inchers at the time), I had enough trouble to wish I'd asked someone to accompany me. To make a long story short, I became gloriously stuck, worked a half-hour to free my buggy using conventional methods (digging) and finally removed the rotor from my buggy's distributor and used the buggy's starter motor to power my way out of trouble.

Although I enjoy walking, I knew no one was home at the ranch behind me, and all other help was far enough away that I didn't want to walk to it. Besides, this is the type of place helping hands tend to shy away from. Consequently, I cut my journey short, returned to Highway #5 (via the Salada's southern terra firma) and home where I made plans for an accompanied trip as soon as I could find someone willing to drive the 100-mile, one-way distance.

There is a distinct beauty in this narrow stretch of mountains displayed by their multi-colored surfaces. The ancient mountains, the Mayor, display a charcoal color shaded by eons of desert varnish. The Cucapah (overlaying an estimated 90 percent of the Mayor) display a significantly lighter color (with a pale rose hue in places).

The Pintas and the Tinajas range in color from bright yellow through orange to a deep blood red. The remaining mountains are comparatively non-distinct as a function of color although all display a variety of more and less desert varnish. In addition to color, there is a distinct lack of covering vegetation in the four northern ranges (Cucapah, Mayor, Tinaja and Pintas), a fact tending to describe their surface chemistry.

The desert flanking the east side of all these mountains displays typical desert growth over a lengthy alluvial fan. There is a preponderance of saltbush, creosote bush, bursage and other salt-tolerant plants. Dramatically different, the floor adorning the west side of the Mayor includes the dreaded Laguna Salada and a wealth of wind-blown dunes while the Valle Chico complex (west of Sierra San Felipe) hosts a variety of normally expected desert plants including cholla, ocotillo and biznaga (barrel cactus).

L-shaped Laguna Salada is slightly more than 60 miles long by 20 miles along its east-west base. Sixty-two miles of pure hell! Nothing grows here; even coyotes avoid the place except to pass when, and only when, seasonal temperature variations permit. Underlain by the outer fringes of the Sea of Cortés the Salada's salt content is refreshed from below by tidal intrusion.

Overlain by wind-driven sand and broiled daily by a relentless sun, the southern ten miles of the Salada's 62 mile length are a study in parched surfaces. Whereas rain can occur, it is so rare the surface is usually adorned with an array of foot-wide octagonal disks of bone-dry crust separated by ever-deepening gaps. It is a surreal scene described in books but seldom encountered in real life.

The southern segment of Laguna Salada is a stage upon which living demons play their tricks with mirages, dust devils, sandstorms and an occasional deluge along its western periphery.

Whereas we once encountered a mile-long portion of this part of the highway covered with two feet of sand, on two occasions we inched our way along the same stretch of highway through blinding Saharan sand storms rather than risk such storms denying us breathable air.

SIERRA TINAJA

The southwestern ten miles of Laguna Salada is bordered by the northern extremity of the brick red Sierra Tinaja. Talk about surrealism! Imagine a grouping that includes the Salada, the Tinaja, Arroyos Jaquegel and Grande and the Sierra Pinta. Surely we've all gone to hell and this is what it's like. Yes, the arroyos exist and yes, surreal waters cut them, but has anyone seen water in them? Not in my lifetime… or is that simply because I wasn't there when it was?

Surrealism? Try to envision the terrain between the Jaquegel and an adjacent unnamed arroyo. Here is a narrow plateau, about ten miles in length, littered with a blanket of deep dark-red (or is it a blending of purple and chocolate?) volcanic stones averaging twelve inches in diameter. Guessing there is one to every square meter of surface, the space between each is paved with smaller stones of the same color and origin ranging from one to four inches in diameter. Have you wondered about living drama? Try walking over this volcanic pavement.

The first time I drove this plateau, it was via a man-made road (the operative word here is "single") that must have taken its creator months to complete. Adding pain or pleasure to the task, the second time I drove it, the first mile of this road was lined, left and right, with white-painted (12-inch diameter) rocks spaced about 20 feet apart. Surely, this must have been done to impress a lady.

Returning to surrealism the question becomes, "Why such a road out here?" I refuse to reply to that question because I know marijuana (and gold) comes from somewhere. In this case, about as far as a body can get from civilization in a civilized country.

For comparison purposes picture a naked woman walking down Main Street: I don't condone it; rather, I do my best to understand it. Therefore, if the harvest is marijuana (rather than gold) don't condemn this place without condemning those responsible for the presence of the same crop in pineapple- and sugar-rich Hawaii (and agriculturally rich Northern California).

Because I had no intention of looking into the business end of a 12-gauge shotgun, I did not take that road to its southern terminus. Instead, I turned from it where it dropped into the Jaquegel. My destination was the base of the Juarez (and home, if I lived to get there).

John Sigala joined me for my second run into the Jaquegel. (John is a bona fide mountain climber from Colorado who once showed me a strip of film depicting him and fellow climbers being swept away by a Swiss mountain avalanche.) Driving from San Felipe I led him through the Pintas via the La Ventana corridor, stopping here and there to point out significant landmarks.

Driving south in Arroyo Grande I took him to Dam #7 and later that afternoon stopped to make camp in the unnamed arroyo. John is four inches taller but 20 pounds lighter. After making camp he demonstrated the benefit of that weight difference by bounding up a nearby hillside to find perspective from an elevated viewpoint. (I went in spirit while the rest of me spent the time gathering firewood from less demanding terrain.)

Later, as the sun disappeared behind the Juarez, fires added atmosphere to a scene depicting two men cooking and enjoying their own dinners in a remotely isolated preserve. (I make campfires wherever I can for the value of the mood they tend to create. In this case, John and I each had our own cooking gear and food and preferred preparing our individual meals without being rushed by the other.)

Conversation included the history of this place, who may have lived in the immediately surrounding region, and a description (based on my topographic maps) of the arroyo we were to explore the following day. Finally, with dishes and cookware cleaned, we retired to lightweight chairs to enjoy the silence of night under a sky likened to a jeweler's tray displaying a wealth of sparkling diamonds.

As the evening wore on, we counted 20 satellites passing overhead in as many directions. Eventually, with conversation waning and eyelids drooped, wearied bones called for sleep and we disappeared into dome-shaped tents zipped closed as protection from the mystery of a desert night.

I'm the early bird. Reveille for me comes any time after 4:00 a.m., and so it was on the following morning. Fully clothed before twilight, I unzipped my tent, crawled into the open and stoked coals to induce a morning fire. With grate and pot in place it was but a short time later that the warmth of fresh-boiled coffee stirred me back to reality.

Ahhhhh, I reminisced as a familiar flavor warmed my insides and morning alertness spread across my brain. Moments later, with darkness fading to the beauty of a new day, I walked the length and breadth of Unnamed Arroyo to find an arrowhead ...a different flower ...a gold-speckled rock. Why does anyone walk in paradise?

I heard John before I saw him, and when he saw me, he said, "Your coffee woke me." I had placed the pot at the edge of the grate where it had heat without boiling away. Because I make stronger coffee than most, the fire's heat had spread a tantalizing aroma omni-directionally in the still morning air. Apparently that tantalizing aroma had forced him out of bed.

We broke camp after breakfast, opted for the left fork of a nearby Y and headed south over the elevated plateau. The right fork would have taken us into the Jaquegel five miles sooner than we actually arrived. Although we stopped along the way to view the arroyo from above (walking over the rocky pavement) when we arrived at the plateau's southern terminus, John took one look at the descent, parked his pickup at the edge of the boulder field and walked. I, on the other hand, was expected to drive the sideways-slanted road he was afraid my buggy would slide from. No hill for a climber, I reasoned: if the man who built this road can do it so can I.

John climbed into my buggy when I'd safely negotiated the 100-meter hazard and away we went (would you believe he walked again during our return to his pickup?). Whereas the final five miles of this arroyo (the northeastern segment) are straight as an arrow, the part we were now in, heading upstream, is a zigzagging watercourse ranging from eight to 50 feet in width.

We entered the arroyo where it makes a 90-degree bend to the west (and the rancher's road disappears up an adjacent hill). From that point onward we found ourselves following a snake-like route through this volcanic mountain range. At one point, a true bottleneck, the rocky surfaces on each side of the riverbed were blackened as though by fire. I can only imagine Mother Nature had been up to one of her tricks because the blackening was soot-like. How strange... in this particular bottleneck only.

Because I have no answer for this enigma, I suggest a storm had piled a density of eroded vegetable matter here, lightning ignited it, and the resulting fire stained the venturi black.

At another point we came upon terrain stained purple by an intensity of heat I presume to have been the core of a (vent?) volcano. It is times like this—the soot, the purple and the silence—that I feel a kinship with Coleridge's Ancient Mariner:

"The many men so beautiful about the decks did die and a thousand thousand slimy things lived on and so did I."

That may be difficult to understand, but I find both beauty and fear in places likened to the bowels of the earth. There is incomparable beauty in such places, but understanding the natural drama that created them causes an occasional shudder. On the one hand, storms out of sight and sound can result in an inescapable wall of water. On the other, this is lions' country and one never knows how hungry or self-confident any particular lion (cougar, actually) may be... an ever-present problem for those who travel alone.

Isolated in the distant folds of the Jaquegel's twisting pathway, we came upon an adjoining, surprisingly deep, waterway. Whereas John ventured into it, he reported it short and impossible for our vehicle. It was (and is) noted because it represents another watershed. Shortly thereafter we came upon an open area (between adjacent hills) so covered with boulders that we decided to call a halt to our run. This is the point where the Jaquegel is intersected by two terminating waterways called Manzanito and de Medio. Manzanito comes almost directly down from the Juarez while de Medio empties the valley-like sandy separation between the Juarez and Tinaja, and the Jaquegel bears off on a west-southwesterly heading. Our choice would have been de Medio, but walking from that boulder-strewn point in well-watered cougar country seemed ill advised.

Did I mention returning here alone? No one in their right mind goes anywhere in the desert alone and yet, time after time I told Freda my travels were like going to a nearby market: I know where I'm going; I know the hazards and I also know how and where to find help. As ignorant as that was, I freely admit my curiosity overcame good sense and I returned to continue my investigation of a land in which my heart and soul resided.

As was bound to happen, friends and neighbors finally got Freda's attention and I am no longer allowed to go into the desert alone. Remember the poem: "I am the master of my fate, …the master of my soul"? Well, I used to be. But because my experiences in the Tinaja were an enjoyable repetition of unending desert drama, including my search for ancient Indian trails and artifacts, rainbows of color, geologic history and mystery, and the solitude I love so dearly, I truly felt a deep-seated need to go. The end result was a feeling like the comfort of donning an overcoat: I was in my own realm; I was a part of it and it was a part of me.

Yes, I went alone as I did to so many other places in those early days when most of our friends felt the Pintas (et al) were too far away. That one fact, being too far, was distressing to me who still feels, considering the entire San Felipe Desert, none of it is as beautiful in its surreal way as the Sierra Pinta-Tinaja region.

Since my visit with John a new road was cut up and over the center of the Tinaja, allowing passage to a swampy interior. That road leads to a water well supplying a commercial gold mine (nearly 20 miles distant) located along the Pintas' southeastern flank. I traveled that road during a reevaluation of my grave-search parameters. I had seen the pipeline to the mine so now it was time to see the water well, the swamp and other Indian trails. (This place—the well and adjacent swamp—is a little more than three miles north of the place John and I investigated.)

We know what this road did for the miners. What is not known is what it did for me: it opened a whole new interior. Carrying my 16th-century friend into a land he never saw, the two of us went up, over and down in search of Indian trails and campsites. We saw the (fenced) well site, skirted the swamp and drove as far as terrain allowed (in a westerly direction).

When boulders stopped us, we went on foot about a mile up-slope to a clearing that could have been an Indian campsite although I found no artifacts. Along the way we spoke of Indians, campfires and the scent of mystery hanging dense in desert air.

During our return I drove north and east to learn whether I could sight the place Henderson may have walked. Shortly thereafter I came upon the road descending the escarpment via Cañón El Mano and, skirting the volcano at the Tinaja's northern terminus, turned east to return to Highway #5 and home. Motoring along I had an exhilarating feeling from my belief I (we) had been in a place non-indigenous men (excepting the well drillers) have ever been.

How neat it was… until Freda ruled the roost. This part of the Juarez was a whole new experience for a ghost and an orthopedics patient but, alas, she laid down the law and I haven't returned since. Although grave seekers asked me to lead them into the Pintas, I had to decline their requests.

SIERRA PINTA

The Sierra Pinta is another narrow range of volcanically uplifted mountains with but limited passage through them. Formed over a five million-year period between 22 and 17 million years ago, their tallest peak stands 4,000 feet in height. Owing to the rate of erosion Freda and I witnessed over the past 17 years, we cannot imagine how high these mountains must have been one, two and …17 million years ago.

If there is a picture of Dante's Inferno, surely it was taken here where the surface of the earth opened many times over those five million years and rivers of lava oozed up and out to form the rock-hard shapes seen in this awesome place today. In some places, particularly along the Pintas' western flank (see below), considerably more than oozing occurred.

In many places I envision streams of molten lava shooting high into the air to fall back to earth in the shape of cinders and rocks of every size. The Pintas' scenery, and that of the adjacent Tinaja, had to have included the most glorious fireworks imaginable.

The standard approach to the Pintas is via Federal Highway #5. Approaching from the north, the first sighting of them occurs while crossing Laguna Salada. That sighting, although unrealized by most, includes remnants of a truly ancient volcano—I call it "El Viejo"—that could have erupted as a single mountainous entity in an equally ancient sea (before creation of the Baja California land-mass). Its age, which is prebatholithic (before the backbone mountain uplift), is described by its color, a desert-varnished charcoal black. Other remnants of this ancient beauty stand several hundred feet west of the highway and are identified by the same shade of black.

Although these western remnants are overlain with considerably younger mountains, they are no less a part of El Viejo. In fact, as one motors through this range, other black surfaces are seen with considerably younger overburden topping them. It is the extent to which the color black is seen in this range that gave me an idea of the original volcano's age and diameter.

Continuing south, as El Viejo disappears in the background, other mountains identify this location as a former volcanic hot spot. Whereas much of this range is stereotypically brick red, at least one mountainous structure, adjacent to the east side of the highway, displays an intense shade of purple indicating to me the core of a mini-volcano. Similarly, in a nearby place there are hues of yellow (sulfur?) and the faintest shades of green (copper ore?).

Approaching the Pintas from the south, justification for their name comes into view where color is a kaleidoscope of reds and yellows separated in several areas by layers of former sea floor. Sierra Pinta: The Painted Mountains—not all, but many colors of the rainbow.

Whereas the Sierra Pinta is a little over 20 miles in length and 10 in width, they are boomerang-shaped with but two passages through them. The first, about a mile from the Pinta's northern terminus, is an unnamed riverbed I call "Rio Payton."

C-shaped, the Payton originates in a bowl-like structure about two miles (line of sight) west of the highway, flows northerly (between mountains) and then east to empty into the Cortés. As a landmark identifying this riverbed, the remnant of a concrete block structure stands along the east side of the highway at the place Rio Payton crosses.

The western flank of the riverbed's originating bowl is alluvial; the true investigator will not only recognize that reality but will find an easy route up, over and out of the bowl leading directly to Arroyo Grande. A more difficult route can be found from the center of this bowl leading uphill in a southerly direction around at least two volcanic outcroppings to another lip over which the Ski Slope comes immediately into view (this is a climb of at least 500 feet). From this elevated place, access to Arroyo Grande is an easy trek down the slope to the west.

The principal passage through the Pintas (mentioned earlier) is the La Ventana corridor. Beginning at Highway #5, we don't actually drive in the waterway; rather, there is an unimproved roadway departing the highway a few feet north of the riverbed's north bank.

Before the gold mine came into being, I followed another ancient waterway into the Pintas rather than through them. That passage led to a bone-dry waterfall (and other interesting scenery) I regret not photographing for, owing to the gold mine, that passage is no longer accessible. There is a similar waterfall, a place I call Diatom Falls, in the Sierra San Felipe. Read about it later in this Part.

Earlier I described the three passages I took through the Pintas. They were the La Ventana corridor, the 12-foot drop to a waterway leading to the Grande, and the Vee with its parabolic passage to the Ski Slope. Now we offer a southern passage between the Pintas and the San Felipe, which is the route the ancient ones (predecessors of the Kiliwa) traveled from the Juarez to the Cortés.

This route begins where the Grande narrows from a mile to less than 100 feet in width. Heading southeasterly an unimproved road disappears in a hodgepodge of gobernadora, cholla and yellow-flowering brittlebush to wind its way along the bank of a small streambed leading to the pass. Along this route we encounter a lung-choking face powder dust my tires kick up to coat everything and everybody it lands upon.

"My God," my soul cries out. "Is there no place in this desert without difficulty?"

"No hill for a climber," comes the reply of dedication, and the first thing we know we are inching our way over semi-sharp rocks in an eight-foot-wide passage. I can reach to my left to touch the Pintas and to my right the San Felipe. Ahead lies relief in the form of a secondary streambed providing a sandy, occasionally rock-strewn passage along a gently curving waterway leading to the Chinero Plain and Federal Highway #5.

This road is divided by a Y at the place it penetrates the Chinero Plain. The left fork leads (at least six miles) east across the cholla-choked plain to intersect Highway #5 at kilometer 135. Beyond highway #5, it skirts El Chinero, a monumental vent volcano, to lead all the way around this tragically famous landmark (see below and the Introduction to Part Four).

The right fork continues along the Sierra Pintas eastern flank to terminate at its intersection with Federal Highway #3 (at Laguna Amarga). Highway #3, the Ensenada Highway, follows an east-west route over gently rolling terrain from its point of origination at

El Chinero to Borrego Pass (at the foot of a landmark volcano named Arrajal).

Beyond Borrego Pass, the highway crosses the northern Santa Clara Valley before leading to the entrance to San Matias Pass. The first of Baja, California's columnar giants, cardón, appear on the north side of the highway at this precise point (the foot of San Matias Pass). This plant does not grow north of the 31st parallel or, with the exception of a tiny parcel of land on Sonora's west coast, anywhere but the Baja, California peninsula and its adjacent islands.

From this point, my choices were to drive six miles east to Federal Highway #5 or five miles south to Federal Highway #3. I drove that southern road once, at night, and vowed never to do it again. The desert plain, on the other hand, is refreshing as it descends ever so gradually to the east. In addition, this road leads past a number of colorful volcanic mounds, adding their individual glory to the scene. I headed for Highway #5.

Cerro Chinero is a vent volcano with an interesting history described by its many contours and the colors of rocks laying on its many surfaces. The hills standing immediately adjacent (both east and west) to the highway are considerably more rounded than each of the other peaks of which Chinero is composed. The color of rocks laying on their upper surfaces is so black they identify an age approximating the time of the backbone mountain uplift.

In contrast, rocks laying on the remainder of these volcanically created hills are so young their colors range entirely within the spectrum of pale to brick red. There is a seismometer located along Chinero's southern flank suggesting the possibility this place may not be completely inactive.

Fourteen miles north of Chinero, along a line paralleling the nearby coast, stand Cerros Lágrimas del Apache (Apache tears) and Pedrera (the quarry) while 21 miles south along the same line stands Cerro Moreno. Each is a vent volcano in a land dotted with them. Twelve miles south of Moreno stand the remains of a pre-batholithic volcano that blew itself apart leaving but two peaks

(Cerros Machorro and Kila) and a mostly-buried layer of lava forming a dramatic foundation to the distant desert community of San Felipe.

Nine miles south of Machorro the Sierra Punta Estrella describe their history as somewhat similar to that of the Mayor: an ancient surface surrounded by considerably younger overburden. Stand anywhere along this coastline, whether at Pedrera, Moreno or Punta Estrella and search the eastern horizon to see Mexico, the land this peninsula was a part of until the San Andreas came along. Recognize it or not, the land you're standing on is moving north (at the approximate rate of one inch per year) while the land you're looking at is moving south (at a similar rate), a surprising reality of the frontier's living desert drama.

SIERRA SAN FELIPE

The Sierra San Felipe, a 63-mile-long mountain range, is believed to have risen from the depths during at least two (tertiary period) geologic uplifts. Separated into two segments by the several mile-wide Borrego Pass (through which Federal Highway #3 passes), the northern segment (see Figure 6a) is but ten miles in length while the southern is 53.

The northern segment includes two significant east-side waterways draining onto the Chinero Plain. The first is an interesting riverbed located one-quarter mile south of Pinta Pass. The second is more like an avenue draining a bowl-shaped structure midway between Pinta Pass and Federal Highway #3.

Since one of the landmarks in Choral Pepper's description of the Díaz gravesite is in this area ("at the center of a 12-mile line drawn between" two nearby mountains), I flew over this northern segment to evaluate the terrain for investigative purposes. I found it distinct, without complication but justifiably excluded it from my search grids.

I explored this northern segment (of the San Felipe) out of context of my search for the Díaz grave. That is, I returned without my search team to this particular segment and spent three days wandering, walking and watching everything that moved. I explored the bowl first because it appeared from the air to be an uncomplicated site. It was.

When I drove to the riverbed (below Pinta Pass), I spent a day and half in it, entirely on foot (and alone with my faithful dog), although this region, too, is considered cougar country. I have fond memories of this half-hidden place but have never taken anyone into it. Similarly, other than John Sigala I took no one into the narrow portion (roughly 75 percent of the whole) of the Grande... primarily because these places are too far away for most of the men and women I might have taken.

On one occasion I invited Norm and Sheri Storm who followed me through the Pintas via La Ventana Corridor but decided it was too rough when we turned onto a north-south roadway. They quit and returned home. On another occasion, I had Neal and Teri Lasansky on that same road and they, too, quit.

Whereas I've never invited anyone else, a mile beyond the place my friends turned around there is a tiny black volcano on a small plateau as pretty as the day is long. That volcano stands like a sentinel at the gateway to Paradise; you've got to see this land to believe it. Once seen, in my opinion, a little discomfort is the price one pays for an incomparable pleasure to be found in but few places on earth. Besides, no one knows where this particular north/south roadway leads...

The southern segment of the Sierra San Felipe is pure drama but drama of a different nature: pleasure. Consequently, comparing accessible features of the backbone mountains to those of the San Felipe is like comparing a place intended for rock hoppers (mountain climbers) with a place intended for dancing.

Before continuing with the San Felipe, I must describe the northern flank of this southern segment that, like Cerro Chinero, is a region of vent volcanoes. Among several others, there are three of these beauties visible from Highway #5 that describe the relief of mountain-building pressures from below. The first of these natural vents is similar to the vent on the west side of the highway at Chinero. That is, it is stereotypical in nature: the shape of an upside down check mark. This is the type of place rock hounds frequent. San Felipe's Lynda Bilyeu, for example, found geodes and other treasures, including Nature's glass, while searching volcanic vents.

In addition to the vents, a major waterway penetrates this watershed region which is composed of an estimated 600 square miles of surface area. During typical desert rain storms, 600 square miles covered with two, three or four inches of rain rushing as it does downhill amounts to a downright dangerous reality.

On one occasion Freda and I were stalled at the place this waterway crosses the highway. About all we could do was climb to the top of the berm channeling the water to the crossing and watch an unbelievable scene of chocolate brown water raging past us with a ferocity I likened to the water hitting the bottom of Niagara Falls.

Within the Sierra San Felipe Mother Nature created a variety of canyons, passes, arroyos and other features for (our) ease of passage. These features include Calamity Canyon, Clamshell Canyons 1 and 2, Power Lines Pass, Diatom Falls, the Chalk Mine, Cañón de Cuevitas, Ram's Head Canyon, Fossil Sites 1 and 2, Hidden Valley (and its northeast extension), the Cloisters, the Gorge, the Connector, Arroyo Chanate, Quartz Mountain, Arroyo Huatamote, Crazy Horse Canyon (sometimes called Arroyo Parral), Apache Tears, the Mud Bank, Sand Canyon, Fossil Site 3, Obsidian Canyon and Arroyo Matomí.

I apologize to no one for giving these places English language names. Those previously named sites bear their names (in this text) in Spanish; those without bear names I've applied. I am neither a cartographer nor working in an official capacity. Rather, I write in English to share my adventures with English speaking readers.

Flanking this southern segment, but no less a part of it, are Valle Chico and the coastal plain. Adding to the San Felipe's majesty, the tiny Sierra Santa Rosa arose alongside a small portion of the San Felipe to form the entrance to and south wall of Hidden

Valley. Half a dozen miles east of the Santa Rosa the boomerang-shaped Sierra Punta Estrella stands as a landmark near Arroyo Huatamote's outlet to the sea to provide a protective cover for San Felipe's "Valley of the Giants" (described under "Sierra Punta Estrella").

At the outset, I suggested God created this land as an experiment not intended for life forms. Now, I suggest this is God's country for here in this land of lost rivers and intolerable temperatures is where the drama of erupting volcanoes, water-carved canyons; deer killers, rattlesnakes and scorpions; Indian shell mounds and animal walkways move us out of the museum and into the classroom (or is it "playground"?).

Figure 6b – Sierra San Felipe, North-Central Section

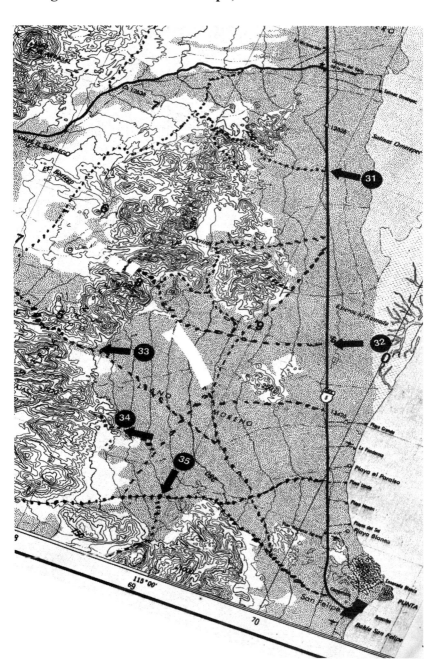

CHAPTER TWO
Sierra San Felipe – North-Central Attractions

CALAMITY CANYON (Figure 6b, Map Key #31)

We approach Calamity Canyon via Federal Highway #5. As we (verbally) motor along that highway, eyes glued to the shrubbery blanketing the six-mile-wide plain to the west, we are mesmerized by the brilliance of an orange colored blanket spread over the land by flowering ocotillo.

Yellow adds pattern to the blanket where flowers of the palo verde poke through. Were we to make this same drive in late spring we would find purple where palo triste, more popularly known as "smoke tree," commands the scene. Alas! With all this beauty how can anyone call it barren?

Access to Calamity Canyon is via the center of three adjacent dirt roads located between highway markers 150 and 151. Having made the turn and now approaching the mouth of the canyon, we cannot help but notice a significant color difference between the mountains on each side of its entrance. That is, the canyon appears to be a dividing line between older and younger mountains. Specifically, the north-side mountains display appreciably less desert varnish than those to the south.

The most plausible explanation for desert varnish seems to be: during sustained hot and dry periods wind-borne pollen containing iron and manganese salts (obtained via plant roots) adhere to surrounding surfaces where temperatures as high as 200°F can cause a polymerization forming this seemingly indestructible plastic coating.

Adding more drama to the scene the desert floor between highway markers 150 and 140 is in the shape of a100-foot deep V rather clearly indicating a significant drainage at some time in the past. In fact, the width of that V (ten kilometers) and its depth tend to suggest the drainage of seawater trapped in Santa Clara Valley (et al) six million years ago.

Consequently, owing to the manner in which the mountains interrupt the V, I believe they were uplifted after that drainage and could have been coincident with a major seismic event (known as the Salton Sink) that occurred two million years ago.

From its 20-meter wide entrance Calamity Canyon road proceeds in a northwesterly direction to a Y intersection. The right leg of that intersection terminates in a relatively narrow channel a mile farther north while the left leg leads through the mountains (to the west) to a point from which there is a commanding view of (and access to) Valle Santa Clara.

This intersection is not readily recognized by the inexperienced. Key landmarks in its immediate vicinity include a significant widening of the waterway, the change in direction of the riverbed's west bank (from northwest to west) and the sudden appearance of a low, mountainous, dark-colored ridge standing in the center of the V portion of that Y.

There is an interesting side trip a short distance ahead along the right fork of this Y. The sharp-eyed investigator will notice tire tracks climbing the bank on the east side of the channel and disappearing around a hill to the east. That road, at least a half-mile in length, leads to a dead end but appears to have been created by a prospector who dug in several discernable sites along the way.

The proper route through Calamity Canyon follows an east-west line understandably twisting left and right as it penetrates the mountains. One-half mile beyond the Y the waterway passes through a red-hued (solid rock) venturi beyond which the canyon opens to reveal a tree-lined lakebed created while the venturi was being cut.

The abundance of mesquite and palo verde in the lakebed is not only surprising but a dramatically beautiful scene. Mesquite in early spring displays tiny pink flowers while palo verde, following shortly thereafter, displays its brilliant yellow balls (of pollen).

One of the reasons we return to this and each of these canyons is the joy we find in viewing such scenery. Not only does it include flowering plants throughout much of each year, but surrounding terrain tends to describe each canyon's history (such as the red rock venturi and the water-carved hills lining the north side of this particular lakebed). In addition, regarding local flora, it should be noted that the greater San Felipe region was once covered with uncountable numbers of ironwood trees. They're gone now for the most part, having been taken by (20th century) woodcutters.

Beyond "Mesquite Lake," Calamity Canyon's waterway continues through a succession of interesting scenery including one place where there appears to be a branch canyon leading south. This is a false canyon while ahead, at a place where the waterway does a squared-S turn (its left and right turns approximating 90 degrees) the sandy surface becomes noticeably deeper. In fact, at this point the sand becomes treacherous and the waterway is split by another Y.

By following the extreme left side of the waterway, visitors are led to an otherwise hidden channel. In contrast, the right side leads to the canyon's west gate from where a view of the Sierra San

Pedro Martir is possible. Between each leg of the Y there is a stand of trees and a rocky surface that, for vehicle safety purposes, is unsafe to negotiate (says the voice of experience).

Apropos of Calamity Canyon, a name I will justify shortly, I broke an axle at the beginning of this squared-S turn during my second visit, and my buggy suffered a blown tire at the entrance to the hidden channel during my fifth visit.

Because Hidden Channel leads to more desert drama, this is not a place for the finicky. Entrance to the channel involves inching over a sharply pointed rocky waterway at its mouth. Once inside, however, the road leads east, ascends a short hill and makes a T. The left leg of the T goes nowhere; the right leg leads to the drama although there are a few ups and downs ('*vados*" in Spanish; "dips" in English) along the way.

Suddenly (that means drive slowly because) we come to a final ascent and—voilà—a rather sheer drop-off of several hundred feet. Believe it or not, it is time to find a parking place, break out the camping gear, set up tables, chairs, tablecloths and cooking equipment and enjoy a well-earned rest during lunch as we observe the distant Sea of Cortés! (I.e., Hidden Channel has turned us around and taken us back to a point 500 feet higher and a mile south of Calamity Canyon's east entrance.)

Continuing west from the squared-S, we come upon an eroded 50 foot tall, naturally occurring monument (on our right side) that none of us would like to have fall on us. (There is debris at its foot that somewhat obviously came from its top.) Beyond the monument we prooceed a short distance to "West Gate," the termination of the canyon and the beginning of a difficult descent to Power Lines Road and the valley floor.

Difficult descent? During our first visit to this canyon with Pepe and Em Garcia, we ran a more or less straight line west out of the canyon, chasing waterway after waterway until we came to a 90-degree turn at the base of a tiny vent volcano. At that precise point I (my buggy) became stuck in loose sand, and behind me the same thing happened to Pepe.

Because the waterway was exceedingly narrow and paved with deep sand, we worked for an hour to free Pepe's buggy first. Meanwhile, the sun was descending to the western horizon and our gasoline gauges were asking for help. With the first buggy free we used it to free the second but then had to find a way around the sand, the volcano, the seemingly impassable lava it had spread and several additional miles of knee-deep sand.

We made it… eventually, coming upon Power Lines Road, Highways #3 and #5 and, without further ado, home. But, because no one knew where we had gone, or where we may have been found, we named the place Calamity Canyon. This ordeal may be considered a close call and exemplary of the mistakes too many desert travelers make. Thank heaven we had the know-how and patience to enable our escape from deep sand, to recognize surrounding terrain (a landmark volcano in the distance along Highway #3) and how to return to the highways.

CLAMSHELL CANYONS 1 and 2 (Map Key #32)

Access to Clamshell Canyon 1 is via a dirt road originating 200 meters south of Highway #5's kilometer marker 166. Although this road is visible from the highway, a lone house on the opposite side of the highway stands as a convenient landmark.

Access to Clamshell Canyon 2 is via a dirt road originating at Highway #5 in the immediate vicinity of marker 155. Depending upon recent rainfall and the amount of traffic this road has recently known this turnoff can be difficult to find. Consequently, for those desiring to experience "Clam Two" the recommended access is via its connector to Clam One. Neither of these sites is a bona fide canyon. Rather, they are naturally eroded features over which water has flowed in excess.

Clam One is approximately eight miles west of the highway. It is a pie-shaped place bordered with high hills and a deepening sandy floor. The mountain forming the south boundary of this triangular basin has a roadway scratched into its surface suggesting the work of a prospector. The west end of the basin follows a rocky riverbed uphill to a V-shaped cut suggesting the ability to see into Santa Clara Valley. But such is not the case in this comparatively remote region strewn with clamshells deposited during the recent ancient sea.

Adding to the drama of this place there are: 1) a caldera-like structure hidden in nearby mountains, 2) a place improperly called "the turquoise mine" (the ore is a sulfide of copper), and 3) a connecting channel to Clamshell Canyon 2. In addition, there is a north-south oriented, volcanically uplifted hill at the entrance to Clam 1 whose west face is adorned with an attractive material I call "extruded rock." This rock is so common throughout the Southwest it is mined and used for construction and landscaping purposes.

I often wonder whether our access road should be named "Clamshell Canyon Road" or "Elephant Tree Road". Shortly after departing the highway the road perpetrates an S turn, crossing a narrow waterway and rises atop a hardened surface lined on its north side with elephant trees. While these are young trees less than two meters high, larger elephants adorn the north end of the Clam 1-2 connector where they are at least five meters high and wide. When there has been sufficient rain, these trees (at the connector) rank among the most beautiful elephant trees I've seen.

There are at least three varieties of elephant tree in the local area: "Colorado" with its smooth dark red bark, "*Bursera hindsiana*" with its smooth gray bark (both the gray-and red-barked elephants are also called "torote"), and "copalquín" with its gold-hued bark with the general appearance of corn flakes peeling from it.

There are two Y intersections along the road to Clam 1. The right fork of the first, three miles west of the highway, provides access to the caldera while leading to the connector (and the secondary access to Clam 1). Driving this route, a waterway, I found an orchid-like flower I've never been able to identify. The size of my thumb, its flowers (white with purple throats) grow at the top of a three- to four-foot stem. I subsequently found others in another waterway that told me the plant is endemic and most likely common to waterways only.

Visitors along this road must exercise a keen eye to find caldera's entrance, hidden by brush but accessible via a narrow, north-south oriented, waterway issuing forth from it. That entrance is another of the many narrow, water-carved (solid rock) portals found in this dramatic region.

Viewing the caldera as a clock with its entrance at position six, it is best described as a circular, bi-level arena with steep outward-tapering sides. The lower level of its floor was eroded by a water-way pouring down from the one o'clock position and is channeled around the caldera's outer perimeter (to the outlet). The upper level, fully a dozen feet above the lower, is composed of perilously soft dirt riddled with ground squirrels' holes. This elevated level occupies more than 75 percent of the caldera's floor.

I love this place for its serenity and the palpable sense of mystery it exudes. There are two lava flows adorning the east wall (at the one and two o'clock positions). What's more, while touring a party around the caldera one day, I came upon animal tracks indicating a mountain sheep fleeing a cougar. Whatever the end of that story told was not in evidence, but what a joy it was to see this tell-tale evidence of geologic and animal activity.

The right fork of the second Y, four miles west of the first, leads directly to Clam 1. The left fork threads its way in a south-westerly direction between cholla, desert sage and ocotillo to a parking area adjacent to the turquoise mine. Spanning a quarter of the distance between the two Ys, two volcanic formations separate the forks of the first. Many of this area's visitors climb one or both of these (50 feet high) red mounds for a view of surrounding terrain. Included in that view is one to the west where arroyos have carved the desert floor in such fashion as to make impossible any thought of reaching the connector by any means other than established roadways.

Entering pie-shaped Clam 1, we find Extruded Rock Hill, a dark brown, 75-foot-high, quarter-mile long volcanic structure forming the base of the pie's triangle. Fossilized clamshells are scattered throughout the sandy, tree-lined floor covering the remainder of the area. The principal road ends in deep sand near the west end of the pie. Another road, intersecting the first at the entrance, cuts across the foot of Extruded Rock Hill, circles around behind it (more deep sand and many trees) and terminates at its intersection with the connector to Clamshell Canyon 2.

The connector opens to a 100-meter-wide, oval-shaped arena riddled with rocks and gullies the truly adventurous will want to investigate. Others will follow the road east and northeast to its intersection with Highway #5 at kilometer 155. Calamity Canyon's (Sea of Cortés) overlook is located 500 feet above the north end of this oval-shaped arena.

Returning now to the turquoise mine, the access road descends slightly as it approaches two perpendicularly arranged mountains flanking the west and south sides of this place. During that descent the road begins a 360 degree turn along which there is ample parking space. At the beginning of the loop the road intersects: a) a north south road coming over from the entrance to Clam 1 and b) another road teeing off and leading in a southwesterly direction. This is a short road terminating in less than a half-mile but takes the eager investigator behind the lower of the two adjacent mountains, crosses a streambed and terminates where the road is cut by a deep arroyo.

From the parking area, walk east to a faint roadway ascending the hill now directly in front of you. Follow this roadway around the hill to a river channel descending from above (from west to east, that is). The ore is found on the sides of this narrow channel.

Freda and I were departing Clam 1, one day, when I decided to cut across the desert towards Cerro Coloradito, a volcano complex with a two-mile-long solidified lava flow extended in a northerly direction. The moment I dropped into the riverbed paralleling the roadway, an adult cougar jumped from behind a nearby bush and dashed away. To this day, I carry a mental picture of that magnificent animal (its color a blend of chocolate and purple) with its legs outstretched fore and aft and three-foot tail straight as an arrow. It is a reminder that this particular carnivore seems to prefer open space to such enclosures as canyons and arroyos.

POWER LINES PASS (Map Key #33)

A difficult place, at best, there is no earthly reason to come here unless you are a racer running a pre-race trial or a bona fide race. Owing to racers the roadway is riddled with moguls over which they literally fly. You and I, on the other hand, must suffer the aggravation of never-ending, somewhat rhythmic, potentially annoying ups and downs that can take a toll on suspension systems.

The pass is narrow; the roadway parallels the power lines running, in general, alongside their square-based steel support towers. North of the pass the road is carved into the west flank of the San Felipe heading ultimately across the north end of Santa Clara Valley on a westerly heading to their point of origination at Rosarito.

South of the pass the road splits with Power Lines Road (used by racers) leading to San Felipe while the left fork follows a north-easterly heading across the desert to pass along the north side of Cerro Coloradito and terminate at Highway #5. This secondary road is a scenic route offering seldom seen views of this remote section of the San Felipe Desert (also known as the Moreno Plain) and all its eroded, vegetative glory.

Owing to the time and trouble it takes to arrive at such a place (the south end of Power Lines Pass) I usually search for a clearing with sufficient firewood to make a (luncheon) fire. Breaking and sorting the wood by size, we need neither paper nor liquid fuel in such places, only a lighter or match we carry as standard equipment. Steaks and sausages are fresh while chicken is always pre-cooked. A green salad dressed with E.V.O.O. (extra virgin olive oil) and balsamic vinegar and, voilà, lunch is an equal part of another fun-filled desert outing.

DIATOM FALLS (Map Key #34)

Another remote place far from the madding crowd, Freda and I escorted a number of friends into this arena to celebrate Easter. In this case it was a late-morning feast that included sliced Polish ham, hard cooked (colored) eggs, a variety of salads and the fluffiest chocolate cupcakes (by Sandy Hackett) I've ever tasted. And what is ham if not accompanied by horseradish, eh?

This is not an easy place to find because it is essentially in the middle of the desert. Access is via a dirt road running straight as an arrow from a point about 100 meters east of Saltito Road's kilometer marker 16 to Highway #5's kilometer 152. Although I've never measured the distance, the turnoff to the falls is at least five miles northeast of Saltito Road but easily recognized by a steep (20-foot) descent to a sandy riverine floor.

A sharp turn to the left (west) at the base of that hill enables visitors to follow tire tracks all the way to the 40-foot falls that are, throughout most of the year, bone-dry. Along the way additional desert drama reveals itself through the presence of a large deposit of pure white calcium carbonate (including crystals). What's more, four miles southwest of this place, the chalk mine, a branch of the same deposit, can be visited via a road branching north from Saltito Road at kilometer 16.

Freda and I, with Pepe and Em Garcia, were driving to Rancho Chinalito early one morning when we came upon an elderly couple walking along Saltito Road. Stopping to ask them why they were walking, we learned they had gone to the chalk mine the day before, buried their pickup truck in sand and opted to remain the night before going for help.

This was a couple that had had a good idea. They'd heard of the chalk mine and thought it would be a fun afternoon outing to visit it and return in time for dinner. They told no one where they were going, had no food with them and he required daily heart medicine he'd left in their trailer. Pressing for more details, I learned they dug sand from around their rear wheels to no avail. But that didn't prepare me for the scene we visited shortly thereafter.

As luck would have it an elderly Mexican rancher came by on his way into San Felipe. I stopped him and asked if he would help us pull the pickup truck out of the sand. The man agreed, the couple got in the truck and away we went (about one mile) to the chalk mine.

The truck was pitched at an angle approximating 45 degrees. That is, this older gentleman and his lady had dug half the distance to hell... and their truck followed. When I questioned the Mexican regarding the rusty length of chain he was about to use (I carry nylon line), an aged length of chain stretched well beyond limits, the 80-year-old replied, in Spanish, "Out of the way, Sonny. It'll pull that and a whole lot more." (I love these old geezers, don't you?)

Diatom Falls' riverine roadway is quite sandy and can be difficult for those with improper (or improperly inflated) tires. As evidenced by tire tracks most traffic passes along the south bank of this east-west waterway although the north bank is well worth trying to avoid previously loosened sand.

The calcium carbonate area offers occasional crystals and crystalline formations to the industrious searcher. What's more, a side trip following a particular ravine (halfway between the falls and the roadway) yields a well-worked mining area with pile after pile of rocks set aside by mechanized equipment. I found the area excellent for photographic purposes with more than ample parking for groups of men and women interested in rock collecting (and a neat picnic spot).

We parked near the falls, set out tables, chairs and tarps for shade, enjoyed the Easter feast and then wandered around to experience the totality of this place. Moments later one of our number called to us from atop the falls. There is a small southwesterly branch to this stream about 100 meters east of the falls. Walking up it, we came upon an attractive eroded gully that makes good photocopy and other eroded features that make rock collectors happy.

CAÑON DE CUEVITAS

This is a low mountain pass (elevation 1,400 feet) allowing easy access to and from Valle Chico. The original road from Ensenada to San Felipe passes through and is in daily use. The east end of this pass displays a low-grade fossil site with decaying seashells hidden in the sand along the west side of a small (seismically uplifted sea floor) hill located at kilometer 19.

This same uplift offers a stage upon which to view the Moreno Plain, the Chinero Plain, the Sierra Pinta, Colorado River Delta, Sea of Cortés and, on a clear day, Sonora's Altar Desert dunes more than 100 miles distant. The stage is composed of Nature's concrete: dissolved seashells (calcium) mixed with sand.

There is a sandy waterway paralleling the north side of the roadway through the entire pass. Bordering the waterway's north flank there are small caves in other uplifted hills in which meat-eating birds (hawks and ravens) leave the larger bones of desert juanchitos they have enjoyed. Here again, we have a brief picture of life in the wilds.

Owing to these bones I am reminded of indigenous man and woman who said a prayer to the bird or animal they were about to kill, hoping it would understand it would find life after death in the Indian's body.

Did anyone say drama? Until someone harvested it there was a beehive in a natural rock cave on the backside of kilometer 19. I took many tourists there to enable them to understand this type of life in the wilds. That hive was eventually harvested and the bees moved to another place.

The left fork of the previously described Y at the west end of this pass (kilometer 21.5) is called East Valley Road while the right fork descends to the valley floor and its dramatic offerings. A higher quality fossil site is located along the right side of East Valley

Road at kilometer 23.25. Here, like teeth on a crosscut saw blade, five uplifted ridges expose fossilized colonies of 6, 7 and 8-million-year-old seashells. Visitors will notice evolutionary differences between many of these and today's shells of the same species.

Although hidden (and difficult to find), a seldom seen continuation of this deposit is located on the east side of the road. Passage to it is nearly impossible but worth the effort of those few desert devotees with other vehicles in company (for safety). Many have looked in vain; the true desert devotee will find and enjoy this remote place… especially for its six-inch clamshells. If they don't, they'll at least drop (literally!) into Ram's Head Canyon and find a convenient way to return to Saltito Road. (See Chapter Three)

Figure 6c – Sierra San Felipe – South-Central Section

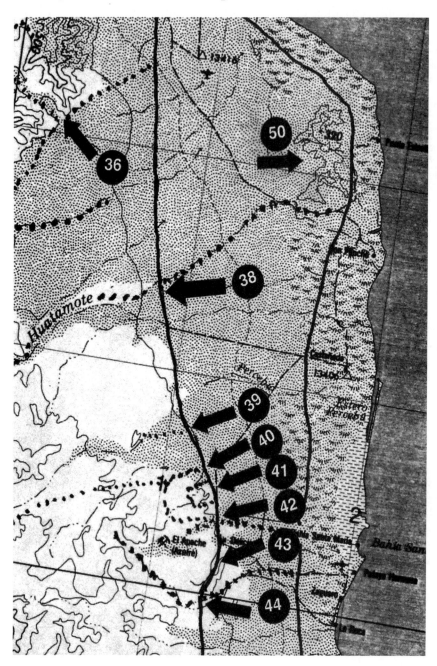

CHAPTER THREE
Sierra San Felipe - Center Attractions

More than any of the others, not only does this mountain range offer San Felipe's visitors a treasure trove… nay, a pleasure trove of places to visit time and time again with family, friends and picnic baskets, its central section is the primary drawing card. To be perfectly candid, San Felipe's visitors have a choice to make between 50 miles of sandy beach and the inland features described herein. Whereas a beach is an environment enjoyed by millions of men, women and children, the desert is another living entity most men and women know nothing about. Therefore, to enable your choice between these two dramatic drawing cards I offer (for prospective desert enthusiasts) Ram's Head Canyon, Hidden Valley (and its northeast extension), Arroyo Chanate, Arroyo Huatamote, Coyote Caves, Cougar Flats and Pumpkin Rock. Remaining (Sierra San Felipe) attractions, equally worth seeing, are described in the following chapter..

RAM'S HEAD CANYON (Figure 6c, Map Key #35)

Access to Ram's Head Canyon is via a dirt road originating about a half-kilometer west of Saltito Road's kilometer marker #13. By turning south on this road (Ram's Head Road) and driving about 400 meters you will come to Red Rock, a 50-foot tall landmark-like red volcanic outcropping. There is an intersection here with another dirt road leading east. (It returns to Saltito Road at another location.) Continuing south along Ram's Head Road, we'll cross two more miles of desert before encountering the canyon's narrow mouth.

Making entry (and exit) difficult, there are three pairs (one behind the other) of deeply anchored rocks in the mouth of this canyon that standard-width automobiles cannot pass. My own vehicle (with Volkswagen axles) is slightly wider than a sandrail but narrower than a standard automobile and must climb the side of at least one of these rocks (in each pair)—a fact requiring muscular coordination (regarding clutch, brake and accelerator pedals) and sufficient skill to avoid damaging tires, wheel rims and running boards.

Beyond the entrance the width of this short, narrow canyon remains constant through its first bend (to the west) and ascent to the desert beyond. The floor of this section, which I'll call "the narrows," is adorned with brittlebush and a variety of desert grasses. Beginning where the narrows fan out to the upper desert taller grasses (similar to pampas grass) are encountered as are a density of other plants including mesquite and an occasional buckbrush (Ceanothus greggii perplexans). Driving south along the upper region the spinosis variety of Ceanothus can make passage painfully difficult (Ouch!).

Whereas the narrows is another attractive demonstration of a water-cut channel through solid rock the upper desert area is quite difficult as there is no bona fide roadway. Passage, therefore, requires following others' tracks or cutting one's own trail. I explored this upper desert area (the width of which spans slightly more than a mile between East Valley Road and the western base of the San Felipe) from the narrows to its southern terminus (an estimated five miles distant).

With head on a swivel as I drove back and forth through this difficult section, I searched for a trouble-free passage to East Valley Road and encountered an unexpected variety of terrain making such passage impossible in most locations and not without difficulty in others.

The Valle Chico uplift (an equal and opposite reaction to the Salton Sink?) occurred two million years ago. At that time the eastern two thirds of the valley (from Saltito Road to the drug rehabilitation center) experienced a tapering uplifted ranging from five hundred feet at the fossil site (km 23.5) to the original desert floor at km 44. A portion of that distance is crowned with a narrow ridge extending from the fossil site to a point some eight kilometers farther south. East Valley Road straddles that crown so that any approach to it from Ram's Head is an uphill battle over rugged, erosion-channeled and densely vegetated terrain.

Near the south end of the Ram's Head region, adding even more drama to it, I came upon a place Indian women used to teach their youngsters how to make axes, scrapers and other cutting tools. Oddly enough, this site is in a small bowl at the east end of an east west oriented ridge with a plenitude of flaked natural sandstone.

Evidence of this ancient school covered an area spanning fifteen feet in diameter. There were tire tracks nearby but they led to what appeared to be a prospect with no indication of discovery of the training site. (So near and yet so far.) From this remote site, I motored at least a third of a mile down the slanted face of that ridge, dodging ocotillo and cholla by the gross, to arrive at East Valley Road (and a relaxing passage home).

How did Ram's Head get its name? The skull of a ram's head (with horns) was found in the narrows by an acquaintance. The first person to tell me about this place wasLester Brickney, a retired engineer I haven't seen in at least fifteen years. When he described the place to me, he knew of no name for it but described its restricting entrance and the hidden fossil site, which was all the bait I needed to check it out.

If you were seeking a name what would you call it? Of course, once you've been there and suffered the indignities it has to offer you may think a better name would be "Impossible Place" but that's a negative term and most of us prefer positives. So, I hereby offer three challenges.

Can you find your way to the southern terminus and describe what it looks like?

Can you find three outlets to East Valley Road?

Can you find the extension of the fossil site (with its 6-inch clamshells) mentioned earlier?

HIDDEN VALLEY (Map Key #36)

Two canyon-like features scar the east face of the mountains flanking the west side of the pueblo of San Felipe. I tried each but was turned back by impenetrable fields of rocks washed from above by erosion. The northern cut, in my opinion, leads to Hidden Valley's northeast extension. The southern cut leads to Hidden Valley (an arroyo, actually) but is blocked by a single row of recently uplifted mountains. Had the mountains not arisen this passage would serve as a shortcut to the arroyo.

Originally, there was no hidden valley... only a broad plain with four riverine drainages pouring onto it from the adjacent Sierra San Felipe. When the Sierra Santa Rosa uplifted, forming a boundary like the Great Wall of China, this "valley" was created and drainage from it shifted from south to southeast. "Let there be mountains," it may have been said, and up came the Sierra Santa Rosa and a series of vent volcanoes adorning adjacent desert floor along their east-southeastern flank. Could this be a rule of tectonic activity? Wherever mountains are uplifted there is pressure relieving volcanic activity along their backside?

While there are two access routes into Hidden Valley, one (I'll call east entrance) is relatively difficult to find while the other (west entrance) is impossible unless you know the terrain better than the back of your hand.

There are two principal arteries leading south from the pueblo of San Felipe. The primary artery is the paved extension of Federal Highway 5 to Puertecitos (and beyond although that segment is not paved). The secondary artery is the original (unimproved) road to the sulfur mines (and Puertecitos) originating at San Felipe's southernmost Pemex (gasoline) service station. East entrance is accessed from this dirt road although there are no maps showing the way. Therefore, visitors must be informed, know what to look for, or forego the pleasure of exploring Hidden Valley. (A future option will be a new map created for sale via the SFARP library.)

Proceeding south (from the Pemex) along Old Puertecitos Road we pass a small agricultural community, several roads leading east and west and then nothing but desert until we come to a highly visible T intersection with an unimproved road leading east to Highway 5 (and a blacktopped extension of it leading to San Felipe's International Airport. Although the proper access to the airport is via that extension, one-quarter mile east from this intersection there is another dirt road leading directly to the airport. It ties into the extension about one hundred feet east of the airport terminal.)

From this point south the terrain on the west side of the road is subdivided into ranchette properties as evidenced by fences and minor structures. This subdivision is known as Ejido Salinas Gortari because it was a land grant during his presidency.

The word "Ejido," pronounced "eh-HEED-oh," came to Mexico with the early Spaniards. It signifies a governmental land grant (usually to a cooperative of at least one hundred families) for agrarian purposes.

There is another dirt road leading west alongside the fence marking the southern boundary of these properties (there is also a huge tractor tire at the southeast corner of that final property). One hundred feet west of this intersection there is a Y with the left fork (ultimately) providing access to Hidden Valley.

Because the intersection between the Sierra San Felipe and Sierra Santa Rosa is not blatantly obvious from any appreciable distance these two mountain ranges appear as one continuous mountain range. As we approach that intersection, the eastern entrance to Hidden Valley remains invisible until it is directly in front of us where, as a complete surprise, a two hundred-meters-wide opening suddenly appears as if from nowhere.

At this precise juncture, I am reminded of an essential activity I neglected through each and every canyon visited to this point. That is, ladies to the right, gentlemen to the left. Or, as Doris Krause insists: Ladies to the right. Gentlemen are never right.

Hidden Valley is seventeen miles in length. The principal scenery, the valley's surrounding mountains, is a mixture of volcanic and granitic formations that, for me, describe an interesting variety of seismic activities. In addition, there is a scattering of mesquite, an occasional ironwood tree, palo verde, gobernadora, seasonal flowers in bloom, a cardonal (a cardón forest, that is), outcroppings of conglomerate rock, riverbanks (indicating the ferocity of previous runoff) and unique eroded formations. In addition, there are six turnoffs including the northeast extension, North Riverbed, Lost Souls Riverbed, the Cloisters, West Gate (the Connector to Arroyo Chanate), and Hidden Valley Gorge.

One mile west of the entrance, there is a sheer rock face with a vertical crack that once housed a beehive. I used to stop there to show the hive to tour participants until the day the bees attacked me. I couldn't believe it: I was being attacked by hundreds of angry bees no matter how fast or far I ran. My arms flailing as they were did little to deter the flying pinpricks from their vengeance. In the end, I reached for double handfuls of sand to spread on my head and every cubic inch of air around it. Either they didn't like my tiny stones or they tired of their sport and returned to base. Why they attacked after so many years of my visitation I do not know. But, I never bothered them again… nor they me.

Beginning at east entrance the southern half of the valley is choked with trees and bushes while the north side is an active waterway forming a sandy platform on which the road is located. Within the second mile, a cardonal stands along the south flank of the pass-plugging mountain mentioned earlier. Beyond that dam-like mountain you will recall a narrow boulder-strewn pass (I once tried to penetrate) and direct access to San Felipe.

Our roadway doglegs left at the cardonal to run a handful of miles in this new direction. Across the valley, other cardón stand in the protective shadow of the Sierra Santa Rosa. I have to believe both these stands were, at one time, a solitary forest. Now, however, the waterway has cleaned a path as neatly as an eraser through chalk on a chalkboard

I visited this place one week after Hurricane Nora and found it as smooth as a slab of marble: No plants, no rocks, no shrubbery of any kind; nothing but a sandy freeway marred by my tracks alone. And such is the power of water. This discovery enabled me to look back, over the millennia, to envision a startling repetition of growth and erasure for as long as this waterway has existed (two million years?).

Still can't handle major chunks of time? Although it is not necessary, that type of comprehension leads to a hands-on understanding of what occurred first, second and third in the greater San Felipe region and, like assembling pieces of a puzzle, tends to make more interesting everything there is to be seen here.

Entrance to the northeast extension appears in the eighth mile. Unmistakable, with an opening spanning fifty meters in width, it is a mile to the first turn, a half to the second, and another mile to terminus: North and east, north and east, and south to road's end.

I love this place because it is quieter, if such a thing is possible. Not that Hidden Valley is noisy but there is, in my opinion, greater tranquility off the beaten path which souls such as mine inure. This is lion country—where they bear their young, that is— for I have seen their tracks here repeatedly.

Driving the extension's first mile, along a wide and sandy plateau, there are no plants save those on adjacent hillsides. At its second turn we find another carved rock venturi, which explains why the sand is so deep beyond it. Racing downhill, that is, runoff scoops sand like a kid scooping bubbles from a bathtub but drops it when slowed by the venturi. And here, in the depth of this loose sand, many of my tour participants voiced a preference to flee to the valley below.

Am I a sinner—for exposing my clients to difficulty—or a saint for protecting the lion's domain? I'll let you answer that question but one day, in this seldom seen corner, I will move enough rocks to clear its northeast passage and create an entrance within sight of San Felipe's Arches. The moment I do, of course, there'll be another Nora and I'll have to start anew.

Too bad I'm not a lion. They go back and forth with impunity via this rocky route. How do I know? San Felipe's missing puppies tell me. That's right; mister and missus lion visit outlying sections of the community for an easy meal… and another animal kingdom display of survival of the fittest.

I led Ken Darsch and Ray Sanders into the extension not long ago and could not believe what we found. The venturi was completely gone. In its place was a seventy-foot wide passage declaring there never had been a venturi. That is, some recent storm deposited so much water that it completely erased a significant part of two adjacent mountains. Further, the place I used to visit while my clients were parked (for lunch) at the extension's southeast terminus was completely blocked. In earlier days I frequently drove up a narrow sandy avenue cresting at least two hundred feet above and a mile east of my clients' parking area to search for animal tracks for it was here, in this upper private reserve, that lion cubs were brought into the world.

A cemented surface I believe to be Cretaceous sea floor adorns the ninth mile. There are clamshells here (and oyster). Parts of this cemented area are rippled like the windblown ripples found along many beaches. This place signals a change in surrounding terrain. Beyond it, stands a narrow, ten-miles-long range of low yellow-colored hills I believe to be cretaceous. They start at the cemented surface site and run in a straight line towards Arroyo Chanate although they terminate about a hundred meters short of that goal.

Aside from their color, a darkened shade of yellow, one other feature drew my attention to them: These hills are dotted with chunks of lava thrown from a nearby volcano. These "chunks" have no matching neighbors along the north side of Hidden Valley's main waterway, only themselves and precious few of them. Where they came from is obvious but why here, why so few, and why nowhere else? I frequently believe Madame Nature enjoys toying with at least one of our human minds.

North River is next, within a quarter mile of the cemented floor site. It is a bona fide riverbed draining a small portion of the valley's northern domain. It is not a dramatic place, only 1/2 mile in length with more than the usual ground cover but it exists and occasional tire tracks demonstrate others' curiosity about it.

Owing to ground cover, in particular, the turnoff for Lost Souls Riverbed is more difficult to find. Once found (its entrance is almost directly across from the entrance to The Cloisters), it becomes an interesting run along a winding waterway to its terminus more than a mile distant. Each side of this run is adorned with a variety of desert growth including the ever-watchful Cardón.

From the moment we clear the entrance, surrounding features call our attention to that difference. I can't put my finger on it, other than plant arrangement. These are the same desert plants— mesquite, spinebush, cholla, an occasional chupa-rosa and cardón—as most other locales but, somehow, it and they are different. Passing through here is as though we were in a showplace… demanding notice.

On the day I named this place, we had passed its hidden entrance when a vehicle horn sounded over and over again. We stopped and waited for whoever it was that somewhat obviously wanted our attention. As it turned out, it was a middle-aged couple in a borrowed jalopy who'd gone out on a morning run, become disoriented and had been spinning circles ever since.

They were not only lost, they were near the panic stage and the sound of our engines was like the Host to a good catholic: Salvation. We gave them water, calmed and reassured them and sent them on their way to the east entrance and home (following our tire tracks). Assuming they made it, I'd bet my seat at the World Series they haven't returned to the desert since.

The entrance to The Cloisters is like the entrance to Lost Souls, you have to have an eye for this terrain and know what you're looking for. The last time I was there I saw no tire tracks, the best evidence there is for a lack of knowledge about such places.

Why me? Because I'm a tracker. I see things in the wilds most men and women don't see. Comparable to the possession of other notable talents (cooking or piano playing, for example), I was granted a keen eye for this type of detail.

Whereas age (forgetfulness) can be detrimental to anyone in this capacity it has not yet raised its ugly head towards me. Oh, I've made mistakes... while on tour... leading folks into a blind canyon during one event and over the wrong road on another. But anyone can do that if he and she haven't been in a given location for a year or two.

My presence in any one of the places described herein occurs on an average of once every two years. I usually describe the places I visit as numbering fifty-six, which is not a false number and may be smaller than the totality of the separately identifiable places I've visited more than once.

The difference between those of us who venture into such places and those who don't is dedication. For me, going into a place for the first time is like attending a lecture: I take copious notes and photographs whether real or mental. Returning to any given site involves referring to those notes and photos. And when I do, I see it and it alone: Scenery returns freshly to mind while all else is blocked from that same mind until called for.

The entrance to the Cloisters is partially blocked by gobernadora. It is a one hundred feet long, twenty feet wide waterway narrowing to eight with two quick turns beyond the entrance.

Strangers will back out thinking there are naught but deepening sand and a wall of (hardened) ancient mud. At the second turn, a 180, the sand is quite deep and can be troublesome. But look what happens the moment we're beyond that trouble: an arena as large as a football stadium enhanced with the Cloisters… a series of eroded vertical formations like no other in the greater San Felipe region.

Beyond the entrance there is a scarcity of plant growth. This is another dramatic scene demanding explanation. Why the formations and why no plant growth? Is it a function of chemistry such as is found in salty (alluvial) sea floor? Yes, it is alluvial and it was seafloor; beyond that I cannot comment except to suggest its elevation has subjected it to land-whittling wind.

The yellow hills run along the southern boundary of this place. In fact, they provide part of a rainbow of color in the southern background. The floor of this hidden basin is sand-colored. Above that, a darker formation behind which the yellow hills stand, then red (the outpouring of an ancient volcano) and the brown-hued tweed of the Santa Rosa.

Look around. In fact, take a walk, as there are a number of water-carved channels here. And, there is scenery in addition to the cloisters. Learn where the yellow hills terminate and whether there is a link between this place and the connector. Learn also that this entire region is barren but for a smattering of scrub.

During one particular visit we discovered a swarm of gold-winged beetles feeding on that scrub as though it was the only food in existence. Leading a tour of twenty-four delighted men and women, I promised the beetles we wouldn't bother them if they didn't bother us. We set up our camping gear, enjoyed a delightful lunch and pleasantly absorbed the drama of surrounding scenery.

The seventeenth mile leads to the western entrance and Hidden Valley Gorge. In fact, the gorge is the valley's western terminus. The waterway makes a 90-degree turn here (the connector is directly ahead and the gorge is to the right). With the east and west banks of the gorge rising right and left as we continue, rocks and trees force us along a narrowing, gently curving path until we can proceed no farther. Parking our vehicles, we walk to experience this narrowing channel until it becomes too far. From that point, we are at least a mile from the gorge's point of origin.

Rules of the road governing the visitation of all such places, whether in this desert or another—this country or another—include the premise "If you carried in it, you carry it out." I found a crumpled beer can stuffed in a narrow crevice here and remember it with every visit. I never say a word about eggshells, sausage casings, bread crusts or fruit peelings because the natural world will dispose of them. Man-made materials, however, are prohibited.

We have an obligation—to ourselves, our children, our neighbors, the code of honor each of us lives by, and the animals whose domain this is—to abide by rules that will guarantee their and our continuing enjoyment of all such places…trash free!

The "west gate" connector is not for everyone. The first quarter-mile of it is as tame as the family cat. Beyond that, it enters upon a domain that saw no man until twenty-five hundred years ago. Since then, almost no one other than indigenous man has passed this way.

The connector is, for ease of description, a Z-shaped passage with the two horizontal parts of the Z representing the (tame) entrance and exit. The vertical piece, then, is the difficult part. That is, it is an avenue of polished rock over which rain runoff found its way to a distant sea. But because erosion causes many forms and frequently involves millions of gallons of water that polished rock pavement is adorned with holes and shelves that may or may not be passable. I, for example, filled some holes with rocks (and others with sand) to enable my passage but Madame Nature, who is constantly changing this incomparable place, easily erases such man-made assistants.

Now, because all that glitters is not gold, once inside this central unit, how does one get out? If there's been no one in here recently there will be no tire tracks to guide newcomers up and over an alluvial embankment to its outlet. Rather, the unlearned will follow the waterway to an impassable place partially blocked by a fifteen-foot boulder. And, inevitably, feeling lost they'll turn around to retrace their tracks to hidden valley (and home).

I found the way because I'm an explorer. I found a passage and followed it from the connector to the Chanate. For me, every canyon, every arroyo, every valley is a road leading somewhere and my curiosity led me into most of them in this region. When I arrived here for the first time I was too happy to be concerned. I simply looked around, followed my curiosity, found what I was looking for and arrived in the Chanate.

How many times have I been in similar backcountry—a thousand miles from nowhere—lost in the annals of that land's history? I love it. Dear God, how I love the beauty of places like this! It may be lion's country, or bobcat's or coyote's, or even Mr. And Mrs. Rattlesnake's but don't forget those who have eyes for such places and the freedom to fantasize.

Do you suppose saber-tooth wandered through here? Where did it come from? What did it eat? Where did it sleep, breed, and have its young?

Did the men and women who harvested shellfish near Villa Marina come this way? How were they dressed? What did they carry? What did they talk about? Believe it or not, the answers are here for other curious souls to find… or fantasize about.

Saber tooth's proper name (the species is Smiledon) is saber-toothed cat, not tiger. He and she arrived a little more than two million years ago, existed at the top of their domain and passed into extinction some ten thousand years ago. So, they're gone but not forgotten because they left us lion, tiger, leopard, panther, puma, cougar (these last three may be the same), cheetah, ocelot, lynx, bobcat and house cat. Such a roster as that reminds me of us (you and me).

Our two-legged species now appears to have arrived between seven and ten million years ago. Whereas we call ourselves "Homo sapiens sapiens," Homo habilis, Homo erectus, Australopithecus, ardipithecus and the newly discovered Toumai came before us. Today there's but four of us (red, black, yellow, and white) but we fondly remember Neanderthal and cannot help wondering how many others there were.

The outlet to the Chanate? Okay. About seventy-five feet south of the polished rock floor there is a sandy four feet high bank on the west side of the channel. Climb this bank (there should be wheel tracks showing the way) and drive about seventy meters ahead to another (tapered) sandy bank. Do not turn left or right. but rather, proceed directly ahead to the very top of this second bank and down the hill following the riverbed roadway to the Chanate.

ARROYO CHANATE (Map Key #37)

Discounting the (near-impossible) connector, there are but two entrances into the Chanate, one via the eastern plain and one via Valle Chico. Between these two options, in my opinion, east entrance is the more dramatic. Primary access to the Chanate's east entrance is via a dirt road teeing from the old Puertecitos road one quarter-mile south of San Felipe's old water wells. (These well sites stand along the west side of the road eleven miles south of San Felipe's south-side Pemex.

Following this west-heading roadway (from the wells), we pass through eight miles of typical desert scenery including an attractive density of orange-flowering desert mallow (Sphaeralcea ambigua). I have taken many cuttings from this plant for bouquets presented to Freda upon my return from desert outings. I did, that is, until we learned they have tiny hairs that cause allergic reactions after handling.

With eyes for the entire passing parade visitors will notice an eroded riverbank at a distance along the north side of this road. The remnant of an alluvial fan, it lends credence to ancient drama played out here by virtue of the fact the Chanate's apron waterway no longer crosses old Puertecitos Road. Although the remnant tends to say it did at one time, most of Chanate's drainage now flows into the nearby Huatamote.

Secondary access, although less desirable, is via Hidden Valley's connector. Western access is via a well-marked turn at Valle Chico's East Valley Road marker #41. Should the word "arroyo" bring to mind a ditch-like structure you may set that aside. Arroyo Chanate is a mountain passage with roadway elevations in excess of 1,500 feet. Throughout most of its seven-mile length, it is a wide, sandy avenue with attractive geologic structures adorning its left and right sides.

Beginning at East Gate, a volcanic structure of pure lava, we are mesmerized by its color, caves, and positioning. It truly is a gate beyond which we find a dazzling display of natural scenery, geologic structures and colors. Whereas this entire avenue is one with ever-deepening sand, there is more lava here, more eroded structures, more cardón cacti, trees and desert shrubbery than in most other canyons. What's more, halfway through the Chanate, a layer of eroding calcium carbonate appears at the four thousand feet level.

At this particular point, at the base of this white-colored layer, there is a stand of weeping mesquite, a variety frequently visited by flying insects including the tarantula killer. This black, winged, finger-size, ant-like insect drinks from the droplets raining from this unique tree, which is a sight to behold, particularly in the midst of an impossibly hot summer day.

From the Chanate turnoff at Valle Chico's East Valley Road (km 41), the distance to West Gate is about one mile. One quarter-mile before that rocky gate we come upon another turnoff (to the south) into a tiny parking area for Quartz Mountain. A remote outcropping, frequented by these who believe gold is a natural companion to quartz. Although there is no gold here, few of the site's visitors depart unhappy because this is an attractive rest stop with ample space to set up tables and chairs for lunch with a trail leading all the way around the hill (for rock collectors).

Suggesting no one, without suitable experience, will find the Hidden Valley Connector from the Chanate, there are two interesting features they may find. That is, should visitors traveling from

East Gate inadvertently bypass the turn-off to West Gate, they will run an additional mile, along a narrowing channel to a surprising dead end. Returning from that end with a red face, they will more than likely make a turn to the west, as I did once, onto a well-traveled waterway running a half-mile west to another dead end.

Such errors can be frightening for the inexperienced who suddenly realize they can't find their way out. To the experienced it is an embarrassing moment during which we return to the main channel, proceed a short distance south, and make the proper turn where a host of tire tracks stand like a kid thumbing his nose at those who missed them earlier. Should you miss that turn you'll probably stick pins in your Bruce doll until you do find your way out.

ARROYO HUATAMOTE (Map Key #38)

Similar to Hidden Valley (with its northeast extension, cretaceous area, cloisters, gorge, and connector), Arroyo Huatamote is another drama center. I think of this place as a classroom in which a half-million years of history appears on its chalkboard. That history is as startling as a prizefighter's one-two punch: It'll get your attention.

There are two entrances to the Huatamote: The western entrance (where the arroyo's cutting action began) and the eastern entrance (from which escaping water flowed to the nearby pre-Baja lake). Because this arroyo contains all the evidence needed to prove the most recent ancient sea existed, we begin this account with the formation of the Sierra San Felipe, the melting of world's glaciers (and subsequent rising of the sea), and the beginning of the reformation of glaciers.

As the sea receded, leaving thousands of landlocked lakes throughout the world, rain and melting snow caused those lakes to overflow. That overflow, thinking of the local region only, began the cutting of mountain canyons, arroyos and other waterways that ultimately made this desert region so dramatically different.

212

Here in the Huatamote, when the final breakthrough occurred, its water was released with such force and volume that it cut a sixty-feet-deep channel through the adjacent desert floor. Standing on top that former sea floor—one mile east of the breakthrough point—we not only see this crescent-shaped cutaway (below our feet) but an additional cutaway indicating the breakthrough point was eroding, as well.

To see what happened next we move a short distance east to the riverbank's second curvature. From here, we have a better feel for the drama of escaping water (we are describing the draining of a 100 miles long lake) by virtue of the width of the downstream riverbed.

As the water crossed the eastern plain, the desert's natural resistance to flow caused it to fan out to such an extent we find it covering an area slightly more than two miles in width. We also learn this debris-laden river deposited its rocky-sandy cargo in a delta-like structure where it poured into what is now the gulf but was then a land-locked lake. When man arrived, twenty-five hundred years ago, he found clams, oysters, and sea snails in such abundance in this sandy delta, he (they) made homes nearby and began a harvest that endured until European man arrived on the scene.

If we enter Arroyo Huatamote via its west gate we tend to flow with the current thereby missing much of what happened here. If, however, we enter from the opposite end we tend to meet the arroyo's six million-year-old drama head on. And so, I selected the Huatamote's intersection with Old Puertecitos Road as our starting point.

Turning west on the road paralleling the arroyo's north bank, and set back a few feet from it, we notice the vertical distance between the desert floor and riverbed to be less than one meter. As we drive along this road, keeping an eye on that vertical distance, it doesn't take long to see a significant increase. In fact, as we approach the mountains we find ourselves looking down on the tops of giant cardón cactus and all the while our roadway appears to be level (which it is not).

At the west end of "Riverbank Road," we come to a difficult eroded ramp on which we descend to the riverbed. From here the road proceeds one-quarter mile southwesterly to the venturi that is the Huatamote's east gate. There is a large rock formation protruding from the north side of this gate approximating the shape of an adult hawk's beak. In fact, I call it "hawk's beak" and use it, for reference purposes, as a landmark.

We stand now in the site of a secondary lake formed while east gate was being cut. This is a rectangular fifty-acre lakebed bordered on all sides by hills. Our road cuts northwesterly across the rectangle to enter a narrow, two miles long, water-carved channel. Before entering the channel, however, we notice the hills forming the north wall of the rectangle. Not only are they volcanic in nature, they are so eroded we realize this was, at one time, the location of a drainage from Arroyo Chanate.

The first time I examined this feeder I chanced upon a particular rock about one cubic meter in size. Three of that rock's six sides were adorned with a total of five morteros worn into them by Indian women grinding seeds. I made the mistake of showing that rock to tour participants over the ensuing year, until it disappeared and in its place were tire tracks of a type made by a truck (with a lifting boom).

That 2,200-pound Indian-modified rock is more than likely adorning a private garden somewhere in the greater San Felipe region (and the rest of humanity will never see it, never experience it, and never get to wonder about the women whose hands created those morteros).

Because runoff rainwater deposited that rock where I found it I often wonder where it came from. If it wasn't from an Indian wintering-over site (which is normally near running water), it must have been near a seed-harvesting site. That is, the women responsible for that rock crossed Valle Chico to harvest and grind what must have been highly prized seeds.

Heading west again, in the channel, the brush-covered hills forming the left and right side boundaries are more than a hundred feet in height. Snakelike, the channel winds north and west over a two-mile course to another secondary lakebed I call Laguna Cardón. A repetition of the reason for the earlier lake, water and sediments rested here while the arroyo's final channel was being cut.

With an area in excess of five hundred-acre feet, there are two additional Chanate-draining channels found here. What's more, there is a domed rock formation at the entrance to east channel with meter-size rocks adorning its upper surface: Another indication of the power of water in motion. But now, as a part of the living drama of this remote place, the top of this dome bears witness to how some rocks are cracked. That is, there are straight-line stains in this dome where, one day, bona fide cracks will appear… and this time our living drama becomes the chemistry of a crack. The overall process is called "erosion by the flaking-off method."

Moving west again, the channel continues from the southwest corner of Laguna Cardón. As we approach that corner we notice a layer of calcium carbonate at the bottom of the mountain along our west side. I found pure calcium crystals among the rocks someone had chipped from that formation.

Next, we negotiate a series of south and west, easy and difficult turns through solid rock in a channel ranging from ten to fifty feet in width and littered with all sizes of rocks. In fact, we inch our way over boulders in more than one place but sail along sandy waterways in others.

Surrounding terrain is a mixture of solid rock, uplifted rock strata and well-weathered lava. Colors range from brick red to charcoal gray. Desert plants adorn every possible place with room enough for roots. There are side channels but nothing of significance as far as investigation is concerned. Every turn brings different scenes that make this run one of the most interesting in the Sierra San Felipe.

When secondary lake number three appears we decide to rest, set up tables and chairs, and prepare lunch. Another large rectangular area this broadened expanse is bordered in the west by a cardonal. There is sufficient deadwood for a fire and before long we have a heap of red-hot coals.

Today's selection begins with sliced mozzarella (buffalo if we can find it), sliced red-ripe tomatoes, a chiffonnade of basil, a dollop of E.V.O.O. and appropriate spicing with coarse salt and freshly ground black pepper. We're having an Italian favorite called "Caprese."

Completing this midday meal we grill skinned, deboned and seasoned chicken thighs under an aluminum foil cover (to minimize heat loss). Lunch involves an hour during which we rest, chat, cook, eat, and leave the place precisely as we found it (after burying our coals). Whether picnicking or dining in the desert, eating outdoors is no excuse for eating poorly nor is there an excuse for leaving trash behind.

The final leg of this twenty-mile run through Arroyo Huatamote takes us through a deep, elongated, sometimes difficult fluvial deposit over which we climb to find our way into Valle Chico. As though it was bidding us farewell, this departure is not without a significant degree of difficulty. The final hill, that is, is so steep and often so eroded it involves another test of driving skill. Fortunately, there is an alternate hill seventy-five meters south of the primary if rain, runoff, erosion or other factors have rendered the main line exit impassable.

To understand this deposit one must understand what happened here as the main lake was drained and through every subsequent storm. Little by little, loosened topsoil was piled here in such a manner it eventually blocked the arroyo's entrance and rainwater runoff is now relegated to a narrow channel south of the roadway and separated from it by a volcanic uplift.

Choices for the homeward leg of this journey include returning via a) the Huatamote, b) Parral Canyon East (the place I call Crazy Horse), c) Arroyo Chanate, or d) Cañón de Cuevitas. Whereas selection usually depends upon where tour participants reside, those from southern locations frequently opt for Crazy Horse Canyon while others opt for Cañón de Cuevitas (the easiest and quickest return to San Felipe and points north). Regardless of the return route, properly planned, this is a seven to eight hour run which allows ample time to enjoy the Huatamote's incomparably dramatic scenery to the fullest.

COYOTE CAVES (Map Key #39)

We were heading to Sulfur Springs when a coyote trotted across the road in front of us. Having frequently wondered where a coyote's trail might lead we did more than wonder this time, we turned... and it led to an amazing place.

Twenty miles south of San Felipe, Coyote Caves is a volcanic mound located on the west side of the old Puertecitos road at its intersection with Laguna Percebú Road. I noticed the place at least a hundred times but never previously investigated it. Now, heading straight for the mound, we found ourselves on a woodcutter's road that made our passage as easy as it must have been for Coyote, which wasn't as hard to follow as one might expect although it disappeared the first time I took my eyes off it.

Unless they're hunting or running from something coyotes have a standard gait (about six miles per hour) enabling them to cover great distances in comparatively short periods of time. As we followed this coyote we arrived at the mound in less than five minutes while our quarry, two hundred meters ahead, finally disappeared from sight. Less enthused about coyotes, my companions went to gather firewood while I returned to the chase and that's when I discovered a path etched into the lava by the toughened pads of a million coyotes' feet over, I presume, as many years.

Although I've seen many animal trails including those cut into the sides of hills and mountains, the cutting of a trail in lava is so rare I abandoned my chase to study it. What I found was a polished fifteen-meters-long path averaging thirteen inches in width. To say coyotes alone had carved it would be as misleading as saying the desert is populated by none but coyotes. Therefore, since the path of least resistance is a rule of nature we may believe everything that ever walked in the area added its feet to this path. Whether man was here is a fact determined by width. Since mans' trails tend to run at least twenty-four inches wide, I discounted him from this trail.

Whereas this path connects a pair of sandy waterways, it stands at the base of a mound mined with caves. Therefore, satisfied my coyote was gone I decided to check the caves and discovered the first had a comparatively small opening but an interior dimension of an estimated one cubic meter. Continuing my trek I discovered caves of every animal size including several larger than a cubic meter and many half that size.

As one might expect in coyote country, I found so many "signs" (droppings) scattered around the mound that suggested colonization or at least birthing rights. Whereas I thought of photographing the scene, I remembered how few find animal droppings as interesting as I do. On the one hand, they tell me who else is in the area. On the other, they tend to describe how many and, to some limited extent, age and gender. Since photography was out, I continued my trek to find the far side of this odd-shaped mound as interesting as the near.

Exploring now by sandrail (while the others prepared lunch), I searched for tracks and the directions they might lead when I came upon a trackway as evident as an animal freeway. To my immediate surprise, this was not a coyote trackway; rather, it was one of animals I envisioned coyotes eating and therein lay the mystery. Remembering films I'd seen showing lions lounging beside a herd of wildebeests, I decided nature knew what she was doing and survival, among animals living side by side, was a function of the fittest.

After lunch, we came upon a cardonal where, standing in their sandy preserves, Cardón share naught but the rays of direct sunlight, the coolness of night and the mercy of wind although when it does rain, they drop as well. Because no two are alike they remind me of people and I often find myself talking to them. And why not? I am the visitor and they who stand and wait the landlords. I walked amongst a thousand of these sentinel-like giants spread over hell's half acre in a desert a hundred degrees hot on a particular November fifth. And, when I asked how old they were, one old fellow told me he was 250 and I believed him for at his feet were desert varnished rocks that substantiated his claim.

The ground I walked upon was littered with tumbled rocks bearing every stage of desert varnish and among them was a variety as interesting as I'd ever seen. Consider a piece of lava resembling a jewelry box with a dozen tiny compartments (for rings and keys and coins). I found another specially crafted rock resembling a birdbath with channels from top to bottom for water to run from one little basin to another.

Before we departed this amazing arena we came upon a tree I thought sufficiently interesting to photograph. The remains of an old mesquite, it had long since died but still stood proud with a stalwart trunk holding branches in picturesque form.

I came, I heard, I saw and the things I saw included a variety of caves where one of the desert's most beautiful creatures has found a home, security, and ample food to keep it here long enough to carve a path through solid rock. I saw cactus that grow naturally nowhere else on earth but are as plentiful as hair on a hound's back.

Because they are the longest-lived life form on the peninsula, cardón are what I look to for wisdom. Many of these old giants saw eighteenth century Spaniards and probably remember the padres of the same century. What's more, their parents and grandparents would have known pre-Hispanic Indians and a plenitude of pre-Hispanic history. The plants I spoke to this day saw the original coming of miners from the north and fishermen from the south.

I saw no rattlesnakes today—I've photographed at least a dozen—although I did see a jackrabbit so large I thought it a kangaroo. Funny thing about being in the desert, you have to look twice to be sure of what you see. When you do, you realize how beautiful the desert is. I saw a possum the other day and a badger the day before. Today, however, I found Coyote Caves in the place I love so much… twenty miles out and a hundred miles from nowhere.

COUGAR FLATS (Map Key #40)

Continuing south, we come upon two nearly identical desert meadows, each with a road leading west. The first, three and half miles south of Coyote Caves, runs two miles west before turning south to disappear into nearby hills. The second, a half-mile farther south, runs west for a mile and separates into two roads. We will return to this second road following our description of Cougar Flats.

A surprisingly flat five-acre rectangle situated a quarter mile south of our access road's 90-degree turn to the south, Cougar Flats is a suitable place to break a desert journey, set up camping gear and prepare lunch for a desert tour or dinner for a larger group. Bordered along its north flank by an old riverbank, and in the south by the presently active riverbed, it is also a place from where to conduct exploratory runs east and west.

Whereas this riverbed originates in the distant (western) mountains the western run is particularly interesting because it offers an opportunity to explore never before seen territory. This is a long run (well over five miles) that, if you started on the north bank, eventually drops down onto the riverbed. Note, however, that this is a run to take with nothing less than a large group because it leads to a most remote residence and, I presume, a marijuana farm. Suffice it to say there is safety in numbers or should I remind readers discretion is the better part of valor. That is, stay the hell out of this place!

Owing to the nature of the terrain beyond Cougar Flats, and most desert travelers' lack of familiarity with it, continuing south from the Flats is also not advised. On the one hand, Cougar Flats Road leads to a small prospect, which is not particularly difficult to find. On the other hand, it passes through relatively dense shrubbery making the roadway difficult to follow.

For those who do follow it, the road eventually turns east to cross an otherwise hidden meadow before entering hills within which it terminates, suddenly, in a dangerous place with a sheer drop-off (at least thirty feet) and insufficient space to turn (safely) around.

When I initially investigated this remote region, Freda got out and walked away with her heart in her throat while I inched my way back and forth on a slippery hill with both feet on the brakes. If you remember how I described our entry into the Jaquegel—when John Sigala refused to ride with me—be advised that roadway was a piece of cake compared to this.

Why do I try such places? Because I am drawn by the magnetic attraction of the desert; because of the desert's indescribable beauty feeding my insatiable curiosity; to enable my sharing of places few have seen, or ever will see, through my writing.

Would you understand if I told you I saw a roadrunner's nest with chicks in it? Like the Hope diamond, hummingbirds' nests are things almost no one sees but because I have the wherewithal to search them out, I can share such finds with you through words on the printed page.

There is a hidden connector to Sulfur Springs North located in the meadow bordering the west flank of these hills requiring trackers' eyes to find. It is difficult because it involves cutting trail through dense shrubbery. And, referring to the name I gave this strangely remote place, it is dangerous… for this, too, is cougar country.

PUMPKIN ROCK (Map Key #40)

Why is it so many of the best places are near impossible to find? This apparent fact seems to apply equally to the neatest shopping areas, the absolute best ethnic eateries and, here in the desert, the most beautiful and challenging tour sites. In this case a ten-mile loop up, over, down, and along some of the most frightening terrain (to newcomers) in the greater San Felipe region.

One half-mile south of the entrance to Cougar Flats there is a similar desert meadow in the center of which a dirt road (Pumpkin Rock Road) leads west. In this case, however, there is a fork in the road with the left fork leading to Pumpkin Rock. (The right fork leads to the riverbed penetrating the hills east of Cougar Flats).

We drop into and cross that riverbed to attain access to the Pumpkin Rock domain which stands, in its own way, unique of all the greater San Felipe's tour sites. Approaching a small hill, we begin a climb in a place giving the appearance of an apple orchard. It isn't an orchard but it has never failed to remind me of one. I suspect it is a facade of beauty placed where it is to ease the hearts and minds of those who fear the unknown.

A sharp left turn, down hill, across a rocky streambed, up a narrow roadway and a brief interlude of meadow-like terrain with a small, perfectly shaped volcano in the western scenery. There is scrub growth here (under your feet) with flowers measuring but one-eighth-inch in diameter. The gray-green leaves of an occasional (February flowering) brittlebush... and lava, the ever-present lava.

The road seems to go right but it doesn't. It is a joke played by the memory of those who prospected here a hundred years ago. No, the road goes left, down slightly and then right to enter upon—left wheels on one side, right wheels on the other—a challenging narrow waterway filled with a host of pointy rocks. Like the false road above, this is a test to learn whether you have the skill to continue.

One man didn't. He stopped, refused to continue and asked for an escort to lead him back to town. When I told him I had no one who knew the way, that he had but another seventy-five meters to go and could brag about his passage thereafter—he gulped, got back in his 4-wheel drive Subaru and continued to the meadow with grinning pride.

The Pumpkin Rock Tour is a challenge. It is a dramatic outing with sufficient difficulty to make drivers think twice before making their moves. It is a memorable outing most participants look forward to year after year and it isn't over as far as this writing is concerned. From this point, we have to cross a rather deep streambed offering another degree of challenge, a right turn, down into deep sand (without getting stuck), over a few rocks and up onto terra firma again to climb another hill.

We're not only halfway there, we're halfway through this blind man's bluff. Ahead of us there is another false lead, more lava, a difficult climb, and a fantastic view of the distant Sea of Cortés (we frequently stop here for lunch). Next, over the crown of a parabolic passage we must cross without falling irretrievably left or right (would you believe I've never lost a client?). Owing to the drama experienced along the way, arrival at Pumpkin Rock is anticlimactic.

Yes, it exists, and yes it is worth seeing. Eight to ten feet in diameter, Pumpkin Rock has two large holes worn into it like the eye sockets of the typical Halloween pumpkin. Parking on another rocky roadway, we have to cross a rock-strewn field and a rocky streambed for a hands-on experience of our goal. (Anyone for photos?)

Anticlimactic? From this point it is less than a five-minute drive to the Old Puertecitos Road. The point being, if you can manage the challenge we'll make your return trip pleasant. What's more, I can have you on blacktop less than twenty minutes later. And, for those who enjoy the celebration of living through such a challenge we frequently stop at Laguna Percebú... where tables, chairs and cocktails offer satisfying relaxation. It is the perfect conclusion to another perfect outing.

Figure 6d– Sierra San Felipe (South)

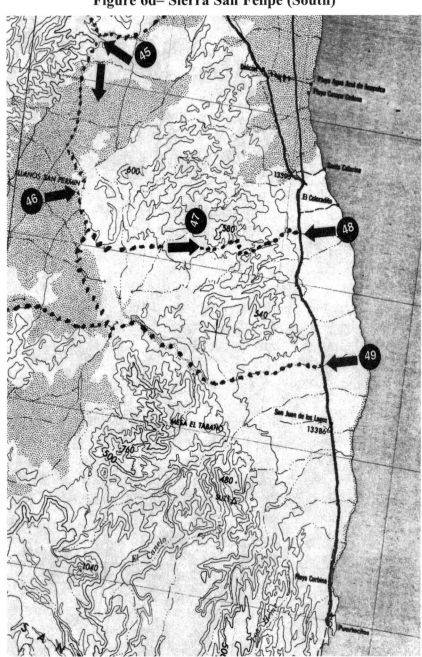

CHAPTER FOUR
Southern Attractions

In the previous chapter you had a taste of the best San Felipe has to offer. If we considered that offering the main dinner course the following must be considered "dessert." But by no means is this the end of tasty reading. That is, "You ain't seen nuttin' 'til you've seen the almost unbelievable Pinacate. We suggest you place another log on the fire, get comfortable again and read on. These southern attractions include Sulfur Springs North and South, the sulfur mines, Crazy Horse Canyon, Apache Tears and Arroyo Matomí.

SULFUR SPRINGS NORTH & SOUTH (See Figure 6c, Map Keys 42 & 44)

To enable an understanding of what could be around the next curve, over the next hill or along a given waterway we include these brief side-trips because they were enjoyable to us and could be for you. Our goal, at this juncture, is not these side trips but the sulfur mining area that follows.

The names "Sulfur Springs North" and "Sulfur Springs South" are nothing more than (hopefully attractive) names rather than indicators of what is found in either of these two remote sites. The northern site is entered via a narrow arroyo running along the northern boundary of the sulfur mining area. Specifically, the arroyo stands a few feet south of the intersection of Old Puertecitos Road and Campo Santa Maria Road (west).

After entering the arroyo, a fifteen feet drop from surrounding desert terrain, we follow its sandy course west between adjacent mountains, along the southern periphery of a tree-lined basin to its terminus where a mountainous watershed empties onto a narrow extension of that basin's floor.

Because this place exists I prefer to believe a thousand similar sites exist and I am constantly on the lookout for them. This and they are natural creations that have nothing to do with mankind. We may believe, however, that members of the animal world found such places thousands of years before you and I and continue to make good use of them for any number of purposes.

The plants that paint this inner basin green grew from seeds brought by birds, rain and wind. There is a density to these plants that tends to tell us (you and I and our vehicles) to stay out. There is also sufficient erosion of the basin to make the western half of it impassible by any means other than walking.

Beginning at the southeastern edge of the basin, where the arroyo opens to it, there was a roadway leading in a north northwesterly direction to enable passage to Cougar flats but weather and plant growth have significantly erased that road. Therefore, because crossing this particular density of plants is unusually difficult, I suggest it be forgotten.

Aside from the possibility of connecting to Cougar flats, Sulfur Springs North is a blind alley. Because it exists, however, tire tracks demonstrate the number of visitors it experiences on a recurring basis. Therefore, as a mile-long blind alley with ample space for minor activities it may be considered a relatively private place to enjoy a relaxing lunch. Because this is cougar country, however, I seriously doubt I would spend a night here.

Access to Sulfur Springs South is via an unimproved roadway leading west from the south flank of the sulfur-mining site. This roadway begins at Highway 5 opposite the north boundary of Campo Nuevo Mazatlán and continues across the Old Puertecitos Road (in the center of a large grassy plain) to its terminus deep within the distant hills.

Because this site penetrates farther into the mountains than the northern site there is more to be seen in this southern area and all of it interesting from a purely investigative standpoint. Things we find in such places are not only pleasing to the eye, mind and soul, they enable us to record natural (and human) history for an understanding of the affect it may have had on adjacent sites.

Vini, vidi, vici: There is purity here where Nature can be herself in whatever form she chooses (rain, mesquite, praying mantis or cougar). We discover this purity, study it, and absorb its information. Specifically, because we investigated we learned; having learned we know and with this knowledge we can plan any number of activities to enable the enjoyment of such remote sites with family, friends, and those we have yet to meet.

Sulfur Springs South is another blind alley internally divided into two remote regions, each with a different character. The eastern region includes a series of low hills with a road traversing it in a manner suggesting some sort of mining activity. The western region is narrower, longer, and more weather-carved although there are places where one or more prospectors left their marks. Call this a neat place to hunt for collectibles.

THE SULFUR MINES (Map key #43)

Twenty-five miles south of downtown San Felipe, the sulfur mining site seems to be confined to a narrow rectangle located between one high and one low mountain spanning three-quarters of a mile. It is an interesting place to ponder the mining activity begun here in the late nineteenth century. Many of its so-called mines appear to be hand-dug glory holes following sulfur veins. In addition, however, hard rock workings, distinguished by their light-colored tailings, are extensive in number and dispersion. Latter day activity shows the effects of scoop loaders and bulldozers. The largest tailings pile in this area, marking the site's southern terminus, demonstrates the extent to which miners removed the overburden to follow a particular vein.

Mining activity appears to follow distinct lineaments of severely altered country rock. In this case, decomposed granites invaded by sulfur-rich hydrothermal fluids along joints and fractures: Sulfurous hot water, actually. These zones, with their (small) intersecting veins, range from thirty to fifty feet in width at the surface. Suggesting the presence of ample or more than ample remaining sulfur. Its odor is as strong as that of a road-killed skunk (particularly on a humid day).

Surrounding landscape is tinted a pale yellow by the site's widespread sulfurous mine tailings and scattered debris. A visible concrete abutment constitutes the remnant of a mill standing about one hundred meters west of Old Puertecitos Road where there are other tailings dumps, as well. Scrounging these dumps, or venturing into the other workings, can occasionally result in exciting specimens. I found a delicate piece of pure white crystalline quartz in one of them. But, I hasten to add, such places are havens for rattlesnakes.

Old Puertecitos road passes through the center of this mining area on a gently rolling bench separating its east and west bordering mountains. In addition, Campo Santa Maria Road (West) and Campo Nuevo Mazatlán Road (West) form the north and south boundaries of the sulfur-mining site. From Highway 5, turn west on Campo Santa Maria Road and travel to its intersection with the Old Puertecitos Road. Turn south to enter the sulfur mining area.

Of equal interest, there is a small rhyolite quarry 1.3 miles west of Highway 5 bordering (north side) this unimproved roadway.

These open diggings feature fine-grained liver-colored rocks with a few darker inclusions. The rocks are glassy in texture (a function of their conchoidal fracturing). This site was discovered and opened centuries ago by native men and women who probably made hundreds of fine, sharp, usable cutting tools from this material.

As is the case with most of the sites described herein we visit the Sulfur Mines about once every two years as a function of the San Felipe Association of Retired Persons' (SFARP) desert touring activities. That is, we bring tour groups here, usually on a desert dining tour, allow them ample time to seek collectibles, gather them for an interesting luncheon and speak on the region's human and geologic history.

I fondly remember Rick and Didi Ferrante and their tendency to become lost during such outings although they found us in a manner likened to a bloodhound finding a scent wafting on a gentle breeze. During their first visit to the mines they arrived late and parked in the assigned parking area. Within seconds of parking, however, Didi was out and gone like a cat seeking a meal.

I watched their arrival, turned to speak to Freda and turned again to see Didi disappear around a distant hillside a half-mile away. I think of her in the same manner I think of ancient Indians: She was a "hunter-gatherer." Now in their eighties, they don't get around as much as before but have fond memories about which we frequently speak.

CRAZY HORSE CANYON (Map Key #45)

The Old Puertecitos Road is quite rocky, quite rough, and cut several times by ever-deepening arroyos for the first mile north and south of the sulfur mines. Two miles south of the mines there is a distinct intersection with another unimproved road leading west (and a minor road leading east via a riverbed to Highway 5).

This new road, leading a mile west and twenty-five south, intersects Arroyo Matomí about twelve miles west of Highway 5. Although it has no proper name we think of it as "Apache Tears

Road" because it passes through that region. One mile west of its intersection with the old Puertecitos road there is a "Y" with the right fork leading to Crazy Horse Canyon, a mountain passage to Valle Chico.

The first seven miles of Crazy Horse Canyon Road are a twisting, turning, drama-packed passage to the summit. Along the way we see a deep vertical layer of slate, several interesting eroded formations, an outcropping of calcium carbonate rock and an interesting stand of cardón cactus where the road narrowly passes between two of them. Stop anywhere along this road to search for collectibles including calcium carbonate on which Freda paints attractive desert scenes.

Several years ago I was a member of a group that traveled through this canyon to Rancho Matomí. Halfway through, while stopped to observe some particular attraction, a participant's buggy had an engine failure. When it refused to start he asked for a jump start and I hopped in my sandrail, turned around and... UGH! I hit a rock that caused the puncturing of my oil filter.

Ever try to patch an oil filter? It can't be done. Either shut up and steer or carry an extra. In this case, I failed to trim an oversized bolt mounted directly below my engine's oil filter. When I hit that rock, it forced my rear bumper assembly upward and the bolt penetrated the filter. Murphy's law states, "If it can happen, sooner or later it will." When I installed that bolt I created the perfect "Murphy." We were towed the remainder of that (150 mile outing).

The summit is a grand place for lunch. It is a relatively open area with a few trees, a few boulders, a few bushes and ample parking to enjoy a lunch break. (If the group is too large a better luncheon site is found two miles farther west in Valle Chico's Parral riverbed.) We have seen Baja's horned mountain sheep from this site (in the mountains forming the summit's northern border) on more than one occasion. It is a grand place from which to view Valle Chico's southern segment and, if there's been recent rain, the ground will be carpeted with a surprisingly beautiful green grass.

Descending to the valley the road traverses a straight line with a barbed wire fence along its north side. The south side is adorned with one of the most beautiful desert scenes in the entire San Felipe region. Why? While it may be a function of soil composition the verbena, lupine, primrose, nightshade, cholla, gobernadora, and mesquite growing here are greener, in greater variety and appear, in general, to be healthier. It is a beautiful desert garden spanning at least ten square miles.

Parral Riverbed stands at the bottom of the hill. This is another grand, sandy but tree-lined place to circle the wagons, set up camping gear, prepare lunch and enjoy friends in a peaceful setting. Remembering the days of old and present-day laws regarding outdoor fires, this is Mexico and firewood is still as plentiful as hair on a hog's back. We seldom stop without taking time to enjoy a campfire around which we relax, chat, and add to the overall enjoyment of the outing.

Continuing the journey we intersect Valle Chico's West Valley Road as we approach the opposite side of the valley. Turning south on that road we head for the place the road begins its descent into Arroyo Matomí but stop short to enjoy the cactus arranged here by departments.

On the east side of the narrowing valley we see a cholla cactus garden at least fifty feet deep. Whereas there are a hundred varieties of cholla (opuntia) we believe these to be either "casarata" or "diamond cholla," both of which throw quite beautiful bright yellow-green blooms. Obviously planned by some master hand a pleasant backdrop to these low plants is a stand of eight- to ten-feet-tall tree cholla.

Cardón adorn the western stage with plants ranging to twenty feet in height alongside the road and thirty to forty feet in the background. This is one of those infrequently seen (magazine) cover-photo spots where dedicated photographers take time to compose photos demonstrating the departmental nature of the scene (particularly when in bloom).

Had we turned right on West Valley Road we would have followed it north and west to Parral Ranch. Continuing north from the ranch it is at least a ninety-minute run to San Felipe.

APACHE TEARS (Map Key #46)

Apache tears are volcanically created pieces of obsidian found in abundance in several local areas. Distant and remote, this is one of the most difficult sites to access (via Apache Tears Road. Although a few "tears" may be found along the first four hundred feet of the Crazy Horse Canyon turnoff, the site is at least five miles farther south.

The road begins innocently enough but changes rather dramatically two miles later where sections of it are subjected to erosion by rivulets following well-worn tire tracks. In fact, I have been here when the roadway was near impassible (and used adjacent desert floor to bypass them).

Four miles into this route, there is a steep descent to a riverbed that, under the best of conditions is not recommended for infrequent visitors. It is so deeply eroded it is dangerous. In this case we use a faintly visible detour leading a quarter-mile east and descend to the riverbed like a kid on a playground slide: Happily.

Once in the riverbed the inexperienced must follow existing tire tracks a quarter-mile west to the access roadway and thence south at least another mile to Apache Tears, which is located on the south bank of a half-mile-wide riverbed. Attractive little stones Apache Tears are frequently used as ground cover to minimize water evaporation from potted plants and small garden plots.

The center of this site sits on an elevated rectangular fifty-acre parcel isolated by one large and one small riverbed. What's more, the access road makes a U-turn near the west end of the island to run a quarter-mile east, cross the smaller riverbed and continue south to Arroyo Matomí.

More adventurous desert wanderers will follow the smaller riverbed along its easterly heading to learn how and where it directs runoff from this backcountry to the Sea of Cortés. Because the riverbed fans out onto a wide level plain (covering at least 1,000 acres), it is best to keep one's eyes on a distant east-west oriented, red-hued mountain forming half of a natural funnel through which runoff escapes.

By committing oneself to the funnel and heading to the place that red mountain connects to another we find a narrow sandy avenue descending into a tiny box canyon. About fifty feet wide, the best descent into this canyon is along its northwest side to avoid a difficult lava bed on its east side.

Once inside, a prominent feature in the center of this hidden place is an ancient (solidified) mud bank about one hundred feet long, twenty feet wide and at least ten feet tall. Standing here, where Freda, Em and I carved our initials a dozen years ago, I joyfully remember a similar site the two of us encountered (with many more carved initials) while prowling around the desert outside Las Vegas. With that spot in mine, I try to envision this place becoming equally carved but that has not yet happened.

An essential of such travel (into funnels) is to remember the possibility of encountering deep pockets of loose sand. Such is the case a few feet beyond the entrance to this place because, one hundred feet farther east, the riverbed turns south to pass through a venturi. In addition to loose sand, there are rock-hard slabs of exposed lava that must be negotiated with care. Beyond the lava, and the venturi, there is a deep pit filled with sand forming a parabola. Passage over this parabolic formation is dependent upon recent rain and erosion. It can be impassible and it can be quite dangerous.

Should it be impassible another exit exists where the waterway turns south towards the venturi. In this case simply climb over the shallow bank along the east side of the right turn and proceed east, about a hundred feet to another lava bed (keep right around it) where you will see an unimproved roadway leading north to connect with Apache Tears Road. In this case, look for the detour over which you earlier descended the riverbank and return to San Felipe. I call this route "Apache Tears Loop Drive."

If passage through the venturi is possible, cross the trouble spot, carefully, turn left and proceed (I've never measured it but believe it is about three quarters of a mile) to Old Puertecitos Road. This place, to O.P. road, is one I call Sand Canyon and is a pleasure to drive (particularly after all you've been through to this point).

In a planning sense, from the moment we decide to return to Apache Tears Road my mind centers on the riverbeds crossing that road. In one place, a mile south of the Crazy Horse turnoff, we come upon a cardón-studded riverbed offering east and west exploration. With a "find a road and follow it" philosophy most riverbeds are roads to me and this one is no different. Where it leads, both east and west, is a dramatic surprise I'll leave for the inquisitive few.

Regardless of where we go along Apache Tears Road, with the single exception of Arroyo Matomí, we pre-plan the run as a 6-hour outing. Therefore, it inevitably involves lunch, which inevitably involves a fire and fires create an ambiance around which story telling is ritual …and a good time is had by all.

ARROYO MATOMI (Map Key #49)

More complex than the Huatamote, Arroyo Matomí is the big kid on the block. Living drama? You haven't lived until you've inched your way down its sharp-pointed, boulder-lined path carved through an isolated solid rock gorge from which there is no escape on a bad day. The good days? The Matomí is a desert explorer's haven.

Accessed via Highway 5, Apache Tears Road or Valle Chico's West Valley Road we prefer Highway 5 to arrive easily, freshly and ready to enjoy what only the Matomí can offer. But, I hasten to add, if it's worth driving an hour to enter this arroyo it is worth making the trek with closest friends, cooking gear, good food and a plan to enjoy the place to the fullest (like over a night or two). Not only do we spend occasional nights here when we plan this run we invite Ken and Sarah Darsch (and others) who love the place as much as Freda and me.

Beginning at km 57 we turn west on a dirt road etched into the riverbed by frequent visitors. If it is early spring the brittlebush will be in bloom displaying its vibrant daisy-like yellow flowers. Desert mallow adds its orange trumpets a few weeks later. In addition, the beauty of lupine shames those who would call the desert "barren" although, less than a month later, huge sections of the desert floor will be paved with nickel-size, purple-flowered, ever-spreading sand verbena.

As we approach the first mountains the road turns north, briefly, to enter a narrow pass I'll call the Matomí's east gate. Beyond this point, a dedicated narrows between adjacent mountains, we find ourselves surrounded by mountains forming a flat-bottomed bowl. The east and south walls of this bowl display deep colorful layers of geologic history so striking either of them is the source of a magazine cover photo. Near the center, protruding through the bowl's sandy floor, are two ten feet tall volcanic formations, locally called "the boobies," surrounded by an interesting variety of collectible rocks. I have one I took from this site that approximates a red and white checkerboard.

Continuing west the terrain changes to volcanic mesas on the south side of the arroyo, alluvial deposits on the north side along with an array of scattered streambeds depositing their runoff here in the Matomí. From the moment we arrive at km 57 we have another site in mind and are on constant lookout for the road to Rio Canelo. That place is so dynamic it is impossible to penetrate this southern region without thinking of the drama to be enjoyed in it.

So where do we go, Coach? The Matomí, Rio Canelo or nearby Rio Blancas? It is a difficult choice when the attractions are equally demanding, equally beautiful and equally unique. For the remainder of this chapter, however, our destination will be the

Matomí while the others must be held in reserve as subject matter for another publication (involving the Sierra Santa Isabel).

About twenty miles west of the highway the gorge is a truly difficult, truly exciting passage. All things considered it is easier to drive west to east than east to west although, like the Huatamote, its scenery seems more visible when driving upstream. Whichever direction one passes through the gorge the driver's eyes must remain glued to the roadway except when his and her vehicles are stopped. Therefore, frequent stops enable all visitors to enjoy its dramatic scenery. In one place, for example, there is an interesting slab of uplifted sandstone protruding at an angle from a northern wall.

A word of caution here because the gorge can be closed by storm water and driving twenty to seventy one-way miles is a long way to go to learn about it. Therefore, owing to other obligations, Freda and I usually see the Matomí but once every two years and always ask those whom we think will know before attempting this run.

Prior to the present day ranch, this was an Indian campsite for what I imagine to have been at least a thousand years. Indian artifacts have been found on the ground (under desert foliage) and in caves adorning adjacent hills.

In one of those caves, there is a one-inch layer of accumulated soot on the ceiling and a floor so loose I have to believe it was dug for artifacts in modern times. On the floor of a nearby cave I found three broken metates but did not touch them because, I presumed, others had seen the same pieces years before me. Few collectors of merit will take such pieces knowing they're of little or no value but by remaining where they were used they continue to tell a story of how the ancient ones lived. Men and women who made a difference in their time deserve to be remembered.

Across the arroyo and over a red, lava-strewn knoll, there is another stream, another stand of blues and two Indian graves. There is water here year round. With the arroyo's headwaters in the mountain to the west, and that mountain catching rain from incoming weather the supply remains as fresh as water can be. No wonder the Indians lived here. There is wildlife here, too. Cougars, for example, are known to parade through our campsite while we sleep.

Now there's a cheery thought: Four, six or eight of us are fast asleep (or, so our visitors think) when in walks cougar sniffing the air to learn what's for supper. He or she smells the perfume, the cologne and all the other odors and knows what to do if it has to. But, because it isn't looking for trouble it concentrates on foodstuff and goes on about its business when satisfied.

I have never eaten cougar but you and I both know the ancient ones did. I guess the real question is, "How many people have cougars eaten?" Regardless of who eats whom there is no waste in the animal world. I wish I could say the same for my world but all too often I find tin cans, beer bottles and plastic bags littering the most remote desert terrain.

CHAPTER FIVE
Valley of the Giants
(Map Key #50)

The San Felipe Desert is a living museum. Within the confines of this museum are an infinite variety of geologic formations, boulders, rocks, gravel, sand, lava, seashells and plants unique to a region like no other in the world. Although a part of the vast Sonora Desert, the San Felipe was given its own name because of its distinctly different characteristics. Surrounded on three sides by mountains and on the fourth by the Sea of Cortés the San Felipe lies in a pocket of sometimes superheated air within which rain is as rare as gold.

Yes, there's a little of each but would you believe one to two inches per year for the water? Every ten or twenty years a chubasco (the local name for a hurricane) churns its maddening way through the region to add to the overall average. But twenty, thirty or forty extra inches of rain over a one hundred year span are almost meaningless in a land where plants long ago learned to absorb moisture from the air.

Driving south from Mexicali the San Felipe is entered through a doorway as distinct as the Laguna Salada and the Sierra Pinta. Or, driving southeasterly from Ensenada the entrance becomes San Matias Pass as the highway twists and turns its way to the desert floor alongside a sometimes-violent waterway. And once in the San Felipe, travelers find themselves in an arboretum as unique and as interesting as Nature has created anywhere.

The land is dotted with bursage, creosote bush (*gobernadora*), mesquite (at least six local varieties), ocotillo (locally used for fencing), *palo chino* (cats claw), *palo triste* (smoke tree), *palo verde* and the rapidly disappearing *palo fiero* (ironwood). A closer look reveals elephant tree, several varieties of *cholla*, candelabra (locally called "*senita*" but also known as "the old man cactus") and there's a taller cactus.

Often mistaken for the stately saguaro (unique to the states of Sonora and Arizona), the world's tallest cactus, Baja California's cardón, grows naturally nowhere else in the world. One of the most beautiful stands is found along the Magdalena Plain where they grow to heights in excess of seventy feet. While the tallest in the greater San Felipe region range between forty and fifty they can be hard to find... until you enter the valley of the giants.

Off the beaten track, not only is it there but, according to the plants themselves, the Valley of the Giants has been there for at least a thousand years. When I first came upon this place I was so struck with their beauty, their numbers and their presence that I left my buggy and started off on foot. I wanted to walk amongst these columnar giants to ascertain their age, their individual beauty and decipher the story they might tell me.

While most of them ranged to thirty feet in height, I found one old timer at least forty-five feet tall and four of them at fifty. There were several with trunks three feet in diameter and one with more than thirty branches. I found some dead, some dying and young-sters no more than one inch tall.

From the living I learned their age, from the dead their structure and from the dying a cause of death. Continuing my walk I began to realize something was wrong. I was awed, at first, by the garden's presence and wanted to get as close to it as possible for I have a thing about being close to Nature. But awakened to the fact that something was wrong I concentrated on it and discovered the problem was a startling absence of youngsters. I saw a few but nothing in comparison to the number of adults.

The more I looked the more I realized that the few youngsters I had seen were nearly impossible to find. That is, they were hidden under the protective cover of a shrub and that, I presumed, is what ensured their survival. Now all I had to do was to find either why there were so few or...

"Where is your nursery," I shouted as I began walking in ever-larger circles until my path led me back to my sandrail and I undertook the search in earnest. To me, the things I was seeing (rather, the things I was not seeing) constituted a mystery and I was going to solve it no matter how long it took. An hour later I came upon the answer when I found the nursery about one-third of a mile northeast of the garden. It was then that I discovered what was happening.

Standing there, staring first at the garden and then to the north and south, I conjured up a vision of other stands I was familiar with including the forests south of El Rosario and the giants along the Magdalena Plain. What I saw was a vision of a group committed to a decision by intelligent choice. These big fellows were desert wanderers who, for one reason or another, had their beginnings on a lonely shelf of land where water is converted from the air and a droplet is seldom seen.

Perhaps it was prevailing winds or perhaps I will never know but they seem to have decided on the north and, having decided, their trek was begun. The largest stands are concentrated south of El Rosario where true cardonales (cardón forests) exist. But, for one reason or another, that northerly trek ceased before they reached the thirty-first parallel.

There are a scattered few near the base of San Matias Pass but there are none farther north. On the one hand, almost nothing grows in the Laguna Salada. On the other, there must be something as identifiable to these magnificent giants as that which enabled cartographers and botanists to place a boundary around the San Felipe Desert for it is that northern boundary that halted cardón's northerly trek. Now, however, speaking of treks, did you know one of these spectacular plants was uprooted, packaged, and shipped to Seville, Spain? For that story see Part Four Chapter Two: "The Pride of San Felipe."

Another interesting fact is found in the history of ocotillo, which is not in the cactus family. About ten thousand years of age ocotillo is the newest addition to Baja California's flora. Little known by most area visitors is the fact that this orange flowering tree has a yellow flowering cousin that is so rare it is protected wherever it grows (in Baja Sur).

Ocotillo is related to the ancient cirio (Idria columnaris), a plant southwestern Indians called "Boojum." Having seen my first many years ago at Arizona's Tonto National Monument, and none since then, I was surprised to find them here. And, as Freda's and my exploration covered more and more ground, we came upon three major stands in central Baja with two of them being protected.

Regarding the stand along the road to Bahia de Los Angeles it is another I consider magazine cover material. These plants, ranging from thirty to sixty feet in height, are adorned with Spanish moss, a spidery lichen draped from plant to plant creating a truly eerie scene.

Another interesting plant is the elephant tree (torote) appearing locally in three varieties. Two of them, the grey-barked torote and the red-barked torote colorado, dwell principally in these northern regions while the blond-barked copalquín appears only occasionally in the greater San Felipe region but is common to Baja Sur.

Maguey is another interesting plant found in profusion along each side of the highway at the northern end of the Santa Clara Valley. Here, in May and June, their ten feet tall shoots are topped with brilliant yellow flowers attracting bats and bees and hummingbirds from all over the desert. A mountain growing variety, giant *maguey* (this is not century plant) is harvested after the flower stalk has dried and sold for household adornment during the fall. The trick to these beauties is to spray newly harvested stalks with a mixture of cold water and detergent and, when dry, apply a thorough coating of hair spray, aerosol lacquer or varnish. A relatively common decoration, you'll find many of them—with Christmas lighting—adorning Southern California homes.

Access to the Valley of the Giants is only with permission and the payment of a token fee to the man guarding the gate a few feet west of Highway 5 at the southern terminus of Sierra Punta Estrella. The giants stand about a mile west of the gate in the protective shadow of the mountains. There is a ramada near the south flank of this cactus garden where we frequently set up cooking gear before conducting a loop-drive tour through the garden.

Following the roadway, we penetrate the garden to find an amazing variety of plants including senita and cholla, in particular. At the garden's northern terminus the road continues via a north-south waterway connector to higher ground and a bona fide roadway to the nursery. This road passes along the north side of a single mountain from where there is a view of the distant international airport.

Proceeding, now in a westerly direction, to the bottom of the hill we find the nursery hidden under bushes lining the south side of our unimproved roadway. Walking through it enables discovery of a number of cardón standing from one- to thirty-six inches tall. Allowing one inch of growth per year (depending entirely on available water) it is amazing to see a fifteen incher and think of it being a teenager... or a five footer being sixty years of age.

The road continues in a westerly direction to a hairpin turn to the south (deep sand here) and thence along a straight-line route (at least three miles) to the east-west roadway back to the ramada. The plant that was removed, packaged and sent to Spain was taken from a spot about one hundred meters southeast of the ramada.

Reflecting on the San Felipe Desert as a whole, it is filled with treasures like the Valley of the Giants. Whereas many of its treasures are highlighted in other chapters, I am humbled by my presence in a seemingly mundane desert where ancient man plodded through life with game, fruit, flowers, seeds and shellfish in abundance amid plants whose ancestors marched some four hundred miles to stand in this community and where another plant displays a flower one day and Christmas ornaments the next.

CHAPTER SIX
Conclusions

The San Felipe desert is filled with treasures more wonderful than most of us realize. After the runoff from a 1968 storm, a local man found Spanish doubloons and two silver goblets laying in a sandy wash. Later, during one of my own outings, I found seashells under a rock 500 feet above sea level. Because one or more Indians walking the same trail 800 years before me had thrown them there I began to realize how wonderful this place truly is. Remember the Indian drawing I described from Oso Canyon (of his encounter with a Spaniard)?

Not only is the San Felipe Desert a place with some of the strangest plants on earth it is the place a steadily increasing number of retirees are calling home. Beginning with a remote garnet mine near the northern terminus of the Sierra Mayor and ending at Matomí gorge, Baja's eastern coastal mountains offer some of the most delightful scenery imaginable. Beyond imagination, there is the reality of hands-on experience.

There is nothing, in my opinion, as thrilling as the drama displayed in the San Felipe's many valleys, canyons, gullies, gorges and arroyos. Think, for example, of the Sierras Tinaja and Pinta, the hundred-miles-long arroyo Grande and the dramatic Arroyo Jaquegel.

There is no joy in finding oneself stuck in sand but giving oneself the opportunity to get stuck, wherever it might occur, is so much more important that this simple problem becomes nothing more than a test of driving skills. And after you or your friends have freed your vehicle you may beam with pride and proceed to the next worrisome place with a newfound knowledge enabling you to see what I see: Pure beauty and unadulterated history.

Think not of sand but of a saber-toothed cat giving birth to two beautiful kittens somewhere in the northeast extension. Imagine ice forming again at the north and south poles, in Ethiopia and northern Montana. Imagine, too, the ancient oceans dropping inch by inch until Valle Chico is an isolated lake and the cutting of the Huatamote is happening. See its water bursting forth to carve a sixty feet deep swath across the eastern plain. Enjoy with fascination the turbulence of that water pouring its sandy cargo into a sea where scallops and snails will soon embed themselves for Pai Pai's ancestors to harvest.

Birds abound; bushes and trees begin to grow. Animals come seeking seeds. Mankind arrives and the region's many shellmounds take shape. The Spaniards come and go but cardón remains to welcome you and me and describe to us the past they witnessed. Join me now, somewhere along San Felipe's Malecón, where we order fresh-cooked carnitas, hot corn tortillas and a frosty beer before sitting to discuss the merits of Pumpkin Rock and the Matomí.

Another subject apropos of this conclusion: The Interface. On the one hand the interface is the land covered and exposed with each high and low tide. On the other, because it is ancient sea floor I will include those hundreds of square miles not covered by today's tides but deposited, nonetheless, during ancient tidal activity.

We drew your attention to it earlier when we described a region bordered east and west by Yuma and the backbone mountains (respectively): The Colorado River Delta. On most maps it appears as a pie-shaped wedge of uninhabited land. From a distance it is a broad expanse of worrisome sand but when you drive upon it, you encounter something considerably more frightening.

This is a previously undescribed land requiring the utmost care and consideration. It is a place of dunes and quicksand. It is a place of leftover lava flows and crusty topsoil. It is a place of flotsam and jetsam from a dim, damn, distant past. It is a place most of you should never attempt for fear of never being able to return. And it extends from the north shore of San Felipe's Cerro Machorro to somewhere in the Imperial Valley.

If you remember "the long-liners," (fishing ships utilizing sixty miles long fishing lines) you may know those lines were supported by glass balls floating on the sea's surface. Storm winds tore those lines, freeing many of the balls, thereby enabling them to drift ashore. *E pluribus unum*, my former partner, Calvin Blessing, gave me one he found on this deserted delta. According to him it was one of many that came to rest in this ghastly ghostly region.

I drove the delta on more than one occasion
    a. Seeking the region's largest shellmound
    b. The pirates' *La Ventana*
    c. To learn of its joy and treachery
    d. To experience Laguna Salada's eastern apron.

Hank Thompson joined me on one such run but we quit as we approached Estero Omotepec. Even so, we saw formations neither of us had seen before which was enough to make me go back for more.

If you'd like an easy sampling of this region (Luke and Sandy Hackett joined Freda and me for this one), I suggest a blacktop run to Cerro Chinero, turn east along its south flank (you'll see the road) and follow it to another road leading onto the delta where you'll find lava, crusty topsoil and treacherous sand dunes all in one. It is a drive you will enjoy and one you wont soon forget. But now, I suggest... turn the page and read about another place: More living drama in a beachside community my sixteenth century Melchior may or may never have seen.

PART FOUR

A DISTANT DESERT COMMUNITY

Figure 7 – San Felipe

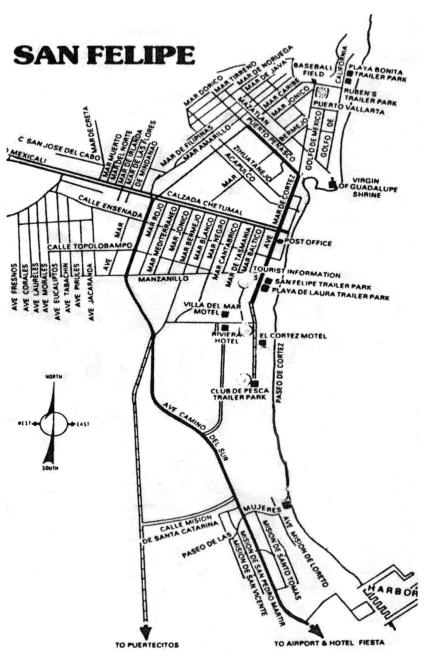

CHAPTER ONE
Introduction to Part Four

Standing in sandals, shorts and a short-sleeved tee at water's edge, I watched as the eastern horizon became a new day. Asleep the day is black but as each new day dawns the black of night dissolves to purple fading to orange until, in the majesty of morning, a tiny speck appears, widens, and swells like a huge orange balloon. It is, in my opinion, the most precious time of life: The daily renewal.

Seagulls announce the dawning like an orchestrated cacophony. A dog sniffs the surf and turns to see its master. A woman scurries by... her swinging arms regulating speed; the swish, swish, swish of her shoes on sand is heard and as quickly fades away. The air is still and I'm standing there in the meditative silence of another magnificent morning.

As heated air rises in some eastern place I can only imagine, cooler air rushes from where I stand to take its place. How many sunrises have there been... or is yesterday a figment of my imagination? Was I born or did I appear out of the darkness of night?

Whether memory or imagination if I was born there was a yesterday and if yesterday happened my father and grandfather were born, and others ...all the way back to...

Shakespeare made Macbeth say, "Tomorrow and tomorrow and tomorrow creeps in this petty pace from day to day until all our yesterdays have lighted fools a way to dusky death." Thanks, Bill, but I find wisdom in each of our yesterdays enabling me to look for the promise of tomorrow. Your writing is classic but is it possible your inner self failed to find the beauty in the dawning of each new day?

Seriously speaking, this is something I've been afflicted with since childhood. My favorite color is the color of dawn. In my late teens I had a chance meeting with the internationally famous soprano Lily Pons who, I was told, was traveling incognito... in her orange skirt and Cadillac. Owing to that color I fell instantly and madly in love with her (and classical music).

IN THE BEGINNING

To have a town, I suppose, we must first have a place to put it. In this case the site was begun with the deposition of Colorado River sediments. When separation of the Baja California peninsula occurred, and the sea of Cortés was created, incoming currents whittled at sedimentary deposits lain at the foot of San Felipe's Cerro Machorro.

This mountain, and adjacent Cerro Kila, is the remnants of a prebatholithic volcano that formed the foundation upon which a desert community was built. Tidal action formed the cove that is San Felipe's claim to fame: A fishing port. Rios Colorado, Sonora, Maya and Fuerte provided nutrients, the Sea of Cortés the medium and the Pacific Ocean more than a thousand varieties of fishes to feed, breed, and multiply within its well-fed depths.

Mar Bermejo, Mar de Cortés, Gulf of California: Baja California's aquatic twin. This liquid desert is the world's richest salt-water aquarium. In my lifetime there were feeding frenzies in this six hundred miles-long pond involving an estimated ten square miles of boiling bloody sea in which every species of fish fed on every other and every sea bird in the region joined the fracas for its fill. As death is a part of life so, too, were these late spring massacres enabling survival of the fittest and renewal of the species.

Because we can count man's presence here in four-digit numbers imagine what these feeding frenzies were like before him. With nutrients endlessly provided by the above-named rivers (the Colorado no longer empties into the gulf unless rainstorm runoff—think of the American monsoon—is so severe it must be released) I cannot help but think of the many tons of phytoplankton that enticed whales and whale sharks into this unique sea. In fact, a resident pod of blue whales is said to have been at the midriff since before the last century.

The first humans to lay eyes on San Felipe are believed to have been the "Painters," an indigenous group who passed this way some three thousand years ago. These men and women, about whom little is known, settled in the general vicinity of Baja Sur's Bahia Concepción where they created paintings in mountain caves from El Arco to Loreto. Fortunately for us, these paintings describe, among other activities, their use of rafts and fishnets.

San Felipe's second visitors are believed to have been hunter-gathers who became Baja's Pericú, Huichiti (also known as Laimón), Guaycura and Cochimí Indians. These were four indigenous groups that settled into and controlled four regions of the peninsula between San José del Cabo and Puertecitos (respectively).

Following them, at least two thousand years ago, San Felipe's next visitors were the predecessors of today's Pai Pai, Kiliwa, Kumeyaay and Cucapah who arrived on the scene, liked what they saw and settled in local mountain regions. It was these men and women who created the shellmounds littering Baja's northeastern shore.

The first Europeans to see San Felipe's cove were (previously described) sixteenth century seamen. Following the coastline north,

Francisco Ulloa discovered he was sailing in an oceanic gulf and that California, the place thought to be an island, was a peninsula extending from the mainland.

Returning along the west side of the gulf he circumnavigated the peninsula as far as the twenty-first parallel before returning to Colima to announce his failure to contact Coronado's men and his discovery of the peninsula. With him was mapmaker Domingo Castillo who created the first chart of the gulf on which either he or Ulloa named every significant location along its two shores. On that chart San Felipe's cove was indicated as "Santa Catarina."

Artifacts discovered near San Felipe following a 1968 hurricane provided evidence of a Spanish presence between 1688 and 1701. Historic records identify that presence as a locally based supply center in support of the planned establishment of nearby missions. Oddly enough, the Franciscans built but one mission before they were recalled to the mainland.

Shortly thereafter, Dominicans arrived in La Paz where a plan was created to settle the land north of the one Franciscan mission (because Russians were known to be penetrating the continent from the north). Departing La Paz by land and sea, two missionary groups headed for San Diego from where their first and twenty additional missions were created between San Diego and Sonoma, California.

Padre Juan de Ugarte arrived in San Felipe's cove in 1721, waded ashore, placed his holy banner in the sand and christened the place Santa Catarina. Twenty-five years later Padre Fernando Konsag arrived, repeated the ritual custom but christened the place "San Felipe de Jesus." (San Felipe was a young Mexican padre martyred in Japan.) Twenty-one miles east of San Felipe a geologically uplifted island bears his name and is a temporary home to many hundreds of migratory seals, pelicans and cormorants. Adding mystique to this tiny guano-stained island in the heat of day (when viewed from shore) it routinely takes the shape of a pyramid, a skyscraper, and an anvil.

Those who approach the island by boat are met by at least a hundred seal pups barking a friendly welcome. Comfortably "seated" on the island's rocky shore successful males are surrounded by their females while the unsuccessful sing their songs of woe from the island's northern terminus. Whereas this small triangular beach is one hundred percent occupied by wildlife, if a pelican moves a seal takes its place and if a seal moves a pelican takes its place. The uplifted rock is adorned with a high number of pelicans, cormorants, boobies and gulls. This is a scene so rich and rewarding that it belongs, in my opinion, in National Geographic.

Padre Wencaslao Link became the first European (known) to reach San Felipe by land (in 1776). José Joaquín Arrillaga, who established a land route between Ensenada and San Felipe through Valle de la Trinidad (seventy miles west-northwest of San Felipe), declared the bay a port in 1792. Long recognized as a habitable site, a commission was granted to one Guillermo Andrade in 1887 to colonize San Felipe but he died during the construction of the original road from Ensenada to San Felipe. Since that road did not materialize until later, the first completed road was built in the early 1900s from Mexicali to San Felipe's sulfur mines.

Records do not clearly indicate when the first fishermen arrived but arrive they did... from Guaymas. (A sketchy history seems to include fishermen's presence in San Felipe between 1901 and 1904). They rowed here, that is, north along the mainland's west coast to Isla Tiburón, across the 22-miles-wide midriff to Baja California, and north (via Canal de Ballenas) to San Felipe, a total distance of three hundred miles.

Campo Uno, San Felipe's first official habitation site, was formed in 1904 under the lee of Cerro Machorro. Because it became a fisherman's paradise it didn't take long for fishermen's wives to arrive albeit by an overland route. The pueblo of San Felipe was officially sanctioned in 1916. The first census, taken in 1928, recorded one hundred names.

Mexicali was settled in the 1890s. Thanks to the Imperial Canal this tiny community began to prosper and was recognized as an agricultural center by 1902. Unfortunately, it didn't take long before this international border town became a lawless boomtown with American dollars supporting gambling, prostitution and drug refining. The city thrived as such during America's prohibition era although gambling was outlawed in 1935 and the city's attention returned to agriculture and industry was added for economic development.

Colonel Esteban Cantú gained control of Mexicali in 1915 when he moved his capital (of northern Baja California) from Ensenada to Mexicali where he governed until 1919. The highway between Mexicali and Tijuana was completed under Cantú's leadership and includes the notorious Rumarosa Grade mentioned earlier in this text.

During this same period, American interests, whose principal product was cotton, owned most of Mexicali's farmland. Thousands of Chinese immigrants were brought into the region to work the fields until 1919 when legislation restricted the practice. By 1935 the Mexican government forced American companies to give up their hold on its land, which they then sold to Mexican farmers.

Of particular interest was the Chinese slave trade, which was run by Mexican and American pirates. There is a prominent vent volcano thirty-three miles north of San Felipe known as "El Chinero." Tragically, its name commemorates the lives of a group of Chinese men being smuggled into the country in a pirate ship. Brutally mistreated during their crossing they gained control of the ship in this locale, beached it and fled into the desert where all but three perished under a blistering desert sun.

IN THE EARLY 1900s

Whereas San Felipe's corvina population has been described as "shoulder to shoulder," the tripe of the giant totoava, a unique variety of sea bass native to the northern Cortés, brought more money than any other fish. These two hundred-pound giants wasted away in the sun after the real treasure (the stomach) was removed, salted and returned to Guaymas for shipment to Chinese markets.

The full potential of the Cortés' marine wealth seems never to have been recognized until the late 1940s when retiring Mexican president Abelardo Rodriquez invited California's Ray Cannon to San Felipe to begin a series of studies of the gulf's commercial fishing potential.

Whereas it was he who identified the majority of the gulf's watery inhabitants, shrimp fleets were formed under Cannon's tutelage and a shrimping industry remains active today south of a line drawn between Puertecitos and Puerto Peñasco with fishing fleets located in Topolobampo, Guaymas and Mazatlán.

Owing largely to Ray Cannon's articles in the Western Outdoor News, gulf sport fishing began and the world beat a path to San Felipe's door. Men like Tony Reyes offered five-day cruises to the midriff islands where game fish abounded. As time passed Mexicali's road to San Felipe became Mexico's Federal Highway 5. Selected streets were paved, electricity came and with it came streetlights and telephones albeit in limited number. Schools came, too... but only as an afterthought.

From a dozen lonely fishermen in 1904 to a population of 100 in '28 to more than twenty thousand by 2002 San Felipe continues to grow. A retired San Diego physicist settled here in '86, captured the telephone company's attention, and that of a Mexicali university, and conducted a demonstration of computer access to the World Wide Web. So successful was that demonstration it resulted in the creation of San Felipe's official Internet Service Provider—The NET—as well as the installation of a thousand additional telephone lines within the community.

Following the 1988 formation of a unique Mexican-American corporation, America's National Pen Company began a campaign of awarding local home sites to a random, computer generated, list of Americans in a newly developing enterprise called El Dorado

Ranch (about eight miles north of San Felipe). Although these home sites were actually located on the side of local mountains they could be exchanged, free of charge, for usable sites in a relatively remote section of local desert. Or, for the payment of a few dollars, better sites could be had in any one of several other communities closer in.

Since the beginning of what many felt was just another real estate scam, El Dorado has grown to more than 5,000 residents with an estimated annual land sales now approximating twenty million dollars. As El Dorado grows, and its influence spreads over old San Felipe, local property values have also grown. Lots initially sold for $199.00 (dollars) are now selling in excess of four thousand and thirty thousand dollar lots are experiencing similar appreciation. In fact, one rumor declares select beachside properties recently sold for one hundred thousand dollars each.

IN THE LATE 1900s

Local businessmen began a San Felipe branch of Rotary International. Following them, local doctors and dentists formed a San Felipe branch of the Lions Club. And, in keeping with public-spirited organizations, Mexican and American housewives in support of the continuing education of San Felipe's children formed an Amigas Club.

Hank and Shirley Thompson settled here in 1987. While he became an avid desert explorer she organized the Friendship Group (in 1991) whose mission was to find, gather and entertain the area's elderly (80s and 90s) men and women during bi-weekly meetings. By agreement with a local hotel manager her group met in the hotel's lounge between ten and noon on first and third Wednesdays. They enjoyed coffee or cocoa and brief presentations by a variety of knowledgeable speakers to keep otherwise shut-in seniors apprised of local news.

In 1994, this pioneering woman invited me to participate in her group as its Director of Activities. Among other things I began a series of narrated 35mm slide presentations depicting my desert exploration. There were eleven attendees at my first presentation, thirty at my second, sixty at my third and… suddenly, we had a problem.

We moved from the hotel's cocktail lounge to its Salon Las Gaviotas, which comfortably sat 150. Freda joined us and we began offering desert tours for those with bona fide desert vehicles. As news of our tours spread those without such vehicles complained so loudly we were forced to initiate specialized tours involving roads their vehicles could conquer. We called these our "Desert Dining Tours"… and fed 157 delighted men and women during one particular event.

Attendance grew exponentially and we began offering monthly festivities, keynote speakers, City Tours (to Yuma, Ensenada and Mexico's Copper Canyon) and a Merchants' Awards program. Our combined total annual participation grew from 168 to 2,750.

TIME Magazine published an article describing (retired) Americans' activities in Mexican border communities including San Felipe. Surprisingly, they not only "scooped" the publishing empire we began receiving telephone calls from as far away as New York City. Suddenly, our distant desert community was in the limelight. The number of (electronic) hits on The NET's web pages tripled overnight; the number of San Felipe's daily visitors soared.

Although TIME's article brought border communities to national attention it was but a flash in the pan: The furor died and tourism returned to a post "9/11" norm. (The American press does its utmost to discourage travel to Mexico via a succession of articles designed to cast a shadow of suspicion on America's southern neighbor.)

If a murder is committed in your hometown it is a horrific tragedy but life goes on. If it happens south of the border it is an international incident and readers prefer to believe an American wife, daughter or teeny, tiny tot could be next. The problem? The press tends to ignore facts in favor of those who pay its bills. Consequently, the general public never learns the truth about crime rates in places like San Felipe and your hometown.

What does that have to do with the twenty million dollars worth of El Dorado's lot sales? We have some awfully nice homes down here and equally nice folks participating in our desert tours. What's more, we think you ought to give it a try in a rapidly growing community where there's peace of mind, you can telephone or email your kids whenever you like, and where many of us start tanning in January.

CHAPTER TWO
The Pride of San Felipe

Gateway to the Sea of Cortés

For many, residents and returning visitors alike, they are a long-awaited sighting. Whether it is absence that makes the heart grow fonder, the hustle and bustle of a trip to metropolis or the two-hour drive across a dramatic desert that first sighting of San Felipe's alabaster arches is a heart-warming experience.

For the newcomer it is an unexpected surprise for who could imagine such a beautiful creation standing way out here? But there's much the newcomer doesn't know. The instant he and she cross the international border, for example, he and she are on the other California. By continuing that penetration to San Felipe they encounter the arches: Mexico's gateway to the Sea of Cortés.

Built in 1980 the arches are the result of a four-state commission created to promote tourism through a continuing program of

A Distant Desert Community

international public awareness of the unparalleled beauty to be found—and enjoyed—along the Gulf of California. Those four states, Baja California, Baja California Sur, Sinaloa and Sonora are the states whose shores enclose this enchanting body of water.

Although there were many sites to choose from, San Felipe was selected to become the portal through which tourists would discover the gulf's many attractions based on its proximity to the thirty-five million men, women and children of Southern California.

Bathed in the rays of a desert sun by day and the brilliance of orange (low pressure sodium lighting) at night, the arches stand tall and proud as they beckon tourists seeking new adventure. As with most monumental creations the arches have an interesting story that was told, in part, by the man whose idea they were, by San Felipe's merchants and by Ismael Soto, the project's Resident Engineer.

Conceived in 1978 by Adolfo Padilla Padilla, a powerhouse of conceptual design, the arches were created under the guidance of one Roberto de la Madrid and designed by Arquitecto Díaz Olmos, the Director of Baja California's S.A.H.O.P.E. (the equivalent of an American Department of Public Works). Their original design was of an all-steel structure at the beachfront terminus of the Mexicali-to-San Felipe highway where they would lend themselves to a startling first view of the Cortés.

Ground was broken in May of '79 but when the site was found to be too soft soil compaction tests were conducted at other sites, emergency conferences were convened and the original hole filled. San Felipe would still have its arches but they would have to sit on solid ground a half-mile west of the sea they introduced.

In addition to the arches the revised plan included construction of a four lane palm-lined boulevard (Calzada Chetumal), the construction of a Malecón (the beachfront drive paralleling San Felipe's principal business district) and altered traffic flow. The end result made the Malecón a one-way thoroughfare north and Avenida Mar de Cortés, San Felipe's principal business thoroughfare, one-way south.

Because the arches' original design included an excessive mass of steel, contractor Alejandro Escobar Huet recommended a change to prestressed steel-reinforced concrete which would involve less material, less time to construct, a reduction in construction hazards, a lower overall cost and substantially greater longevity. Approval was granted, ground was broken at the new site, the soil prepared, and a two-inch bed of concrete was poured.

Anchored to this bed the foundation for each arch leg is composed of one block of steel-reinforced concrete six meters square by three meters thick. Each leg is one and one-half meters wide by three meters long. The outside dimension of each arch is ten meters while the inside is seven. Each of the four arch legs is hollow but one of the four, a center column, contains a circular stairway leading to a connecting bridge near the top of the two arches. Measuring twenty meters in height, the north arch is two meters taller than the south and the view from the top is spectacular.

Construction of the boulevard was begun as the arches neared completion. A forty-feet wide, two-lane street suddenly became a divided four-lane boulevard. Adding tropical beauty to the boulevard, palm trees were purchased and trucked to San Felipe from Palm Springs, California.

Spaced twenty-five feet apart each tree originally bore two colored spot lamps illuminating an area of adjacent roadway. With alternating colors of red, green and blue evenings along the Chetumal brought a beautiful sight to behold.

Next came the Malecón and the widening of Avenida Mar de Cortés, which was closed for two months. Since these were projects undertaken during July and August, San Felipe's slowest business period, affected merchants suffered less than they might have during other times of the year.

Finally, on October 29, 1980, President José Lopez Portillo led the inauguration ceremonies during a four-day Fiesta del Mar de Cortés. Conducted on land now occupied by George's and Puerto Padre Restaurants the fiesta included a twenty-foot high replica of the arches. Special coins were minted and sold with the monies realized going to each of the four states as a partial payment for the newly completed project.

A few years later, in 1984, the world's Western Hemisphere was hit by a blight that killed an unbelievable percentage of its magnificent palms. San Felipe lost as many as most other locations and the few surviving palms made an ugly appearance until they began to grow again. In the interim, those red, blue and green spotlights were replaced by modern streetlights of low-pressure sodium design.

Visible from twenty miles at sea, the fishermen's shrine in downtown San Felipe (atop a volcanic outcropping) and from ten to fifteen miles into the southern desert, the arches are more than Mexico's gateway to the Sea of Cortés, they are the pride of San Felipe!

In 1992, for example, when a giant cardón cactus was offered as Baja California's gift to the World's Fair in Seville, Spain, the packaged plant were trucked to the arches where a bona fide celebration of departure was enjoyed to the strains of Las Golondrinas.

At the conclusion of that ceremony, with music playing and the truck beginning its departure, there were lumps in onlookers' throats as the meaning of the moment struck home. The San Felipe Giant, now rolling slowly past the Arches, was about to take it place on a stage in far off Seville, home of history's Hadrian, the operatic Carmen and the 1992 World's Fair.

Completing the story from Seville, an acquaintance sent a photograph of the giant standing at the entrance to the Mexico pavilion. As if sending a message home there were blossoms on its many branches. Men and women who had never heard of San Felipe may have begun to wonder... and six thousand miles farther west, those alabaster arches, from whence that stalwart giant originated, stand as the Pride of San Felipe.

The San Felipe Giant - A previously unrecognized plant takes its place on a world's stage

Seville, Spain: Site of the 1992 World's Fair. Popular with tourists for its associations with Don Juan, Doña Elvira and Figaro, Seville was the site of the tobacco factory in the opera Carmen, as well. The history of this imposing city began long before Carmen, however, and includes capture by Julius Caesar in 45 B. C., the Moors in 721 AD and a return to Christendom in 1248.

This important seaport located on Spain's Guadálquivir River is famous for the magnificence of the many processions and ceremonies conducted during Holy Week and the gaieties of its post-Easter "Feria" (fair) when it comes alive with bright costumes, gypsy music, flamenco dancing, and many important bullfights.

With more than one hundred twenty countries participating in Seville's World's Fair, beautiful pavilions were constructed for the display of important products, scientific achievements, and national treasures. Designers of Mexico's Pavilion placed a botanical garden at its main entrance featuring plants from each of its twenty-six states. One of those plants, representing the state of Baja California, was a cardón cactus, which was excavated, prepared and shipped from a natural cactus garden nine miles south of San Felipe.

Baja California's cardón (Pachycereus pringlei) is frequently mistaken for Arizona's saguaro (Carnegiea gigantea), a symbol of the American southwest. Cardón is, therefore, an essentially unknown species except to the most devoted of Baja California's admirers.

Whereas saguaros grow naturally only in northern Sonora and southern Arizona, cardón are limited to the Baja California peninsula, on most islands in the Sea of Cortés and along a narrow coastal strip of Sonora (between El Socorro and Guaymas).

These massive plants bear a multiplicity of columnar branches reaching to the sky. Most of Baja's cardón range to fifty feet in height while along Baja Sur's Magdalena Plain a unique stand of the world's tallest grow to seventy-five.

Having a normal life span of three hundred years, the one hundred fifty-year-old giant selected for Seville was forty–two feet tall, had a six-foot root cluster and was estimated to weigh eighteen (metric) tons (39,600 pounds).

At the beginning of this project, the owner of the property from which the giant was ultimately removed spent a week searching for the proper plant in the proper location. Having found it, and with agreement from the local plant committee, workers cut, cleared and compacted a circular area one hundred feet in diameter (around the base of the cactus) for the men, tools and equipment needed to prepare the plant for shipment.

As the project progressed an angle steel framework seemed to grow out of the ground to enclose the giant for lifting and transporting to the Fair. Support for the trunk, and each of its branches, was provided by a series of foam-padded steel rings held rigidly in place by braces welded to the outer frame.

When excavation began the stabilizing roots, extending twenty to thirty feet beyond the plant's drip line, were pruned and the frame's four large triangular feet were bolted firmly in place. With feet in place the feeder roots were excavated (by hand) and, suddenly, the plant hung in suspension. The feeders were cleaned, sealed with a fumigant and enclosed with burlap and a Styrofoam-filled protective sheet-metal housing.

A crane arrived during the afternoon of March 11. The following morning a tractor-trailer arrived that was to transport the giant to Altamira, a deep-water port on Mexico's east coast from where it would be loaded onto a cargo vessel and transported to Seville.

Initially the trailer appeared too small for the task until, with a few grunts and groans of the tractor's diesel engine, the bed of this specially constructed unit was lengthened to forty-eight feet. Only then did I notice it's five steerable axles. In combination with the three-axle tractor this was a heavy-duty thirty wheeler!

Nothing of this import could occur without the arousal of public interest and sightseers came by the dozens. School busses arrived and youngsters poured forth for individual and group photos at the base of the symbolic giant. Men and women who had never before ventured into the desert found themselves staring at a steel–encased cactus destined to stand, a few days hence, in a garden somewhere beyond the horizon.

Cars of every description ringed the site where folding chairs, ice chests, and portable grills enabled observation of the ongoing preparations in relaxed comfort. And in the center of that ring, at 9:30 the following morning, a welder climbed to the top where he worked without a break until four that afternoon to complete the structure.

We were there because we believed the giant was to be lowered by mid-morning. As morning and afternoon wore on, shadows crept slowly across the desert floor and we gained a fuller appreciation for the dedication under which this job was progressing. The San Felipe Giant would stand until, in every respect, properly prepared for lowering and transport.

This humble plant from the land of cactus giants represents the people of Mexico, the men, women and children of Baja California, and the residents of San Felipe. What a fitting representation—this Mexican plant on Spanish soil—for the first European to set foot on the New World's mainland was a Spaniard. What followed, good and bad, is history. We cannot change history but we can learn from it and the San Felipe Giant represents a proud posture of learning.

At 9:45 a.m. Friday, March 13, 1992—four hundred seventy-three years after Hernán Cortés landed at Tabasco, four hundred fifty-nine years after Fortún Jiménez discovered La Isla de Perlas and four hundred fifty-two years after Melchior Díaz set foot on Baja California—the crane lowered its hook to lift the eighteen ton giant. A purchase was made, bolts were removed and, one by one the four triangular feet were carried way.

But the project was not to end without problems. As tension was applied the lifting sling snapped and progress came to a halt. Engineers conferred, a foreman commanded and workmen returned aloft. Four hours later—repairs completed and a new lifting sling in place—the operator pulled a lever and tension was applied again…

but this time it was the crane that balked and a second crane was ordered.

As if that wasn't enough that special tractor–trailer buried itself in sand while maneuvering into loading position. But problems were taken in stride, as they are among professionals, the second crane arrived, the truck was freed and work resumed. By now, three tension–filled days into the final stage of removal, a kinship had developed that resulted in observers becoming a part of the team.

As the second crane moved into position, the site engineer requested observers' automobile headlights turned on to provide illumination to supplement the light of a late afternoon sun. But fate dealt another hand and lowering was postponed to the following morning.

Monday, 15 March 1992. The morning dawned cool with a typical Baja California sunrise painting the land a brilliant shade of orange. No need to rush, crane number two was stuck with no visible way to free it on site. We arrived at 9:30, paid our respects to the workmen we'd come to know and other observers as much a part of scene as they.

Morning minutes ticked away during which workmen began jacking the crane for the placement of boards under its rear wheels; first one side, then the other. Finally, with boards in place the operator backed his rig slowly until, thirty minutes later, his rig was in lifting position.

The structure was inspected again... and again... and again. Lifting slings were adjusted and at 2:54 p.m. crane operators mounted their rigs, started engines, and began to lift. The San Felipe Giant seemed to groan as it leaned one degree, then five, six and ten....

Shouting commands, one voice rose above the sound of the engines. "Bájele! (Lower it!) Bájele! Bájele!" Onlookers were frozen in a trance created by the making of history. Twenty degrees... twenty-one... twenty-two....

Heavier than anticipated, the second crane's left front jack–stand settled into already compacted earth. The operator, nicknamed "El Negro," suddenly realized he was lifting one of the heaviest loads of his professional career. His heart, he admitted later, was in his mouth.

"Bájele! ...Bájele!" Forty–five degrees... fifty.... I was perched on a rocky hillside a hundred meters away, my hands and fingers poised to capture on film any and every event as it did or might have happened. Eighty–five degrees... eighty–six... eighty-seven...

The crowd of three hundred men, women and children from different parts of Mexico, America and Canada burst into a roar of applause as the San Felipe Giant, the king of all the world's cactus, destined to take its place on a stage previously acted upon by Julius Caesar, Hadrian, Amerigo Vespuci and Sebastian Cabot, came gently to rest upon the ground. It was an emotional moment with tears dampening a surprising number of cheeks!

"El Rey descansa (the king is resting)," I thought as I descended to offer my congratulations to the man upon whose shoulders the weight of this project rested. I shook the Chief Engineer's hand, himself shaking like a leaf but smiling like a proud new papa. El Negro told me what had happened and re-estimated the weight at twenty-five metric tons: 55,000 pounds. The owner of a local restaurant told me he'd suggested (to proper authority) the making of this site into a national park.

Owing to the strictest safety precautions loading of the package was delayed until the following afternoon. So now, with the giant lying on its side and the crowd rapidly dissipating, the need for additional ringed supports was identified. Plans were modified, the supports were added during the night and the giant was loaded early the following morning. In fact, the loaded package was ready for shipment by sunrise.

At 8:00 a.m. this truly unique gift was rolled to San Felipe's alabaster Arches where, to the strains of Las Golondrinas the townsfolk paid their respect with a traditional farewell. The San

Felipe Giant was down, out and gone on the first leg of a six thousand mile journey from San Felipe… to Altamira… to Seville! But fate intervened again, a few days later, and another decision was made.

Stopping in Hermosillo, Sonora, after a tortuous, four-hundred-mile journey involving several flat tires, planners at the international level intervened and an airplane was obtained to fly the giant to Seville. The driver of that special tractor-trailer had told his wife he was going to San Felipe and Altamira. She could expect him to return in two weeks. Instead, he drove his monstrous package into an equally monstrous Russian cargo plane, flew to Seville, encountered unbelievable problems snaking through ancient narrow streets and arrived—finally—at the 1992 World's Fair grounds. When he had a moment, he telephoned his wife to tell her he'd be a little late.

Today, that humble cardón, that solitary lord over all it surveys, stands tall and proud at the entrance to a pavilion where men and women from all over the world can observe it, admire it, and marvel at its grandeur. Those same ladies and gentlemen may even wonder about the land of the giants and the place from whence it came: A natural cactus garden nine miles south of a budding seaside resort called San Felipe.

CHAPTER THREE
San Felipe

ONE

Technically speaking San Felipe is a "barrio" of "El Municipio de Mexicali." That is, San Felipe is a neighborhood within the city of Mexicali's geographic limits. Mexicali's mayor is entitled "El Presidente del Municipio," and San Felipe's senior governmental official is El Presidente's "delegado" (his delegate).

Aside from technicalities San Felipe has its own fire department, two police departments (judicial and municipal), a water department, a tourist department, a post office and most other governmental offices one might expect in such a (remote) community.

The telephone company is headquartered in Mexicali but maintains local business and maintenance offices. In addition, there are two cellular telephone companies, two satellite television companies, three purified water companies, a propane gas company and four gasoline service stations with diesel available at three of them.

There are six hotels, a dozen motels, and half a dozen bed and breakfast inns. There are ten recreational vehicle parks and at least twenty beachside "campos" accommodating visitors with leasable lots. There are thirty-five restaurants, five pharmacies and fifteen grocery stores.

There are two coffee shops, one American bookstore, two copy centers, one bank, half a dozen liquor stores, three veterinary services, two ice cream parlors, at least five bakeries, a drapery and carpet center and a public library. There are a dozen tire repair shops, a radiator repair shop, several automotive mechanics, four auto parts stores and a recreation vehicle parts store.

There is one high school, two grade schools, one handicapped children's school and a day care center. Several religions are celebrated in a variety of local churches. There is a Red Cross center, several medical clinics, a (new) hospital, two medical laboratories, more than a dozen local doctors (including a pediatrician, an orthopedist, a gynecologist and several doctors of internal medicine) and a like number of dentists including at least one dental surgeon.

There are architects, a house designer, several house construction contractors, three hardware stores, one bona fide paint store and both new and used lumberyards. (Used lumber is best for construction in our local climate—it doesn't warp.) Rounding out the picture there are electricians, plumbers, glaziers, tile setters and construction laborers.

Recurring annual events include a Mariners' Day (celebrating the men of the local fishing industry), a Shrimp Festival (celebrating the shrimp fleet's harvest), a Snowbird Festival (celebrating San Felipe's winter visitors) and Mexico's national holiday celebrations including a Juán's Day. Need I say there are many men named Juán in Mexico.

Residence for foreigners leasing, renting or buying Mexican property (whether full- or part-time) requires the acquisition of the FM-3 visa (to enable the federal government to know who is in its country). Employment necessitates a special stamp on the FM-3 or an FM-2 visa.

Temporary visitors residing in hotels, motels and recreation vehicles parked at bona fide RV parks need not apply for the FM-3 although they are expected to have the FM-1 (another visa) unless visiting for a period of less than 72 hours and traveling no farther into the country than San Felipe (Maneadero on Baja's west coast and Puerto Peñasco in western Sonora).

San Felipe's rainfall has been quoted as one to two inches per year but recent storms have literally drowned those figures. Storms on September 6 and 13, 1991 dropped a total of ten inches. Hurricane Nora dropped twenty-six inches and the following year's Hurricane Isis dropped fourteen. Assuming at least one 8-inch rain every ten years, I'm inclined to abandon the lesser figures and depend on the basic qualification for a desert classification: Less than ten inches per year to describe San Felipe's average annual rain fall (on a one hundred year basis).

What is it like to live in San Felipe? It is precisely what its' inhabitants make of it in an environment experiencing six months of wind (mid-November to mid-May), the rarity of freezing temperatures, summers in excess of one hundred degrees, idyllic Spring and Fall temperatures and sun from morning to evening throughout most days.

The majority of San Felipe's American and Canadian visitors are seniors enjoying the fulfillment of retirement. Consequently, life includes a modicum of household chores, the enjoyment of one's neighbors and time to celebrate one's hobbies and other niceties postponed during working years.

Seasonal visitors include Mexican and other Latin American tourists from each side of the border although there are but a few from western Baja. In an understandable manner of speaking San Felipe is Mexicali's playland at the beach.

TWO

San Felipe is not for everyone. Among the many are those who dream of being dot-com millionaires in America's ever-changing environment. In essence, these are the men and women who seem to think all environments should be exactly like the one they prefer. Whereas it is natural to compare, it is unnatural to expect any country, any given environment or any particular community to be like the one in their dreams. There is but one bus line in San Felipe, owned and operated by El Dorado Ranch, and you'll find no posted schedule for it… anywhere. Although counter-productive, facts like this deeply annoy the class of men and women referred to in this paragraph.

Similarly, there are many who would be happier in their American and Canadian homes than standing in a local store arguing with a man or woman who doesn't speak their language. In Europe, owing to the close proximity of its several countries, many of its citizens speak two or more languages. In America it is rare to find one out of ten who speaks anything but English. Whereas Canada has Quebec and its French language the number of Canadians who speak French, I suspect, equates to the number of Americans (per capita) who speak Spanish. The crux of the matter is the bulk of San Felipe's visitors do not speak Spanish and among them are those who thoroughly enjoy time spent here and those who do not.

Mexico is a third-world nation with a dramatically different history than that of America or Canada. It is home to more than eighty-eight million men, women and children who, on a one-to-one basis, are some of the most pleasant, most sharing and most friendly of all the world's people. In fact, Freda and I have a rule we learned from Mexicans every time we encountered a stranger (whether walking or riding). That is, smile and wave. Although I speak Spanish and Freda does not those who do not know us may be amazed to learn of the number of Mexican friends we have.

Many years ago the American military introduced a "People to People" program under which emphasis was placed on each of its members to open their minds to the fact that men and women of different cultures are different. Among the many differences are skin color, facial structure, language and the fact that foreigners think differently than Americans.

By maintaining an open mind military members were expected to allow reality to color their thoughts and, because so many of them were traveling world-wide, it was of the utmost importance to make the best possible impression on men and women who had no other contact with Americans. That philosophy, the fact that there are differences between the world's many people, is as valid today—and as applicable to San Felipe's visitors—as it is to America's military men and women.

So there are differences, eh? Well then, let's review a few of them. The first thing I realized when Freda and I moved to San Felipe was that I couldn't estimate distances correctly... because the air I was looking through was different from the air I was used to looking through. Can you imagine breathing pure air? Can you imagine seeing the horizon in its natural state rather than a shade of misty brown?

In its article on border communities TIME magazine intimated San Felipe was different but if you read the article you know a local man described our difference as "No bad days" and that's about as different from wherever you live as communities can be.

—Luis Escamilla owns a corner restaurant in the center of town (Los Mandiles) and wants me to help him produce a news magazine that could make a difference for our local populace (both Mexican and American).

—Across the street, Octavio Ascolani makes a difference with his Marino Liquors, a 7-11 type of store. Next door he has a motel named El Pescador (The Fisherman) and next door to that he has an eatery called "Del Mar." —Across the street from the Del Mar is a bakery that makes a difference for SFARP. It is one of several bakeries from which they buy the bakery items they give away during their meetings (see Chapter 4).

—Across the Chetumal from Los Mandiles, Juaquín Sahagún makes a difference with his curios shop and money exchange businesses. Did you know a Sahagún accompanied Coronado during his Cíbola expedition?

—Across the street from Juaquín is a leather shop in which you can have your passport photos taken or rolls of film developed.

Above it there is a coffee shop with fresh-baked "out of this world" rolls. Next door to the coffee shop is our local bookstore. Next door to that is a computer repair shop.

—Two blocks south of the leather shop, Yolanda Tafoya makes a difference with her YET MAIL business. Not only does she offer a daily U.S. mail forwarding service, she and her staff will assist with the origination or renewal of visas such as the FM-3.

So there's a difference, eh?

- Not only is the language different but the money as well… and the coins are heavier. Paper money is available in increments of five, ten, twenty, fifty, one hundred, two hundred, and five hundred peso notes. In coinage you'll find twenty, ten, five, two, and one peso coins plus smaller units amounting to fifty centavos, twenty centavos, ten centavos, two centavos and one centavo. (Like American pennies there are one hundred centavos to a peso.)

- Aside from the money Mexico's food is different, too. Have you heard of birria, synchronizados, mole or chilorio? You'll learn more about these differences below and after reading about them we suggest you c'mon down and enjoy each of them (and more).

THREE

The number of San Felipe's medical clinics was mentioned above but what wasn't mentioned is a problem each of these clinics endure as a result of the failure of too many of San Felipe's visitors to travel with copies of their medical records. Without them, particularly in response to an emergency, doctors' hands are tied by a lack of information.

For example, what heart medicine is he or she on? What other medication(s)? Does this man or woman have diabetes? Does this patient have one or more prostheses for which a special antibiotic may be required? Is this patient allergic to anything? Who are his or her next of kin? As they hope you will understand there is a plethora of information needed and each of San Felipe's visitors is the key to its presence or absence.

Because accidents happen with predictable regularity—this is a tourist town where American euphoria contributes significantly to the accident rate—many are so critically serious that the need for emergency medical evacuation is an unfortunate reality. Does your insurance company provide such coverage while traveling in foreign countries? What about your dependents? Are they covered, too? And your vehicle, whether recreational or standard? How is it to be returned to America or Canada in case of your incapacitation?

Whether you know it or not there are American and Canadian companies providing such coverage quite cost effectively. If you're completely in the dark on this subject check with Air Ambulance companies located at major airports throughout America. They can provide the name, address, and telephone numbers of many of these unique "insurance" companies. Sky Med, headquartered in Scottsdale, Arizona, is but one of them.

FOUR

Mexican food is wonderful. In fact, it is not only wonderful it is a world-class cuisine with flavors developed to the fullest. Because today's Mexican food is the product of two different culinary traditions—that of the Mediterranean and that of Native Mexico—I think of it as I do Cajun food, another delightful combination of differing cultures.

As in other cultures Mexican cuisine varies widely from region to region but has characteristics that give it unity. Foremost among these unifying characteristics is the tortilla. ("Tortilla" in Spain is a kind of potato omelet sometimes called a "torta.") Mexican tortillas are flat breads made of wheat or corn flours. (Mexican tortas are sandwiches.)

Flour tortillas are a combination of flour, lard, salt and water pressed flat and fried on a "comal" (grill). Corn tortillas are made of corn that has been soaked, cooked with lime or ashes, ground into a flour, mixed with water, shaped and cooked in a special oven.

Tortillas are seldom eaten alone. Rather, they are frequently used as a single ingredient in a wide variety of foods. They also serve as eating utensils. Fold a tortilla around any other food and you have a taco. Tacos in the Mexican culture can be hard-fried or soft, folded or rolled and wrapped around (almost any) food. Larger hand-rolled tacos are often called flautas (flutes) and are usually served with guacamole, a delightful sauce made of avocados, onions and cilantro with a dash of salt (and tiny chunks of tomato).

Talk about different: When I was a kid living in Yuma my buddies and I frequently drove to Algodones (a tiny border town west of Yuma) where we bought flautas filled with strips of beef, chicken or pork, deep fried and served with a spicy sauce. In those days, however, they were called "tacos rellenos" (refilled tacos) and we ordered and ate them by the dozen. Hmm, such fond memories!

Fry a corn tortilla until it is crisp, heap shredded lettuce, chopped onions and tomatoes on it and you have a tostada. If you cooked a corn tortilla lightly in a red chile sauce and rolled it around pieces of meat or cheese and then cooked it in more sauce, you'd have an "en-chi-lada," a name referring to the process of cooking and serving in a chile sauce.

Pointing to regional differences between many the country's foods, Sonora's "flat enchiladas" aren't like those of other Mexican states. They are thick cakes of corn masa (dough), red chilies and a local cheese, which are fried and served in a special red sauce.

Let standard corn tortillas get slightly stale, cut them into strips, fry them ever so lightly, serve them in any one of several sauces and, voilà, you have "chilaquiles," a favored breakfast dish (which I prefer with chunks of cooked chicken breast). Let corn tortillas get stale, cut them into triangles (three equi-spaced cuts through each tortilla's center), fry them crisp and you have totopos (tortilla chips), which are frequently enjoyed with a dipping sauce during Happy Hour.

Facts like these hold true over much of Mexico but there's a special wrinkle here in the northwest that has been a wheat-growing region since Father Eusebio Francisco Kino introduced wheat (and beef cattle) in the late 1600s. In Sonora, tortillas are made from wheat as well as corn. Of particular importance is the fact that Sonoran wheat tortillas are huge, often over twenty inches in diameter. Wrapped around some sort of filling they are called "burros" or "burritos," depending on the size. Burros can be filled with anything (teenagers in the upper Santa Cruz Valley have for years made and consumed them with peanut butter and jelly).

Should you deep-fry a burro it becomes a "chimichanga," a truly local dish from northern Sonora. There are many legends concerning the origin of the chimichanga, which is, apparently, a meaningless name. Whether that is true or false we'd rather eat the things than argue their origin. (My favorite chimichanga is filled with beef machaca—see below—and a chiffonnade of vegetables.)

A crisped flour tortilla with something added to it becomes a tostada (as it did with the corn tortilla). Often topped with melted cheese they are called "cheese crisps" in English, and, Heaven help us, "Mexican pizzas!" Have you ever seen a Mexican grilled cheese sandwich? Take a fresh flour tortilla, add cheese, fold it in half and fry it lightly and you have a "quesadilla." Add tiny bits of beef to the cheese and it becomes a "synchronizado."

Whereas the above seems to exhaust the possibilities of the tortilla, to whatever extent it is possible to categorize and circumscribe such a versatile folk-food, it is time to move on to Padre Kino's other great introduction to this region: Beef.

Sonora is beef country and the traditional Mexican diet to this day includes lots of beef. Slice beef thin and cook it over a comal and it becomes carne asada. ("Carne" is meat in general and the verb "asar" means "to fry.") It is said that a high Mexican government official in the 1920s described Sonora as the place "where civilization ends and carne asada begins."

Chop beef into cubes and cook it with a red chile sauce and it becomes "carne de chile colorado," a mainstay since at least the 1750s. Beef can also be cooked with green chilies but it isn't as popular in the north as it is in other states. Cut beef into thin strips, dry it, shred it and cook it with chilies, onions, garlic and tomatoes and you have carne seca or "dry meat." In some localities carne seca is also called "machaca" although most machaca is seasoned boiled beef (or pork) shredded (with two forks) and served with a vegetable chiffonnade and scrambled eggs. (Machaca is also made from selected seafood such as stingray.)

Cook beef or pork machaca with special spices to make "birria," a delightful breakfast soup served with chopped cilantro, chopped onions, oregano, a hot sauce, and piping hot corn tortillas.

Sonoran ranch families have a reputation for using every part of the critter except the moo. The head can be cooked and turned into a wonderful taco filling while the marrow and intestines, called tripas de leche, are slowly grilled as a wonderful picnic treat. Tripe, and at times the feet, are thoroughly cleaned and prepared with hominy as "menudo," a soup to be compared with Philadelphia pepper pot soup and surprisingly similar soups from European countries.

There are no halfway measures with menudo; folks either like it or they don't. Menudo is typically served for breakfast on Saturday or Sunday. In fact, many restaurants prepare it only on those days. It is a wonderfully hearty dish especially with the addition of cilantro, bits of chile, chopped onion, a little oregano, a squeeze of Mexican limejuice and a dash of hot sauce. Accompany all this with a stack of piping hot corn tortillas and it becomes a breakfast feast.

Although menudo in Sonora is traditionally made in a white color Texans and many southern Mexicans prefer to cook it with red chilies. Many restaurants serve both types and list them as "blanco" and "rojo." Menudo also has a reputation as a sovereign hangover cure and is sometimes jokingly referred to as the "breakfast of champions."

Mention of menudo leads us into the topic of Sonoran soups. These household staples have only recently begun to appear in restaurants throughout the country but they are well worth seeking out. Called "caldos" or "sopas" in Spanish there are several popular varieties, each made with a slightly different flavor depending upon the cook.

Some of the most popular are: Caldo de queso (cheese and potato soup), sopa de albóndigas (meatball soup), sopa de tortillas (tortilla soup), cazuelas (made with machaca), pozole (a hominy and meat stew), cocido (a vegetable soup), and caldo de rés (a hearty soup with chunks of beef, potatoes, carrots, cabbage and half an ear of corn).

The word "cazuela" is the name of the Mexican frying pan, which is made of a particular red clay called "barro." The word "rés" is the Spanish word for beef.

Pork is another important food in Mexico. Perhaps the most commonly known pork dish is "chorizo," a form of sausage in many guises. Spanish chorizo, for example, is comparable to Italian pepperoni. Indian chorizos are softer and slightly spicier. A similar dish is "chilorio" which is fine-ground pork blended with selected spices and formed into a baloney-like loaf. Cut from the loaf in slices, fried to render its fat, drained and served on corn tortillas it makes an enjoyable taco treat. Fried with scrambled eggs it becomes a popular breakfast dish.

Tamales, for a change of pace, are a truly ancient Mexican food. Eaten in great variety for centuries before Columbus crossed the ocean, tamales are made with masa spread onto dried corn-husks, filled with a flavoring agent (beef, pork, a black olive or pineapple chunks), folded over and steamed. They vary from one end of Mexico to the other. In the southern state of Oaxaca, for example, they are wrapped in banana leaves. In other coastal areas they can be filled with seafood while in San Felipe many are filled with beef or chicken.

Tamales are traditionally made in huge quantities throughout Mexico at Christmas time. Among the many, one of the most popular is the "red tamal" which includes shredded beef (cooked in red chile) and an olive. But there's another kind of tamal that's made at a completely different time of year. This is the green corn tamal consisting of ground fresh white corn with a little cheese mixed into the masa and a strip of green chile in the center. These are wrapped in fresh corn shucks, steamed and thoroughly enjoyed.

Mexican bakeries provide another bit of Mexico's history. If tamales remind us of Mexico's Indian heritage baked goods remind us Europe is an important part of the overall equation. Legacies of Spain (and perhaps of 19th-Century France) Mexican bakeries produce a wonderful, traditional variety of breads and cookies. Although many Mexican pastries may be bland by American tastes don't give up on them. I've enjoyed Mexican cinnamon rolls as tall and flavorful (and as delightfully gooey) as any I've seen anywhere. Another called "concha" (shell), is round, cake-like and frequently appears in a variety of (coconut dusted) colors. The best bet is to sample them all and find the ones you enjoy most.

Beans are an equally important Mexican staple. Called "frijoles" they are prepared and served in wide variety of dishes. Frijoles de la olla are cooked in a broth with onions and other wonderful ingredients. Frijoles refritos, "refried beans," are more accurately described as "well-fried beans," which can vary greatly in quality. I, for example, have eaten refried beans that were fit for sticking pages together. Others are delicately crisp with wonderful additions of cheese or milk. Pinto beans are the most common although blacks, kidneys and pinks play equally important roles while many other varieties are found throughout the country.

Finally, something wet and something sweet to top off the foregoing. Try some of the wonderful "refrescos naturales" (also called "aguas"), which are natural soft drinks. The most common are horchata, made of rice water and cinnamon; tamarindo, made of tamarind squeezings; and jamaica, a sweetened product of hibiscus flowers. Try them all for they are wonderfully refreshing drinks for a summer afternoon.

For dessert, what could be better than "almendrado," a tricolored almond confection that was invented, according to one story, in Tucson in the 1920s. Naturally, in a volume such as this, we haven't looked into all Mexican foods that span the gamut from seafood to carne asada to birria to "moles" (MO-lace), which are different types of stew.

I haven't called the roll of all the different chilies used in Mexican cooking, much less embarked on an analysis of the myriad variations of salsas. Nor have I mentioned Mexican beer, tequila or mescal, which are parts of another story. But, whatever I've accomplished in these paragraphs I have certainly managed to make myself hungry. Buén provecho!

FIVE

Because there are more than thirty restaurants in San Felipe, many of them visible along Avenida Mar de Cortés, we suggest a visit to one or more of the smaller establishments and their truly delightful "in-country" food.

Somewhat hidden in an alley behind Liquors and More (on the Chetumal) you'll find "El Minuto" where Señora Alba, in my opinion, makes the best menudo rojo in town. Of course there's always caldo de rés, chicharones con salsa verde (deep-fried pork skins softened in a delightful green sauce) or one of her daily specials. Whichever you choose you cannot go wrong.

At Los Gemelos, near Bancomer, try machaca de rés, taquitos de chilorio, mole poblano (a culinary blending of chocolate, chiles and chicken), chilaquiles (crisped corn tortilla wedges in a light cheese sauce with or without tender chunks of chicken or beef), or camarrón ranchero (fresh-cooked shrimp in a garlicky tomato-vegetable sauce).

A half-mile south the Pemex Circle, Freddie Limón's "Asadero El General" serves the best "frijoles charros," (a bean soup) and the tastiest fried chicken in San Felipe along with truly wonderful carne asada whether enjoyed in taquitos or a full dinner serving. And, if all else fails, there's always the Saturday night special (rib eye steak) at Pete's Camp (eight miles north of town) where you'll meet local (American and Canadian) men and women who can tell you what it's like to live in Paradise.

SIX

Fishing, as you learned in the segment on Tony Reyes, was San Felipe's principal source of income until surpassed, in recent years, by tourism. Nowadays, more noticeably since commercial fishing was banned in the northern Sea of Cortés, not only is this community's principal income from tourism it can be stated that about a fourth of it (an estimated seven million American dollars) is provided by resident tourists (remaining six to twelve months annually), one-fourth by more transient tourists (residing one to four months annually), one-fourth by weekend visitors (including sports fishermen and women) and an estimated one-fourth by the commercial fishing industry.

With such a significant change in this community's sources of income, national and local governmental planners must maintain a close watch on the national economy, the American economy, international affairs and trends in tourism based on each of these influential factors. These trends, basically stated, depict a majority of American and Canadian residents returning to San Felipe between October and December while May through September witnesses the annual return of Latin American visitors.

The recession of 1991–'94 cost local merchants dearly. Similarly, "9/11" caused a major reduction in local tourism although its effects were comparatively short-lived. With such international uncertainty, including America's war with Iraq, merchants and their employees tighten their belts and pray for a return of the 250,000 annual visitors San Felipe used to enjoy. El Dorado Ranch has made a difference and, it is hoped, will continue to do so as an increasing number of American and Canadian retirees discover this distant desert community many local residents see as Paradise.

Fifty years ago (if my memory serves me correctly) Doris Day told us, "Qué será será, whatever will be will be. The future's not ours to see, qué será será."

CHAPTER FOUR
The San Felipe Association of Retired Persons

PART ONE – How my lust for the desert spun out of control

Shirley Thompson created The Friendship Group. Three years later, with Freda's help, I changed this tiny organization's name to the San Felipe Association of Retired Persons. As we envisioned it, SFARP was to become a considerably larger organization of men and women committed to promoting volunteerism and conducting a program of entertaining activities for any and all San Felipe visitors. Its purpose was educational and recreational.

Seeking a cohesive group of all senior ages we enlisted the help of men and women who believed in "community" as deeply as each of us. To motivate others to participate in our activities we tackled the problem involving the basic fact that most of us have attended far too many meetings to participate in those some "clazy glingo" is convening in a far-off Mexican community. Add fees to the equation and you have an even better reason to say NO! That is, by the time most men and women become seniors they've paid too much money for whatever it was they did.

Because we were the first to say no we decided on two basic rules upon which our association would be built. That is, all fees would be maintained at the lowest possible level to enable us to conduct our business. And, owing to an inherent problem of younger men and women not trusting, liking, or believing older men and women, we made our motto "Your presence in San Felipe makes you a member of our informal organization" and invited everyone to participate as little or as much as they cared.

Another factor that entered into our planning was: Meetings are all bout the little touches—the details that make such gatherings into special occasions. Beyond the basics we wanted nothing but the most interesting activities, speakers, tours, foods, and information that would, in and of themselves, attract meeting and activity participants. Finally, having agreed on how to go about the task, we created an Association that grew almost astronomically over its first five years. And, when Hank and Shirley Thompson saw what we were doing…

-We brought the desert indoors with narrated 35mm slide programs.

-We conducted tours into outlying desert regions.

-We created "festivities" to give wintering-over visitors something to do besides drink or sit and count the days until they returned to their (snow country) homes.

-We invited knowledgeable speakers to provide the latest information on Mexican banking and investing, health care and insurance, personal and community security, southwestern and in-country touring (and a host of other subjects).

-We created a library from which we sold general information brochures (twenty-five cents each or five for a dollar) and reproduced topographic maps of our region.

…they contributed a site they call "The Lodge" for our unlimited use. Located at Campo Ocotillos (4.2 miles north of San Felipe's Arches) the Lodge is a brick structure with ample parking space, a kitchen, two dining areas (one is used as our meeting room), men's and ladies' restrooms and a storage area plus inside and outside gaming and activity areas.

Dumbfounded by their kindness we undertook a major redevelopment of its kitchen facilities to enable the preparation and serving of anything we may desire.

-We bought and installed a (used) gas grill.

-We designed and had specialized (wall and floor) cabinetry built and installed for food service needs.

-We designed and will shortly have a small cantina built and installed.

-We purchased tables and chairs to accommodate our membership during Lodge events. In addition, several of our members contributed chairs.

-We bought and installed a barn-type roof ventilator to eliminate cooking heat and odors.

-We created pancake and French toast breakfasts (with all the appropriate trimmings) at an affordable price. (Is $3.00 too much?)

-We created a Parade of Homes activity and invited local architects and contractors to a post-Parade (lodge) meeting to enable our membership to learn of their services and the cost-effective resolution to related problems.

During SFARP's seven-month meeting season (October through April), it conducts:

-Thirteen meetings (most with guest speakers)

-Seven desert tours (at least one each month)

-Five dining tours (Nov, Dec, Jan, Feb & Mar)

-Seven pancake or French toast breakfasts

-A Fall Festival (our free Thanksgiving Dinner at the Lodge)

-A Christmas Dinner (at a local hotel)

-A Parade of Homes (ending at the Lodge)

-A City Tour (to almost anywhere in Mexico)

-A "Senior Sunday" (six hours of non-stop entertainment including lunch)
-A Funny Hat Parade and (free) Ice Cream Social
-An April Dinner Dance (at a local restaurant)

We claim to be the best English language information resource in town by virtue of the fact we can answer any question asked about the enjoyment of life in our community. Subject matter ranges from real estate to house construction (whether brick or concrete block, wood or metal stud-framed, straw bale or other energy-efficient building material), from solar electric systems to potable water systems, telephone systems, radio communications, local and distant shopping, mail handling, Internet access, local banking and investing, local medical and dental services, taxation, required visas and their preparation, Mexican wills and any other subject related to local residence including maid service.

Guest speakers are invited from wherever we find them including San Felipe, Mexicali, California and Arizona. Meeting attendance fees are $2.00 per person and include free coffee, tea, cocoa (and water), and fresh-baked pastries. Those two dollars go into our treasury to cover our cost of operations. Eighty (and more) years old ladies and gentlemen are admitted free to all meetings and at half-price to all other events. We identify these wonderful folks as our "Goldeneers" and introduce those in attendance during each meeting.

Desert tour sites are selected from the many discovered during the years Freda and I spent in the desert. In addition, however, new sites are developed as often as possible to maintain a fresh supply of interesting places to visit and enjoy. Volunteers are solicited to assist each tour. If Freda and I aren't present, for any number of reasons, Hank Thompson frequently guides these groups to destination. Gene Krause, an outstanding Master at Arms, helps immeasurably during ticket taking and parking evolutions. And others come forward willingly to assist with cooking, serving and cleaning chores.

Yes, I'm a certified nut about the desert. One morning, I concocted the idea of bringing the desert indoors by way of a series of personally narrated 35mm slide shows and the rest is history. Attendance exploded from a dozen at prior meetings to one hundred fifty (and more). These shows brought forth a plea for added desert tours and away we went like… "ask and ye shall receive." What we didn't anticipate were the demands by those who couldn't participate in our desert tours. Consequently…

Desert Dining Events give us an opportunity to attract participants from all over the community. So long as possible we hope to continue these on-the-spot barbecued baby-back rib, flame grilled filet mignon, barbecued chicken breast, thighs and/or hot wings dinners. Although our (rock-bottom) price does not include beverages, it does include a freshly made tossed green salad, fresh rolls (with butter or margarine), a freshly cooked vegetable (when practicable) and dessert whether purchased or homemade.

Whereas we formerly conducted dining tours to remote locations over a wide range of local desert, a particularly generous Mexican gentleman invited us to use his beachside facility for the purpose. Consequently, because this site is but a dozen (paved) miles from town, we accepted his generosity but charged one additional dollar to cover his costs for water and paper products our guests used. We insisted on doing our own cleaning to insure we never lost our sense of responsibility to all concerned.

Our annual **Fall Festival**, convened the Thursday before Thanksgiving, is a free turkey dinner with all the trimmings, which we offer as a payback to the community that serves us so well.

Christmas Dinners are a traditional gathering to celebrate friendship. Although it is not required, we suggest each participant bring a wrapped gift, with a maximum value of five dollars, intended for a man or woman. Those gifts are exchanged between participating members during dinner, usually by our Master of Ceremonies who could be a local musician treating us with appropriate music.

Our **Parade of Homes** is an annual event designed to provide newcomers an opportunity to see local homes. During this event participants meet local home owners, see the results of their designs (and neighborhoods), discuss property acquisition and construction problems and learn as much as possible from these new contacts before they blunder into the inevitable mistakes made by newcomers. It has often been said, "Give a man a mustache, a smile, and a tiny bit of guile and he'll have your wife or your money in a minute." Mexican men, although there are exceptions, are mustachioed gentlemen who can be quite beguiling.

The annual **City Tour** is an exciting travel adventure whether to Ensenada (and its Guadalupe Valley wineries), Copper Canyon, Mazatlán, La Paz, Guadalajara, Teotihuacán, Oaxaca (and its many archeological sites), Palenque, Villa Hermosa or, as we did last year, a 17-day travel adventure to Guanajuato. Descriptions of selected annual tours follow in Chapter Six.

It is not uncommon for workingmen and women to ask, "What am I going to do in retirement?" Equally good questions relate to a determination of whether prospective retirees are emotionally and financially prepared for retirement? Whether you are is none of our business but our city tours offer participants an opportunity to see places they might otherwise never see. And, because we speak the language, get hungry two or three times each day and love sight seeing at least as much as you, we do our best to find the most interesting (not the most expensive) places wherever they may be. We also seek the highest quality for the prices paid.

Senior Sunday is the dream of Shirley Thompson. It is the day we celebrate ourselves through a program of entertainment including a crafts display, singers, folkloric dancers, musicians, and one or more comedic skits. This six-hour program is convened at the lodge, includes a cantina for refreshments and a hot lunch.

The Spring Festival is an all day outdoor affair involving competitive games, driving events and more than ample food including one or more spit or pit-roasted pigs (or goats). As this festive day gains popularity we are hoping to land sponsors representing local telephone companies, wineries and breweries

The Hat Parade is a competitive activity for anyone silly enough to want to participate. The audience selects the winners who are awarded special ribbons following which free ice cream is offered as another payback to our membership. This is also the day members of our Board of Directors are elected to office. Terms of office are one year although any incumbent can be reelected as many times as he and she agree to the membership's desire(s).

The April Dinner Dance is a season-ending activity conducted at a local restaurant giving us an opportunity to wish our members God-speed before they rush off to enjoy the remainder of the year with family and friends.

Finally, all the above is planned and conducted by men and women who seek and gain nothing for their efforts. SFARP's Board of Directors are elected volunteers willing to work their buns to the bone to produce an annual activities calendar, general information brochures, the above-listed activities and anything else they may dream up for nothing more than the praise of their fellow men and women.

At the risk of being repetitive, what are you going to do in retirement?

PART TWO – A Beach Run

The following describes what we call "an extra," a special desert run with our closest companions. It is during runs like this that we discover new places we frequently add to our Desert Tours list. In fact, shortly after the outing described below we conducted a dining tour involving carnitas at the same location. During our first carnitas event we fed one hundred fifty-seven delighted attendees (and sold leftovers). During our second, we committed an unforgivable error: We scheduled it on the same day as an off-road race and fed but one hundred.

"How about a beach run?" she asked.

"Which way?" I ventured. "North or south?"

"South," came Freda's reply, "More shells down that way."

"Make it Saturday and I'll see who else wants to go."

"Okay, but what should we prepare?" she asked, knowing my preference would be a seafood salad.

Because my picnic favorites include tuna, salmon, crab and shrimp, I replied, "Jale-tuña, what else?" (jale-tuña is a word I concocted from "jalapeño" and "tuna.")

Departing home at 7:00 a.m., we met our friends at a pre-arranged spot. There were eleven of us in five sandrails. Our destination? A place Freda and I learned about two years earlier but had told no one.

We discovered this amazing place through a chance encounter with a man stalled on the road to Puertecitos. It was one of those beautiful summer days when it was fine to be out but trouble for anyone with a breakdown.

He was taking a load of building materials to a beachside campo where he and his wife were building a small cottage. His engine had overheated and he'd stopped to allow it to cool. Freda and I were returning from Gonzaga Bay (one hundred miles south of San Felipe) when, with plenty of water on hand, we stopped, talked, and took the time to insure the stranger arrived safely at his destination.

Grateful for our kindness, he offered beer and showed us his beachside project, which was adjacent to a hidden campo nestled in a low-lying riverbed. Our host called himself "Baja Max." The place he and his wife were building is more like the Winchester Mystery House than a beachside cottage.

Although we enjoyed Max, of greater interest to us was that hidden campo and its trees, the most beautiful stand of tamaracks we'd ever seen. This is a man-made arena with trees planted to provide a completely shaded five-acre campsite with car and trailer parking between tree rows.

The unceasing action of the Cortés mounded sand so high in front of the place it is impossible to see it from the shore. Similarly, 20-feet high, river-carved dunes block the view from the west and north. Although Freda and I have camped there on several occasions since that day of discovery, we have never again seen Max. It is as though our meeting, one that occurred on a 120-degree day, was a figment of our imagination!

(Returning to our Saturday morning group,) we made a sharp turn to the left, headed down a sandy hill and out across the beach. Running in convoy is fun but, owing to each driver's need to keep his and her eyes on the road ahead, our copilots have the responsibility for the car behind. That is, if it stops we stop thereby preventing separation and separation-related problems. Another aspect of our desert travels, since each of us has the added responsibility of finding what there is to enjoy in the desert, both pilot and copilot must have their heads on swivels.

Our first stop was near San Felipe's Punta Faro (Lighthouse Point) where a mile-long, one hundred feet thick sedimentary deposit stands on an ancient layer of lava. Putting that into perspective, it is impossible to overlook mounts Machorro and Kila standing guard from San Felipe's north shore. They are both pre-batholithic (suggesting an age of at least 115,000,000 years), and both surrounded by lava. In my opinion, they are the remnants of one ancient volcano that poured its fury upon the land and, in a final submissive act, blew itself apart.

A mile farther south, Punta Radar is a local promontory comprised of a mixture of lava and shell-impregnated sandstone. The adjacent Sierra Punta Estrella is equally interesting with a visible section of country rock (original land surface).

To the east, between Punta Radar and Punta Diggs, stand some fifty magnificent Cardón. To the west, in the lee of the sierra, stands the cactus garden where a thousand of these incomparable giants stand tall and proud.

Except during low tide, there is no beach-level passage between Punta Radar and Punta Diggs (punta means "point") although there is a trail up and over the dune and here the hidden youngster in each of us comes into focus. This particular trail is likened to a racecourse with sharp left and right turns and as many ups and downs. It is a place for caution lest you damage your vehicle's suspension. It is a place for patience lest you lose your desire to traverse it. It is a place for fun where practiced application of throttle and brake yields a smile that says 'anyone can if they try.'

A quarter-mile north of Diggs there is a place to return to the beach to traverse a curiously interesting cove where we discovered twenty whale vertebra and a variety of other bones. Finds like this describe a tiny portion of the story of life in the wilds and serve to make our outings interesting.

Most of us have gardens and patios with souvenirs including rope, seashells, bones, miners' tools, ore specimens, other rocks and cactus. I sometimes wonder whether we're in a race to determine who can dress (or litter) his and her house the fastest.

After Punta Diggs, the shore traces semi-circles as it dances between the outlets for Rios Huatamote and Parral. But, because crossing the *estero* (swamp) south of Laguna Percebú can be a problem, a tide calendar is a must. The alternative is to travel via the highway.

Whereas the entire region south of Punta Faro is primitive, there are an estimated one thousand homes lining the beach between it and Puertecitos. Driving the southern beach provides an opportunity to view those homes. While some are shanties, some attractive shells built around trailers, others are cottages and a surprising number are really nice homes.

As the morning wore on, I remembered that Freda and I, busy with outing preparations, had failed to take breakfast. Now, having stopped for photography, whalebones, seashells and coffee, we decided it was time for brunch. So, taking the lead, we headed for the highway with the others following along behind.

Fifteen minutes later I slowed, signaled a turn to the left and pointed my sandrail into a sandy, tree-lined riverbed. There's a roadway there, of sorts, but you have to have an eye for it. Following overhead, a raven might have seen five colored sandrails twisting and turning their way along that sandy road until they came to a stand of trees: Hundreds of them… thirty, forty, even fifty feet tall.

We drove to the east end of the campground where, after paying the daily use fee, we came upon unoccupied picnic tables, parked and assembled our nest. While some prepared lunch, others wandered in amazement. Not only was this campo beautiful, it was quiet and cool with a pleasant breeze wafting in from the sea.

"I'll bet I've passed this place a hundred times…" became the statement of the hour.

"Join the club," Freda replied as she described our meeting with Max.

Campo Nuevo Mazatlán is a place nature chose to hide. Although easy to find once you know how, it is a place you don't tell others about for fear of it being ruined. It is also a place where you can enjoy the warmth of friendship in beautiful surroundings.

"Come and get it," someone called. "We've got barbecued beef and pork, grilled turkey sandwiches with jalapeño, onion, lettuce and tomato; a green chile casserole; smoked salmon salad; crudités in blue cheese; garlic-stuffed olives, melons, mangoes and papayas; coffee, coke, beer, red wine and a partridge in a pear tree."

We were five rails, eleven friendly souls (and three dogs) on a beach run… to Shangri La.

PART THREE – Veterans' Day

Walt Jones is a retired U.S. Marine residing in San Felipe's South Beach Community. In the year 2000, he planned and convened a (first ever) Veteran's Day celebration in the South Beach Community Hall (about 35 miles south of San Felipe). The following year Junio invited Freda and me (and many other veterans) to participate in their 2001 Veterans Day celebration. We arrived with 23 attendees (total attendance was 93) and shared a truly enjoyable afternoon.

Whereas all attendees were bona fide military veterans, they included one woman from the Army Nurse Corps, a retired Homicide Detective, two firemen, a man from the Mexican army, and a man who served under Hollywood's own Jimmy Stewart who was, at the time, a full Colonel in the Army Air Corps. During that event, Junio gave me a copy of a poem she found on the Internet. A copy of that poem appears below.

Beginning in 2003, SFARP will conduct its own Veterans Day celebrations which will include introduction of all attending veterans by military service, service number (if remembered) and a brief description of how, when and where they served. These will be potluck dinners with background music including each service's hymn. Copies of the poem will be available for distribution to any and all. Concluding ceremonies will include a prayer for our fallen brothers and sisters and the playing of Taps during a minute of complete silence.

A Veteran Died Today

(Author Unknown)

He was getting old and gray
With a little bit of fat,
And he told a lot of stories
That were mostly of the past.

And though sometimes,
To his neighbors,
His tales became a joke,
His buddies knew whereof he spoke.

But we'll hear his tales no longer,
For he has passed away,
And the world's a little poorer,
For a veteran died today.

No he won't be mourned by many,
Just his children and his wife.
For he lived an ordinary
Very quiet sort of life.

He held a job, and raised a family,
Quietly going on his way,
And the world won't know his passing,
Though a veteran died today.

When politicians leave this earth,
Their bodies lie in state,
While thousands note their passing,
And proclaim they were so great.

Papers tell their stories,
From the time they were young,
While the passing of a veteran,
Goes unnoticed and unsung.

The politician's stipend,
And the style in which they live,
Are sometimes disproportionate
To the service that they give.

While the ordinary veteran,
Who has offered up his all,
Is paid with but a medal,
And perhaps a pension small.

It was not the politicians
And their compromise and ploys
Who won for us the freedom
That our country now enjoys.

While he was proud to be a veteran,
And his ranks are growing thin,
His presence should remind us
We may need his like again.

For when countries are in conflict
We find the Military's part,
Is to clean up all the troubles
That others seem to start.

If we cannot do him honor
While he's here to hear the praise
Then at least let's give him homage
At the ending of his days.

Perhaps a simple headline
In a paper that might say
"Our Country is in Mourning,
For a Veteran Died Today."

CHAPTER FIVE
City Tours

Copper Canyon

The train stopped at a dirt road crossing and we were told to get off and wait for a van. Standing there, seven thousand feet above sea level at three o'clock on a chilly February afternoon, I looked at the road and then at the train. What I saw was a miserable, rock–strewn trail disappearing into nowhere and, as the train's caboose disappeared around a distant curve, a rusty little sign announcing…AREPONAPUCHIC.

I know… I had the same problem but it grows on you, especially when you realize places like this exist nowhere but in heaven. Of course, standing as we were—high and dry on a remote Mexican mountaintop—we hadn't yet learned about heaven.

When the van arrived, a vintage thing that had long–since forgotten what water was, it was driven by a pint-sized levi–clad woman who slammed on the brakes, jumped to the ground, barked a few orders and began loading our bags in the rear of the van. Those orders, in a language approximating "Areponapuchic," were directed at us and meant, somewhat specifically, "Hop in."

We hopped in and she (the only one who knew how) slammed the doors, returned to the driver's seat, coaxed her dusty coach into gear—leaving half our number standing by the tracks—and headed back along that rock–strewn road from whence she had come.

Travel is like that, you know. Everything, in a strange sort of way, is different no matter how many times you've done it. The woman, for example—I had to look twice to make sure—was just another woman but somehow she radiated an incomparable beauty that—as we learned more about her—identified her as a part of heaven, too.

She rounded a curve, pointed the van uphill and, a minute or so later, brought a castle into view: A real–life honest–to–God castle high on another remote mountaintop in the Mexican state of Chihuahua. It was the Mansión Tarahumara and she—our driver, maitre d'hôtel, bartender, chef par excellence and our waitress—was Maria, its owner and we were on the edge of a whole new world.

This whole affair started, I suppose, in San Felipe when I invited the owner of a tour company to make a presentation to our local version of the American Association of Retired Persons. I had read about the canyon, the Chihuahua–to–Los Mochis railway and two or three of our tour company's competitors (companies, that is, offering a lot more comfort, even better food, but a great deal less for a whale of a lot more money). Two weeks later twenty of us boarded his private Pullman rail car in Mexicali.

As the train glided out of the Mexicali station, rocking from side to side as it picked up speed, we settled back to stare at the passing scene—peek-a-boo glimpses of yards and cars and people frozen in solitary moments of time. We savored the sunlit desert and multi–colored mountains as we crossed the western fringe of the Altar Desert, passed through Puerto Peñasco, Caborca, Benjamin Hill, Hermosillo, Guaymas and Obregón. At three the following morning our private car was dropped by the wayside to await the train that would take us to heaven. At sunrise, not only were we attached to the east-bound train, we had a specially cleaned and modified gondola in which we could ride, if we chose, to see the passing countryside without dirty windows to blur our vision.

As far as rivers were concerned—for it was rivers that had created the little bit of heaven we were going to see—we crossed the Sonora, the Moctezuma and the Yaqui but followed the Fuerte to its junction with the Septentrión. These were unpretentious liquid ribbons, stretching from high in the northern Sierra Madre to a distant western shoreline that had carved their individual places in history.

It was while standing on the north bank of the Yaqui, for example, that Cabeza de Vaca discovered his six horrifying years as a slave was nearing an end. When it did, sixteenth century Mexico was electrified with the news of buffalo and northern Indian pueblos overflowing with gold. Three years later it was the Rio Sonora that provided the path upon which the first Europeans entered Southwestern America.

Departing the pueblo of Sufragio with the Fuerte River to our left, we crossed a cactus–studded (geologic) bench laid out before the mountains like an apron on a woman's lap. A few hours later we began to climb, now following Rio Septentrión, but at this juncture I must ask how often you may have seen railroad tracks climbing mountains? Or a train, for that matter?

With eighty-five tunnels and uncounted bridges this unbelievable rail route has to be the eighth wonder of the world as it climbs from sea level to eight thousand feet passing places as mystical as the route itself. Try to imagine Témoris and Cerocahuí, Bahuichivo, Cuiteco and Areponapuchic. These are Indian names for here and now we were in the land of the Tarahumara (the world's fastest humans).

Copper Canyon (Las Barrancas del Cobre) is a misnomer. Yes, there is a Copper Canyon but that implies a singular place while the Spanish name "barrancas" tends to describe the truth of the matter:

Plurality. Las Barrancas del Cobre is a complexity of five canyons (carved by five distinctly separate rivers) frequently compared to Arizona's Grand Canyon. Combined, they encompass an area four times larger than the Grand although, owing to significant differences between the two, they should never be compared.

When I climbed to the top of the mountain upon which Mansión Tarahumara is perched I saw a view as spectacular as the views from the Grand Canyon's north and south rims. But the sum and substance of these remote mountain canyons is significantly different... like two dramatic sunsets: There is no comparison. Each has its own spectacular beauty and, because nothing is gained by the declaration "mine is bigger than yours," the matter should be forgotten: They exist; they are different; they are magnificent in their individual ways.

The following day, we were bussed to Divisadero where our private rail cars (our Pullman and gondola) stood on a siding. Our next stop was Creel, the place from which we would motor to the bottom of Batopilas Canyon.

The primary jumping–off point for tours into the canyons, Creel is a quaint little village (3,000 inhabitants) where, spanning two days and nights, Freda and I discovered food as good as it gets. Here again I should put another misleading foible to rest: Mexican foods, and the development of their distinctive flavors, are as world class as the culinary arts can produce.

We dined on filleted breast of chicken over a delicate Chihuahua cheese sauce. We enjoyed a mole poblano as fragile as any dish in the world. We succumbed to a sautéed sirloin steak in a reduction of chiles and wine. We marveled at a menudo that, like the Barrancas del Cobre, was beyond compare.

Batopilas originated as a sixteenth century mining town. Four centuries later we came along—over a seven–hour–long, zee–shaped road chiseled into the side of near–vertical mountains—to experience its Brigadoon beauty.

This is a place where a gentleman had his children pick papaya for the two of us as gifts, where naranjitas (love oranges) are the size of cherry tomatoes and the river cuts an S–shaped path beside a quiet little town as long and narrow as it.

How can I convey beauty... the natural beauty we saw and felt? The reaction to real beauty—the stuff we saw—is a feeling that can only be shared with what or whomever you believe in. From the moment we laid eyes on the castle, Creel, the Tarahumara men and women, the beauty and tragedy of the caves they live in, the rivers, the canyons, the Mexicans we met and shared our days with, the scenery, the mission... we experienced that special feeling.

A mile or two south of Batopilas there is an old Spanish mission no one seems to know anything about. Generally referred to as the Lost Mission its name is *Satevó* and it is located in as pretty a setting as ever you want to see.

Our first sighting of it was from a quarter-mile away when we rounded a curve and there, in the pastoral distance it stood... as it has for the past four hundred years. Typical in structure to most early Spanish missions it rested on a narrow fertile plain with the river flowing along one side and a mountain bordering the other. On its interior walls we found faded paintings of a chalice out of which corn appeared to be growing.

I found a message in that chalice... of respect for men and women to whom corn was a source of life. They never understood Christianity but they accepted it to allow what was proposed as a meaningful marriage. The painting is still there and so is its message. It is the people who painted it who are gone... but not forgotten.

Home again—home again—neither will I.
Think of riding in a gondola,
A bus too big for the road,
The Indian trails we saw on other mountains.
A man carrying a hundred pound load up a near vertical trail,
A girl tending goats on a cactus–studded plain
The woman I had to look at twice
River–carved grandeur,

The food and, like the chalice and corn,
An incomparable place called Copper Canyon.

January Blues

I awoke to the humdrum sound of a motor. Struggling for some sense of reality, a conversation came to mind involving four feet of snow. It was a phone call from a daughter who delights in the seasonal change of pace.

More singularly minded than she, Freda and I prefer but one season. In fact, we suffer from a thing we call "The January Blues." That is, the humdrum sound of my awakening came from an air conditioner while the blues are the colors of a lobster-laden sea and a sun-drenched sky hanging so beautifully over... Mazatlán, Old Mexico.

There are, of course, other blues including marlin, shrimp and the emotion stirred by the wail of a distant train's whistle. But those are dreams brought on by the reality of separation while the blues we know are realities of a southwestern January sun.

Seven hundred miles south of the international border at Nogales (Arizona), Mazatlán has always been a fishing port. Originally a Nahuatl Indian community dating to a time before Columbus, the city's original name, "Mazatl," means "place of the deer" and so it was until modern man conquered and occupied the land. Rather than deer he produces bananas, mangoes, papaya and pineapple; cattle, coffee, cotton and a plenitude of condos, hotels and housing with 24-hour security.

When we went to look, during a tour of the city, we found a community as inviting as any we've seen anywhere. The marble floored house we inspected was selling for a negotiable three hundred thousand American dollars. But if you think that's high, consider a brick-walled property with landscaped front and back yards, a double–wide carport, a temperature controlled Jacuzzi plus wading and diving pools, a weather-protected boat mooring, a family room, a separate barroom with its own half bath and closeted storage area, a breakfast bar separating a nicely designed kitchen from a pleasant but informal dining area, a formal dining area, a curved marble and mahogany stairway leading to three adequately sized bedrooms, a central upper bathroom and an amazing master suite occupying more than a quarter of the upper floor.

Comparing this house to a host of others we've inspected we felt it was not just worth the price of admission but between two and three times that much in selected California localities. Twenty-four hour security was quoted at $70 per month while property taxes were $2000. By the way, the "$" stands for pesos, not dollars; the taxes are per year and pesos, for your information, were 7.3 to the dollar when this was written.

If you think you could live with that, then buy the place now and put it back on the market three to five years later for what I believe could be a handsome profit. You see, Mazatlán seems destined to become the next Puerta Vallarta!

The original city site stands at the foot of the world's second highest light house (Gibraltar is the highest) where a sixteenth century church continues to celebrate daily mass. Overlooking the entirety of Mazatlán from a ledge near the top of the lighthouse we saw a seventeenth century church and an eighteenth century cathedral.

Of the two luxury liners I could see, the Song of Norway was standing into port from Alaska within minutes of the ferry from La Paz. Having landed from the ferry, we hailed a cab and cruised the Malecón—and a heartful of its tempting restaurants—before heading for Old Town and Mercado Pino Suarez. An exhilarating place, it may best be described…

With dusters and dresses and drinking cups,
Fishes and cheese and beef enough to please,
A host of hogs and hearts
And chicken to fill every shopper's cart.

I love these old markets as I do the streets that surround them for it is here—where the populace does its shopping—that we measure the pulse of a people we'd otherwise never know. Yes, it is here in the marketplace that some of our most memorable mixing has occurred and it is here that we find the best bargains. Consider, for example, the miniature cups we bought for a single peso each. In any other location, and especially in America, these very same cups would have cost more than fifteen times that amount.

Known for the quality of its bull fighting, Mexico, too, has its professional and "leaky roof" circuits. Whereas Mazatlán's fights are on weekends from January thru April, this professional-circuit city features some of the most prominent toreadors during Carnaval when tourists from every part of the world fill the bedrooms reserved as long as a year in advance.

Boasting cool (not cold) winter nights, Mazatlán's year-round 70- and 80-degree daytime temperatures make it one of the most desirable tourist spots on earth. Reinforcing this incomparable city's desirability, we found an abundance of hearty lobster dinners for nine dollars each while a tour of the city—enjoyably experienced in a Volkswagen-engine-powered, open air, Jeep-like "Pulmonia"—cost but two hundred forty. Four of us, that is, paid fifteen pesos per hour to a man who seemed to know about everything.

Finally, because our schedule precluded a tour of the nearby jungle (our choices were Mazatlán or San Blás), we promised to include them when we return to this city by the sea where a little bit of heaven offers a whale of lot... of January Blues.

The Guanajuato Adventure

Freda and I spent one year planning this adventure. At the end of that year we sought the assistance of a Mexicali-based travel agent who arranged our transportation, hotel reservations, and ferry crossing from Mazatlán to La Paz.

Because we had heard good reports of bus travel throughout Mexico we leased a bus that would carry us from start to finish. That bus, driven throughout this adventure by Sr. Raul Sanchéz, the bus company's owner, and José Neria, a professional bus driver, met us at San Felipe's Campo Ocotillos so that each tour participant could leave his and her car in a secure location at the camp and have that car immediately available upon our return.

We departed San Felipe at 2:00 p.m. Thursday, February 20, 2003 with thirty tour participants. This 17-day adventure involved hotels in each scheduled location and four nights sleeping on the bus while traveling long distances between key points. Those key points included (the following are each city and state it or they are located in) Alamos, Sonora; Guadalajara, Jalisco; León, Guanajuato, Santa Rosa de Lima, Dolores Hidalgo and San Miguel de Allende (in the state of Guanajuato); Mazatlán, Sinaloa (where we boarded a ferry to La Paz, Baja California Sur), Puerto Escondido and Guerrero Negro, B.C.S.; and Ensenada, Baja California.

Our first stop was for dinner at El Herradero Restaurant in San Luis, Sonora. Afterwards, we enjoyed a movie (in the bus) before drifting off to sleep as our bus advanced through the dramatic Altar Desert region of western Sonora to Sonoita and thence to Hermosillo, Obregón and Navajoa where we stopped for coffee early the next morning.

In Alamos, we enjoyed two restful nights at Hotel Los Tesoros whose spacious rooms included a fireplace and firewood. Our first and lasting impressions of this quaint colonial city stemmed from its immaculate state of cleanliness and its graveyard, which dates from the16th century.

In this hallowed ground lay the remains of a large number of men, women and children sacrificed for the freedom of their country. This one message, the sustenance of freedom in a country whose populace has not enjoyed life, liberty and the pursuit of happiness such as our own country enjoys, was to be reinforced throughout this adventure.

From Alamos we returned to Navajoa and then south via Culiacán to Mazatlán where we enjoyed supper. Back on the bus again, we enjoyed another movie before drifting off to sleep.

Arriving at our Guadalajara hotel at 7:00 a.m. we were graciously received and assigned our rooms thanks in no small part to our program manager (in Mexicali). After breakfast, several of us set off to see the highlights of this major metropolitan city but returned for a pre-arranged walking tour of the city's historic center under the control of an English-speaking guide.

Departing Guadalajara the following morning we visited Tlaquepaque where many of our numbers were surprised to find such a magnificent shopping center for art (of all kinds), furniture and clothing. Because Freda and I had been there before we enjoyed El Patio Restaurant where we found the absolute best birria de rés imaginable. This is a place to list in your travel records as a must when visiting Tlaquepaque.

Departing Tlaquepaque in mid-afternoon our next stop was in León, Mexico's leather center. Our drivers displayed an incomparable expertise negotiating streets barely as wide as our bus to place us as close as possible (within one hundred feet) to our hotel. That evening we enjoyed dinner at an outdoor restaurant (Howard Johnson's) on the city's Historic Plaza. After dinner we found an Internet café on that same plaza enabling many of us to communicate with loved ones back home.

Following next morning's breakfast we were driven to the leather shopping center, which is adjacent to city center. Here, purchasers reveled in belts, wallets, purses, shoes and coats. In addition, because our bus drivers parked adjacent to what may be the best outdoor, fast food, seafood restaurant in Mexico we enjoyed the freshest seafood available from a delightful luncheon menu on the heels of traipsing an unknown number of cobble stoned streets through "leathersville."

Within one block of the city's central bus terminal, this place, Pancho's Sea Food, is another MUST to be added to your list when visiting León. Whether cocktails or entrees each contained more seafood and less filler material than ever before experienced.

From León we were driven to Guanajuato, which is advertised as Mexico's most beautiful city. Truly delightful, it must be experienced to understand that claim. From our experience, I rated it "one of many" but hasten to add it has an incomparable charm and unique design that may be unmatched in the entire world.

Its history is legendary with Alhóndiga de Granaditas the place where the heads of four principal revolutionaries were on display (impaled at each corner of this fortress-like structure) for 10 agonizing years. Suffice it to say there are three significant parts to this art-filled city to place it in perspective:

a) The Guanajuato River runs in a tunnel under the city.

b) Seventeen mine tunnels were widened and supported to create the avenues through which much of the city's automotive traffic runs.

c) There are "old" and "new" sections of this five-hundred-years old city to enable expansion without changing the original city's form or charm.

The old section, the most beautiful part of this continually enlarging city, was built on hill and mountain sides so that most all walking is up or down rather than horizontal. There is an opera house, many churches (each with its own history), a central marketplace, an endless array of stores, many historic statues and a world-renowned university. We enjoyed three days here when a week, in my opinion, is insufficient time to see and understand this historic treasure.

Departing Guanajuato, we visited an off-the-beaten-track mountain community where we discovered a pottery factory (Majolica Santa Rosa) producing high quality merchandise comparable to Mexico's ever-popular Talaveras. One hour later, in Dolores Hidalgo, we were shocked to learn how large this historic pueblo really is.

We were equally shocked to learn the full extent of its (pottery) shopping areas. In addition to the fact the 1810 revolution began here, Hidalgo offers a plethora of visitors as many as one hundred flavors of locally made ice cream. I, for example, enjoyed never before dreamed of flavors of corn, capote, and montecado ice creams. Of these, montecado, a buttery prune ice cream with huge prune chunks, was the best but try to imagine the others including garlic, rum, jalapeño and a dozen varieties of chocolate ice cream

San Miguel de Allende was the coup de gras where as many as half its residents are American and European. While a dozen churches were in full view from our hotel room, shopping centers and hot springs add to this quaint little city, as did its magnificent restaurants. One of them, Harry Bisset's New Orleans Restaurant, proved to be another of our MUST ENJOY locations.

In addition to churches, statuary (including Ignacio Allende and Cristoforo Colón) and restaurants, we found an internet café and the central market place where home décor products are considerably less expensive than in many (if not most) of Mexico's other tourist cities. Freda, for example, bought an attractive hand-crafted mirror for 240 pesos. She saw the same mirror selling in Ensenada for P950.00.

Returning to Mazatlán, we stopped for supper at El Arriero, an Argentine restaurant in La Piedad de Cavados, Michoacán. Another MUST ENJOY restaurant where service, cleanliness and food quality were incomparable (its wine cellar visible through a glass floor). Later, with but a few hours to spare in Mazatlán (following our 7:00 a.m. arrival), we visited the central marketplace to renew a long-held nostalgia and enjoyed freshly smoked marlin before boarding the ferry to La Paz.

Our crossing (of the Sea of Cortés) was pleasant, providing a relaxing change of pace after what many may call a whirlwind adventure. Upon arrival in La Paz we stopped at a supermarket to purchase foods and beverages for a picnic to be enjoyed along the route to Guerrero Negro. That is, owing to the distance we had to travel, and the scarcity of restaurants capable of feeding thirty-two hungry travelers on a timely basis, our drivers recommended a picnic and selected a beautiful location to enjoy it.

Our picnic stop, at Puerto Escondido, was another memorable highlight. Hidden as its name suggests, it is a gem location surrounded by eroded volcanic mountains many of us likened to

Hawaii's natural beauty. A shallow water port naturally protected from the open sea contained anchored sailboats adding charm to an idyllic scene where the waterfront is encased in concrete, a lamp-lined boulevard directs incoming cars to its inner beauty, two arched bridges provide (low) passage for boats to backwater moorings and an RV park completes the scene.

That evening's dinner was enjoyed at Mama Espinosa's restaurant in El Rosario. And, following a full-length movie and a 60-minute short, we arrived at our hotel for the night on the outskirts of Guerrero Negro. Long noted as a seasonal whale watching haven, a part of our group signed up for and departed early the next morning on a whale watching adventure. Later that day, one of our participants told me the thrill she enjoyed that morning (try to imagine a 21-foot panga surrounded by six cavorting grey whales) was exceeded only by the birth of her two children.

Ensenada was our final destination and the place we invited our drivers to dinner (at El Rey Sol restaurant) so that we might express our gratitude for their professionalism, the security we had enjoyed, their many kindnesses and their continued assurance of our complete enjoyment throughout this memorable trek.

During our "Guanajuato Adventure" we enjoyed blue skies and starry nights, dined on excellent food in truly outstanding restaurants, drove 5,754 kilometers (3,575.5 miles), paid $10,000.00 (pesos) in highway tolls while our bus consumed 2,000 liters of diesel fuel. We traveled through eight Mexican states (including Baja California, Sonora, Sinaloa, Nayarit, Jalisco, Guanajuato, Michoacán and Baja California Sur), left the driving to them and had such an enjoyable travel adventure we are now planning another (to Chihuahua, Zacatecas, Teotihuacán, Oaxaca, Palenque and Villahermosa).

CHAPTER SIX
Conclusions

The history of San Felipe is as interesting as the mystery surrounding the location of the Melchior Díaz grave. Whether Díaz actually ventured this far south is of little consequence (to recorded history) because other Spaniards arrived in the late 1600s and early 1700s. Previously mentioned visitors include Padres Ugarte, Link and Konsag. Not previously mentioned are:

Padre Kino who came some seventy years before the Dominican padres, was recalled to Sonora and became famous for his missionary work with Indians there and in Southern Arizona.

Padre Junipero Serra, who became famous for his missionary work in California, walked from La Paz to San Diego. This trek involved difficulties that nearly ended his life prematurely.

Wherever they came from indigenous man also walked and here we add even more drama because those men and women, known as the Painters, are bound to have passed this way some 3,000 years ago.

For anyone with interests as deep as mine our local shell-mounds speak as loudly as a textbook describing how and where the ancient ones fished. Although scattered by at least two thousand years of tidal and storm activity the stories these mounds tell involve indigenous women and children as well as their ubiquitous men.

Once boat traffic began between Guaymas and the northern tip of the Cortés reports of spectacular fish sightings were carried back to Guaymas from where San Felipe's pioneers originated. From that moment forward San Felipe's future seems to have been guaranteed. The first settlers rowed here, their women walked and a lasting presence grew from a handful to more than twenty thousand.

There has never been a natural supply of fresh water in San Felipe although there was one brackish well in pioneering days and a reasonably good well on the same property where Costa Brava lumberyard now stands. Other wells were drilled and served the community on a limited basis until the first truly significant wells were drilled eleven miles south of town (along the original road to the sulfur mines. When they began to fail new wells were drilled alongside Rio Huatamote (three miles farther south) and the pueblo now boasts an unlimited fresh water supply.

Why San Felipe? Fish was the original answer although the income now realized from tourism surpasses that of today's local fishing industry by at least three fold. Whereas the arches are a substantial drawing card they are a monumental introduction to a place where the inquisitive may ascertain whether to venture farther into Mexico.

Still known as a fishing port San Felipe has never been as popular as nearby resorts. It is no Palm Springs nor does it have a multitude of golf courses. San Felipe is San Felipe. It is a distant desert community with its feet in the water. Its primary access is via Federal Highway 5 (from Mexicali) with an alternate route via

Federal Highway 3 (from Ensenada to its intersection with 5).

Rather than a super highway over which its visitors might arrive without concern, Highway 5 is a "good" two-lane road supporting typical highway speeds. Highway 3, in contrast, is less frequently maintained and, therefore, can be so problematic that many would-be visitors opt to remain in west coast communities.

Whichever route you take San Felipe's visitors have the option of enjoying more than fifty miles of broad and narrow beach along which no breakers disturb its tranquility. A perfect place for seashell collectors these beaches are normally quiet as a church mouse while four somewhat phenomenal tides per day vary from zero to twenty-three feet in height. The most dramatic affect is enjoyed during the lowest tides when a quarter-mile of sea floor is exposed.

San Felipe is a humble place with humble men and women seeking little more than the sustenance of a humble life. For those who know it best…

It is a playland at the beach.

It is a paradise with pure air.

It is a place where winter begins in November, tanning in January and fishing is as good as it gets.

Like a natural sauna the Sea of Cortés' temperature soars to 80°F in June and late spring visitors flock to it by the hundreds.

San Felipe's desert is an attractive playground, an historic place to study, a great place to hunt for buried treasure and a peacefully colorful place to picnic with family and friends.

When you think of San Felipe think of retirement in pleasant surroundings and of being away from the madding crowd. With a brilliant spring sun shining on me as I write we are but a two-hour drive from Mexicali, three from Yuma, five from San Diego, six from Tucson, seven from Phoenix and Los Angeles and considerably less than that from your airport to ours.

The Arches are a surprise for those who want to be surprised and home for those who cannot wait to see them. This is a peaceful place with no prevailing buzz of local activity. Fishermen rise early, go to their boats before sunrise, and spend most days earning their living.

Women prepare kids for school, clean house, wash clothes and shop. Retirees arise, relax over morning coffee and plan a day in Paradise. Summers are hot, autumn and spring are perfect, and winter is warm with a gentle breeze although about every ten years we are inundated with a hurricane.

What do San Felipe's retirees do? Precisely what they feel like including thinking about the kids they once sent to school, planning their days with friends and neighbors, volunteering their time, energies and knowledge, and exploring an incomparable desert region where indigenous man left his mark in more than 8,000 (relatively) nearby locations.

Our kids think we're crazy, "bats," completely out of our minds but they've never tasted retirement. Remember, as a grandparent, not only do most of us never have to say "NO" again, we should be free to do what we want. Crazy? "Say it with flowers," the expression goes. Our house frequently displays flowers I pick in the desert including one resembling an orchid.

Why San Felipe? Why not?

PART FIVE

TURBULENCE

Figure 8 – El Marmol - Santa Catarina Region

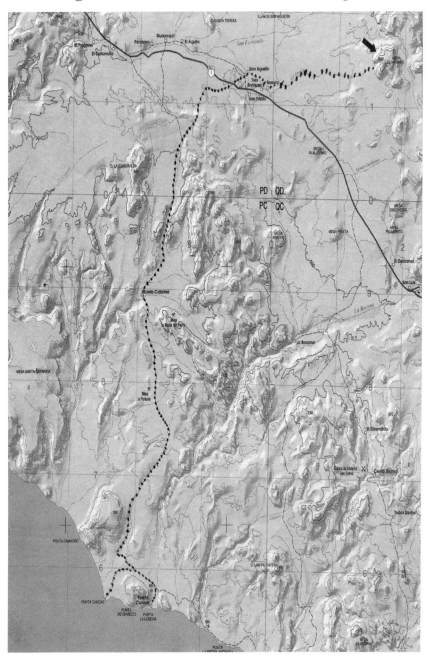

CHAPTER ONE
Introduction to Part Five

This Part was entitled TURBULENCE because, with the exception of an event appearing in Chapter Five, it presents events, or the results of events that occurred millions of years before present. The article in Chapter Five describes an activity that occurred in the space of half-a-dozen seconds while Freda and I were driving north out of San Felipe at 65 miles per hour. It is a tale I had to include in this book because it describes life in the wilds as it truly is, not like many of us tend to think it is.

This part of the book is not intended to minimize the relative importance of the uplifting of Baja's backbone mountains, the cutting of their canyons or the impact and beauty of its eastern ranges. Rather, it is to dramatize regions we tend to pass, while our minds are on other matters, without lending credence to our surroundings.

Who, for example, whether driving north or south along Mexico's Transpeninsular Highway, takes the time to imagine yesteryear's mining operation at El Marmol? No less important was the transportation and shipping of that mine's onyx to market.

When I think of it, involving the road to Santa Catarina, I cannot help but think of the reasons America has OSHA, the lives and limbs OSHA has saved and the needless waste of lives in the absence of such an organization.

There is no condemnation here, especially since that operation concluded many years ago, but if you drive the road to that former seaport you'll know what I mean. And while you're in the mood, drive Baja California's Rumarosa Grade, Berkeley, California's Marin Avenue or Utah's Dugway Grade and you may begin to wonder why man seems to love steep grades.

Chapter Two describes an event Freda and I participated in at a remote location somewhere along the road to Santa Catarina. In addition, the two of us explored a larger section of this west-central region with Frank and Debbie Albrecht half a dozen years before this event. During that trek through a remote region known for its turquoise, we stopped at a nondescript place a dozen miles west of Highway 1. During a discussion about exploration the girls decided they'd had enough and preferred waiting where they were while Frank and I ran ahead to find what might lie around the next two or three hundred curves.

Picture a typical desert scene of gently rolling hills blanketed with cholla and gobernadora. The sun is high, the sky blue, the land is carved with two barely visible roads heading only God knows where. Now place two middle-aged women alongside one of those roads, add an ice chest and two folding chairs and you have what Frank and I left in the middle of nowhere.

I look back on scenes like this with fond memories of places we've been and things we've done. While Frank and I (or Pepe and I) scouted the countryside the two of them sat and chatted as women have done throughout history... waiting for their men to return. And because of those memories I can honestly tell you (within reason) I have seen almost every square inch of Baja Norte while Freda waited (in many cases) in some of the most desolate places on earth. Can you imagine what faith we had? Me in my buggy and she in me.

Chapter Three touches on the Sea of Cortés. This is a six hundred miles long body of water ranging to ninety miles in width with no tides of its own.

The story that is not told in this chapter is that of the "sea gypsies," a powerful saga describing waterborne hermits entirely alone on the world's most prolific sea. That is a tale involving an era that ended about the time Freda and I landed in Baja. Anyone with sufficient curiosity should seek information about them via Internet search engines and local libraries.

Whereas I spent the better part of sixteen years at sea, my shipmates and I survived typhoons, hurricanes, waterspouts, torrential downpours, dense fog and the blazing sun. During those years I saw the sea as every color in the rainbow. In the South China Sea I saw one-meter-wide jellyfish blanketing the surface as far as the eye could see. I saw sharks twenty feet in length and participated in the recovery of a rib cage that, but minutes before, was a living, breathing 180-pound man.

Following the penetrating rays of a bright noonday sun I have seen as far into a sea as is humanly possible. Holding on for dear life I once looked up, from the flight deck of an aircraft carrier to see the top of an adjacent wave. As I came to know the Cortés she is as attractive as a calendar girl, as mean as the wicked witch of the west and as sure to get you as any other sea... if you ever turn your back on 'er.

Chapter Four describes a place I fell in love with, a place I met fear face to face and a place like no other on the planet. Talk about remote; it is but sixty miles east of Sonora's San Luís (Rio Colorado) and yet it is a million miles from nowhere. Artifacts found here place man in the Sierra Pinacate twenty-five thousand years before he was supposed to have crossed the Alaskan land bridge.

If this place isn't haunted no place is. Drive north or south from "Elegante" and see what you find besides black. Look for tracks and about all you'll see is cougar. Look for food and you'll starve to death. Seek drama and you'll hit the jackpot: The living drama of a sea of sand, a dozen incomparable craters and the land of the six hundred. El Desierto del Altar-Sierra Pinacate region: Frightening... unique... the most starkly beautiful place in the Mexican Frontier.

CHAPTER TWO
The Road to Santa Catarina

The first time I drove the road to Santa Catarina, Freda, Peso (our dog) and I were in a borrowed pickup truck with an improperly mounted camper. So bad was that installation that the camper leaned from one side to the other as we inched our way over a twisting, rutted, 6- or 7-percent downgrade I preferred not to be on. At one point in that descent, while I was focused on the road, my hands glued to the steering wheel and daylight rapidly disappearing, Freda mumbled something about a thousand foot drop-off to our right. My unsympathetic reply was, "Not now, sweetheart. I'm busy!" Not only was she frightened (she told me later) our dog was frightened too.

We'd been invited by Glen Conklin to participate in one of his annual ammonite digs. Whereas directions to the ammonite site are difficult to describe I have a feeling the Mexican government would be happier if I refrained from that description because good ammonites command three thousand to five thousand dollars on the open market (and more on the black market). What's more, law prohibits the removal of these treasures from this or any comparable site.

Suffice it to say there is an ammonite site somewhere along the road to Santa Catarina. Paleontologists know where it is, and there are several of them at San Diego's Museum of Natural History. (There is also an anthropologist in the nearby Museum of Man who helped me with my study of the area's early Indians.)

Our campsite was about fifty meters from the digging site. In fact, camp was in the lee of a mesa around which Glen and I walked daily during lunch breaks. You haven't walked, I suggest, until you've walked a "Conklin Mile." When this six-foot man started walking it was at the rate of about four miles per hour (depending on terrain). Glen was happiest, I believe, when walking.

Of all the walkers I've known there has been only one like him: My older sister (when we were kids). She took me by the hand and away we went at a speed and distance I came to know as a Conklin Mile. I never told Glen but if it hadn't for Sis I would never have been able to keep up with him. But now, with the shoe on the other foot, I freely admit when I began conducting tours in the greater San Felipe region many of my clients had to threaten me to slow me down. Somewhat obviously, there is something to the pleasure of walking that warms the soul.

Santa Catarina, a frequently encountered name in Baja California, was a west coast port from which onyx was shipped to market. Onyx, "marmol" in Spanish, was mined in a place called El Marmol and trucked to this man-made port.

Digging for ammonites is like digging for nineteenth century bottles (my mother was a bottle digger). Diggers start with a narrow steel rod that is gently but firmly forced into the soil until it comes in contact with something solid. Hopefully, in this case, that something will be a concretion: A volleyball-, basketball- or larger-shaped, rock hard, chemically produced "shell" usually encountered several feet below the surface. (Those several feet relate to sixty-five and more million years of soil deposition and its subsequent erosion.) Once contact is made its overburden is removed (like digging a grave) and the object is exposed.

I found a concretion, after digging for the better part of an hour, that contained a chunk of redwood. About the time my redwood came into sight the man working next to me found a perfectly shaped Nautilus in the concretion he'd uncovered and opened. In fact, that eighty million-year-old nautilus was so perfect it came apart and reassembled exactly like a puzzle (or a modern-day laboratory specimen).

Opening a concretion involves the use of one or more chisels, a four-pound mall and a ton of patience as the rock is struck time and time again around a marked circumference while hoping it will open in even halves.

Not only did Glen have permission to dig in this site he always invited scientists (from each side of the border) whom he showed how to dig for these historic treasures. In my opinion, he found and delivered at least fifty ammonites (and the fossilized jawbone of a mososaur) to selected Mexican and other western museums.

An Ammonite is a prehistoric marine animal from the Cephalopod family. Nautilus is the earliest of the cephalopods initially appearing in the Upper Cambrian period. The name "ammonite" is derived from the Greek word "Ammon," the Egyptian ram-headed deity resembling a ram's twisted, ribbed horn. Oddly enough, their shape reminds me of a tuba (coiled in a flat spiral although rarely more than eighteen inches in diameter) from which a multi-tentacled, squid-like body extended for feeding purposes.

Whereas ammonites first appeared about 300 million years ago the sites in which their fossilized remains are found are apparently limited to Germany, England, North Dakota and Baja California. Their shells, according to papers I read about them, were well engineered for survival as bottom feeders but poorly engineered to survive predation. They became extinct some sixty-five million years ago.

The formation of concretions is a complex chemical process explained within the scientific field of petrology. When I think about the life and death of ammonites in the Mesozoic era, I am reminded of Baja California's geologic history: The collision of major crustal plates, mountain building, sea floor thickness, subterranean heat and a turbulent past unmatched in all the world.

In addition to this remote site, I am reminded of El Marmol and the ruins of houses, offices and a school built entirely of onyx. When Frank, Debbie, Freda and I camped there, Frank and I left the girls to dig for collectible onyx specimens while he and I followed the site's one road east. We came upon an outcropping of quartz, another mining site and a dramatic waterway where pre-Columbian Indians created drawings in a cave at least fifteen feet above the riverbed. At that point, I fondly remember, we were less than twenty miles from Baja's eastern shore.

Other interesting information about the greater Puerto Catarina region includes the existence of an estimated four thousand Indian drawings, the ruins of an eighteenth century Spanish mission and a road leading from the mission to the beach. The true investigator will find the trail from that beach (about a two-hour hike) into the mountains where the drawings are located. If unsuccessful, ask local Mexicans about the drawings site.

I once owned an early copy of AAA's Baja California handbook that contained descriptions of each of the peninsula's (twenty-one) Spanish mission sites. A search through old bookstores should produce that edition and the wealth of information it contains. Not long after Graham Mackintosh walked the perimeter of Baja California (see his book "Into a Desert Place") he walked the peninsula's backbone in an effort to see each of those twenty-one sites. Reports of his findings appeared in the Discover Baja newsletter all during that trek.

I met Graham at one of Glen and Betty Conklin's annual Baja aficionado dinners and asked if he'd be willing to write a monthly article for the magazine I was then publishing. Although he agreed quite happily that was days before the recession of ' 91 struck and my advertisers could no longer afford the expense.

328

CHAPTER THREE
The Vermillion Sea

One of the most despised men in the new world Hernán Cortés built ships throughout the late 1520s and early 1530s for the purpose of exploring (and mapping) the continent's western shore and the body of water they called "the Southern Sea" (the Pacific Ocean). Whereas one of those ships made the first "American" contact with the Far East, at least one other was involved in a mutiny and the discovery of the Baja California peninsula although, at the time, the place was thought to be an island.

Sixteen months later Cortés named the body of water he sailed through (between the island and the mainland) "Mar Bermejo" in reaction to its color. "Bermejo" translates to "vermillion," a brilliant shade of red caused by the presence of a rare species of phytoplankton natural to this sea alone. These phytoplankton existed at the bottom of a food chain so complete this incomparable sea was the world's most prolific salt-water aquarium.

Sailing in 1539 Francisco Ulloa, the man who changed the sea's name to "Mar de Cortés," discovered California was a peninsula rather than an island. Unexplained in historic records I studied Ulloa's discovery was ignored until Hernando de Alarcón verified his finding during a 1540 cruise in support of Coronado's expedition to the seven cities of Cíbola.

"Mar Bermejo," "Mar de Cortés," "Gulf of California." There is such a unique beauty to this magnificent body of water it warrants a closer look. Created when the Baja California peninsula was ripped from mainland Mexico, as the separation between these two landmasses increased, and Pacific Ocean seawater filled that separation, a major mountain range was broken and submerged forming as many as fifty islands. Of them, Islas Tiburón and La Guarda are so close (twenty-two miles) they form a venturi known locally as the "midriff." Caused by in-rushing and out-flowing tides, this is a region of extreme turbulence.

The inrushing water filled trenches formed south of the midriff—some of them more than six thousand feet deep—. Prior to this separation the Colorado River poured a seemingly endless stream of water and eroded debris into the Imperial and Mexicali Valley regions (from Bishop, California to Mexico's coastal city of Guaymas) creating a truly monstrous lake.

When that inland lake overflowed its land-locking boundary it appears to have found an outlet to the Pacific Ocean as evidenced by western Baja California soil strata. But, as separation continued (the new peninsula sliding northwesterly) the Colorado's drainage was diverted to the ever-widening gulf, which is now a six hundred miles long sea.

Fed by the Colorado, Sonora, Maya, Fuerte and other Mexican river systems, the temperature of this newly formed sea promoted such unusual growth that north and south Pacific fishes (of all sizes) discovered a haven they couldn't refuse. The result is the world's richest salt-water aquarium.

When sea floor spreading began between La Paz and Mazatlán, another trench was created and has been sounded at ten thousand five hundred feet making the Cortés the world's deepest oceanic gulf. Not large enough for its own tides the Cortés is filled and drained twice each day by the Pacific Ocean resulting, during each new and full moon phase, in a vertical rise and fall of water in excess of twenty-three feet.

At the Midriff currents racing in from the Pacific climb the sides of underwater mountains creating, when they break the surface, mushroom-shaped upwellings so powerful they can stand a boat on end. These same currents, having stirred the gulf's bottom, provide a mixture of warm and cold nutrient-rich water in which the smallest to largest marine animals feed to their hearts' content.

A few miles north of Guaymas is the sleepy little town of San Carlos, an unspoiled Mexican beach community. Fishing from its nearby Isla San Pedro Nolasco yields a delightful harvest of sierra, dorado and snapper demonstrating the extraordinary benefit of these nutrient-rich waters.

The sun is responsible for a variety of seasonal winds that can plague the length and breadth of the gulf. There are times in every month when boating in the Cortés is a risky proposition. During July, August and September the Chubasco, a tropical hurricane, is always possible.

Beyond the powers of weather the Vermillion Sea—still fed by Mexico's Sonora, Maya and Fuerte Rivers—provides the medium for the world's richest aquatic pasture. From microscopic plankton to the eight-ton finback whale to the monstrous whale shark the Sea of Cortés is home for more than eight hundred varieties of fish, shellfish and other marine creatures.

For at least the past three million years great schools of fishes are believed to have migrated from the North and South Pacific Oceans to feast upon the Cortés' seemingly endless food chain. To the sports fisherman this means marlin, sailfish, spoonbill, roosterfish and yellowfin tuna. It also means more than a hundred other varieties of fighters and non-fighters alike. From needlefish, barracuda and albacore; ladyfish, pompano, orange-mouth corvina and crevalle; to snapper, cabrilla, milkfish, dorado and croaker. There are many varieties of shark and at least two of sea turtle. Comparable to the Gulf's lobsters in succulence, the Cortés is famous for its yellow, white and blue varieties of shrimp.

With a heart that beats for the desert I am anything but a fisherman although I have taken a fish a minute while standing on Bahia Conzaga's sandy shore. What's more, I accompanied friends and accepted invitations to fishing ventures on each side of this azure pond. Whether fishing from a northern or southern port it is a rewarding experience to savor a catch at a beachside campfire while flocks of the winged community glide gracefully overhead. Yes, above the sea but no less a part of it are thousands of resident and migratory pelicans, terns, boobies, gulls, and frigates; eagles, ospreys, vultures and fish-eating owls; herons, egrets, sandpipers and cranes.

I have witnessed great feeding orgies covering an acre or two of water in the Gulf of Mexico where schools of gamefish feasted upon schools of baitfish and seabirds added to the milieu. But nowhere on earth have I seen the frenzy of larger species feeding on the smaller as there used to be in the Cortés in April and May. So rich were these waters that Nature's feeding forays frequently and invariably involved two, three and four square miles of pure slaughter.

And today? The Cortés has been diminished but not depleted. When Jacques Cousteau sailed Halcyon into its southern deeps he found an underwater world of sand slides, canyons, encrusted wrecks and fishing vessels (known as "long liners) raping a formerly virginal sea. He also found a way to recover; the long-liners are gone now as is San Felipe's fishing fleet. And, slowly but surely, this incomparable body of water is replenishing itself.

I am fortunate to have lived when I did for I remember when rock oysters were as plentiful as pebbles in a stream and the midriff boiled with fishes feasting on each other. Having seen rock paintings of mantas leaping high into the air, I will never forget the formation of fifty mantas gliding swiftly beneath me (standing on a ferry at the entrance to the La Paz bay) in the rays of an early morning sun.

I have studied Baja's pearling industry and watched a coyote taking crab with its tail. On one occasion a whale nudged our boat. On another I fed dolphins begging for herring. I've come home with a hundred squid, a boatload of seven-pound corvina and on one occasion with 170 two and three pound dorado. (There were three of us in that boat.)

I fished Cabo, Buena Vista, Mazatlán, Topolobampo and Loreto. I worked the waters of La Raza, Bahia de Los Angeles and from Punta Final to Puertecitos. I've been blown off course and on, into the water and out. I saw a man literally standing on it in a storm (you can do almost anything when your life's at stake). I learned to eat snails and wept over an orca lying dead on the beach.

I see the Cortés as a waveless azure sea surrounded by turquoise-colored coves; its placid waters lapping gently on beaches of beige, orange, black and pure white sand eroded from the volcano-strewn land. Like the dramatic stage and its faces of tragedy and comedy the Cortés displays faces of terror and tranquility. I see the gulf as one of the most beautiful bodies of water on earth. I see it as home for a pod of blue whales and the rapidly disappearing totoava. I have seen it as it was and see it now as it is: The Gulf of California, the Sea of Cortés, El Mar Bermejo: Baja California's aquatic twin.

Figure 9 – Sierra Pinacate, North-Central Region

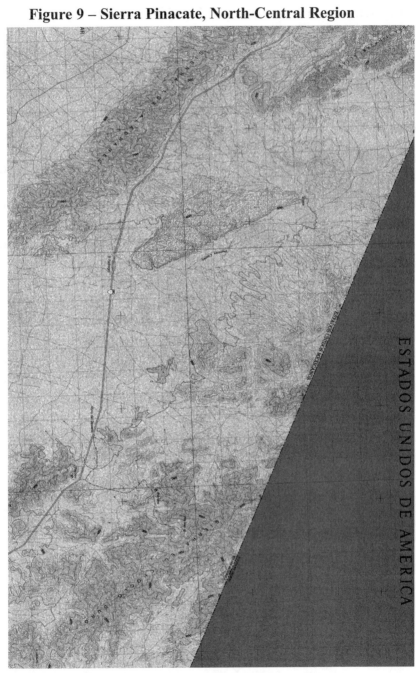

CHAPTER FOUR
Desierto del Altar and Sierra Pinacate

Have you ever seen a sunrise o'er the Mexican frontier? The first rays strike Baja's backbone mountains, painting them orange. The eastern desert plain is next… and the Sea of Cortés. By the time the sun has erased the memory of the night before it has illuminated the Altar's sea of sand, a dozen craters, the mystery of jet-black lava, six hundred volcanoes and Volcán Pinacate.

Can you imagine six hundred volcanoes? If you've seen Hawaii's Kiluaea—pouring its never-ending stream(s) of lava upon the land—you can imagine how this region must have appeared when active. Stream after stream of molten lava geysering, gushing, oozing from the six hundred… its rivers of death spreading across the land like an orange-colored syrup over pancakes.

There are cinder cones here standing 4,500 feet high. There are lava floes, lava tubes and strangely quiet cinder fields. Remember me calling another place "Indian country?" I call this place "no man's land" for I truly believe it is one of God's experimental laboratories.

Anyone who has explored the Pinacate will understand why it was called "The Black Desert." Aside from El Desierto del Altar whose color and surface are Saharan, the Pinacate is another of those mysteriously eerie places like the cirio forest on the road to Bahia de Los Angeles. In place of ancient plants and Spanish moss this region is covered with black sand, black cinder cones, black (rocky) pavement, black dust and black lava floes.

One of those places, north of Federal Highway 2, made me feel as if I'd suddenly been transported to the Black Hole of Calcutta. I've never been to Calcutta but that name tends to describe a feeling of inescapable doom that came over me during one of my (solo) explorations.

There are places here where exploration is a thrill a minute. Exactly the opposite there are places here where fear rules and chills run their gamut up and down the (human) spine. These are those deathly quiet, deadly remote, volcanically blackened regions where cougar rules and the only other occupants are seasonal antelope (wintering over from the north) and an occasional investigator in an orange-colored sandrail.

I was following a river of ancient lava towering some twenty feet over my head when I came upon what I presumed to be an antelope's femur. (Figure 9 encompasses a region including Sierras Las Alacranes, Sierra Tinajas Atlas, Sierra El Choclo Duro, and Sierra El Aguila. The experience described here happened in the region between Sierra Tinajas Atlas and Sierra El Choclo Duro.) A short while later I saw lion tracks (the ever watchful, ever roaming cougar) and its droppings. Suddenly surrounded by an inexplicable silence a chill ran up my spine in a place where black rendered my surroundings as far from civilization as man can possibly find himself and I thought of my bones and a similar pile of dung being all that was left of me.

At that same moment—try to imagine those final seconds when a goner knows he's a goner—I had another thought: "Civilization exists by geologic consent." This is not easy for me to admit because I've been in many places I call lion country but for some reason I had a sudden urge to change that cliché to, "Bruce exists by cougar's consent." Of all the places I would revisit in a heartbeat, I cannot recommend this silently peaceful place as black as a predator's heart. I think of those moments as Yea, tho I walk through the valley of the shadow of death the black hole of the Pinacate is a place where doubt obscures confidence and skepticism erodes trust. It scared me and I'm unshakable.

Those who have driven El Camino del Diablo (an early Indian trail between the Pinacate and the Gila River valley) know what I mean for if they've been along that road the chances are they explored this nearby region, as well. "If the cactus doesn't get you the lava will."

The world's largest lava fields are in India and Russia, respectively. In addition, however, there are huge deposits in eastern Oregon, north of Alamagordo, New Mexico, and east of Compostela, Sinaloa (Old Mexico). But the Pinacate may be the world's' most-unique volcanic region. In addition to the miles of jet-black pavement (largely along the north side of Highway 2), Volcán Pinacate (south of Highway 2) has spread the land with lava in a manner including two lava tubes I know of. In addition, there are the black sand desert, cinder fields, other lava flows and a dozen craters.

Freda and I were seated at Glen and Betty Conklin's dinner table one evening when, reminiscing, I began to describe a trek we made from Elegante to El Pinacate. Somewhat apologetically, Glen interrupted to ask whether I'd seen the Pinacate's lava tubes. When I told him 'yes,' he told me he and a friend had been lowered into one of them. Thirty feet below the desert floor, they walked along a dismally dark corridor he likened to a subway tunnel. At one place, on a ledge in that tunnel, they came upon an antelope's skeleton from which two carved lengths of ocotillo protruded.

That scene, the sacrificed antelope, is a tiny glimpse of early man's past. Assuming that skeleton has never been touched it describes one of the holiest of indigenous man's holy events. In this case it was not a sacrifice to the sun or to some heavenly god. This event took place in the bowels of the earth where, sometime between now and thirty-nine thousand years before now, indigenous man sacrificed an animal to the spirit of Volcán Pinacate.

Try to envision how these long-ago-vanished men and women lived, believed and prayed. And, for whatever reason, they entered the same lava tube Glen walked in but conducted a ceremony as meaningful to them as mass in a Catholic cathedral. In this case, they offered the life and blood of a living animal to the great god of the underworld, the spirit of darkness and all that is concealed by the color of night. But there is more to the Pinacate than this individual treasure.

The trek around the Pinacate is difficult, at best, impossible for most. The reward for perseverance is sighting of the giant intaglios, in particular, which are as old as the sacrificed antelope. The shapes are difficult to decipher but appear to represent both human and animal figures among others I did not recognize. Suffice it to say they are man made, ancient and irreplaceable.

Entering the Pinacate from its southeastern approach (along the road from Sonoita to Puerto Peñasco), Freda and I had passengers who described the place in a single word: Inhospitable. Although there are residents at Los Vidrios (and along the old gold field adjacent to Highway 2 near San Luis), the Pinacate knows no interior residents other than scorpions, black widows, gila monsters, rattlesnakes, antelope and cougars.

This particular drive began as a request by friends of ours in Yuma. They'd heard us speak of the black desert and suddenly showed an interest in it and the Pinacate's intaglios. Because I had a circle route in mind, I opted for the eastern entrance to avoid backtracking. But here, in a place I have a fondness for, our passengers saw it as a wasteland because it was covered with cholla.

Unfortunately, owing to the density of cholla along its southeastern flank, Volcán Pinacate was inaccessible from this direction and, therefore, so were the intaglios. To force the issue (because I

Figure 10 – Sierra Pinacate Craters Region

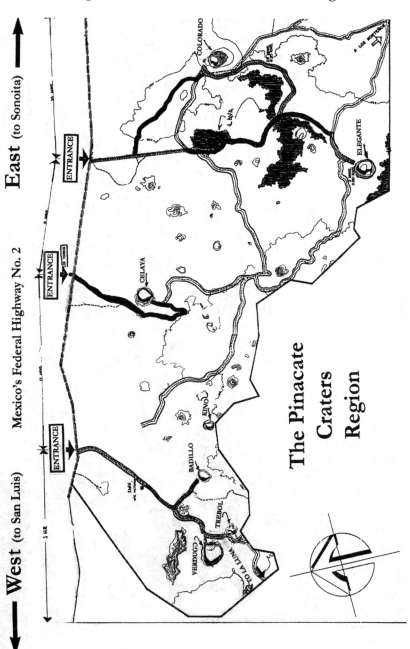

normally don't hesitate to cut trail) would have been detrimental to our tires and we were a long way from tire repair centers.

Consequently, we assigned that run to the future and proceeded to the black dunes and Mt. Tecolote, another Pinacate volcano.

The first of the region's black sand appears fifteen miles west of the southeastern entrance. Like that forbidding northern area, this part of the Pinacate is a truly ethereal experience. Adding to the strangeness of black sand, black lava flows encompass this inner region like tentacles of a giant squid.

Half an hour later, during which our friends could not believe what they were seeing, we made a bee-line to Elegante crater, parked at its base and climbed to the top from where we marveled at its stadium-like interior: Six-tenths of a kilometer in diameter, Elegante is the largest of this region's twelve craters.

Standing on its eastern rim, our view into the crater was a scene to behold. Dotted here and there with saguaro cactus the otherwise barren floor was at least fifty feet below us. Adding to the beauty of the moment our elevated vantage point provided an unrestricted view of an immense desert region without a sign of another living creature.

It is a strange feeling—loneliness—unless one truly understands the beauty of "solitude." I mention this because of the immensity of the silent drama surrounding us at this moment but with our friends in company we were anything but alone. And, because we were here many years after the fact, we were bathed in the stark beauty of a place none but a comparative few have experienced.

Another crater, Colorado, is at least a mile east-northeast of Elegante while the remainder are several miles west. Called "Maar" craters in English and "volcanes" in Spanish they were created when magma from subterranean wells came in contact with underground pools of water. Here again, I suggest an imaginary vision of an atomic-like blast involving the eruption of surrounding overburden and billowing clouds of steam. First one, then another, and... at least a dozen.

The Sierra Pinacate-Desierto del Altar region includes more than 600 square miles of volcanoes, lava, cinders and cinder cones. So unique is this region it is resistant to weathering. That is to say nearly everything ever dropped upon it remains where it came to rest. Consequently, archeologists dated some of early man's habitation sites (sleeping circles, tools, cairns and his twenty giant intaglios) to as long ago as 39,000 years.

A friend gave me a copy of a manuscript entitled Archeology of the Sierra "El Pinacate" Sonora, Mexico that describes evidence of man's habitation in this region for most of those years. That evidence includes choppers and scrapers found on the desert floor. In addition there were many notched tools including simple spoke shaves, which tend to imply woodworking.

Sleeping circles and trail shrines are described in the manuscript, as are the intaglios. These intaglios, best described as a variety of ghostly shapes, were created by scraping elements of desert pavement to one side or the other to expose a yellow-colored undersoil in foot-wide strips.

I have often wondered how, so many years ago, ancient man and woman established this isolated place as sacred. Water is an obvious reason for here in the Sierra Pinacate there are natural bowl-shaped reservoirs called "tinajas." But it cannot have been the primary object of their devotion. For this, I rely on such obscurities as the six hundred and an incomparable region of blackness but prefer to believe they saw the soul of Volcán Pinacate as the creator of the world and all life within it.

Considerably more recent inhabitants, the "Pinacateños" sold water to Arizona's Pima Indians when they traveled back and forth between their homeland (along the Gila River) and the coast for fish, shellfish and seashells (used by the Pinacateños for money and jewelry).

Owing to a seasonal presence of antelope in this region I imagine early man enjoyed meat as a respite from his regular diet of rattlesnake, seeds, an occasional fish and other native appetizers. Try to see this land through the Indians' eyes for there is beauty here—

intense beauty—in black, a hundred shades of brown and a sparsity of green. And as you look around try to understand how and why this strangely unique place exists.

NASA found this place so unique it sought and received permission for America's early lunar astronauts to train in the area known as Cerro de la Morusa (about half-way from Highway 2 to Elegante), which is now being mined for agricultural purposes.

Although a network of roads are shown on Figure 13, prospective visitors to this area are advised to use topographic maps which provide markedly greater detail. Topos, as they are commonly called, can be purchased from San Diego's "Map Center" as well as map centers in Encinitas and Los Angeles, California. (Check local telephone books for map centers in your area.) Ask for Mexican topographic map H12A12... for starters.

Whereas, a few paragraphs ago, we drove to Elegante from the southeast, craters Colorado, Elegante, Celaya, Kino (this one involves a little more walking), Badillo, Verdugo (another big daddy), Trebol (which could be classified as a multi-crater site) and La Luna are easily accessible from Highway 2. What's more, the cinders volcano standing a few hundred meters west of Celaya is an interesting feature. (When found in abundance, Freda uses cinders as a garden ground cover.)

Equally interesting is the lava field between Colorado and Elegante. Readers are cautioned, however, to exercise extreme caution in this area. As beautiful as it is to the two of us it is loaded with spiders, bugs and snakes. What's more, its surface can cut like broken glass.

Having said that, I would be the last person on earth to say anything about the beauty of a piece of this lava on a home table or bookshelf because its removal from the site would be contrary to Mexican law. (Now that's food for thought. Imagine the federal government setting up roadside stands at scattered locations along Highway 2 for the sale of various-sized chunks of this ancient stuff.)

El Desierto Del Altar occupies a rectangular area encompassing the Sierra Pinacate. For the novice an agonizing death lurks in its Saharan sea of sand where directions without a compass are impossible except when he or she can see distant mountains. Forty miles wide by a hundred in length, the Pimas paid the Pinacateños for the use of their trail to the shore (ending near Puerto Peñasco) rather than risk this treacherous place.

If you think misery likes companying wait until you're stuck in the middle of these dunes and the nearest conceivable help is seventy miles in any direction. Opposed to such misery there is a world of joy waiting along the western edge of these dunes for those who enjoy clams, oysters, mussels, sea snails and scallops.

Located on the Sonora-Baja California border (twenty miles south of San Luis) is the agricultural town of Coahuila. Forty-three miles south of Coahuila stands a fish camp, Santa Clara, as vibrant as it was in yesteryear (my first visit was in 1946). Run the beach south of Santa Clara—you'll know when you get there—and you'll find a peaceful place free of the sights and sounds of man.

Isolated in that particular place—the only human within a thirty, forty or fifty-mile radius—there is an opportunity to understand the intrinsic beauty of the desert and its dependence on the sea and sun. In reality, it is more than an opportunity, it is a blessing, for me at least, when I can observe the dawning, the actions of local animals, creatures of the sea and even myself. There is purity in solitude that I find contagious. The two of us (Freda and I) come here, occasionally, for renewal.

Standing on that southeastern shore as the sun dips behind Baja's backbone mountains we have gazed at a reddened sky and given thanks for the pleasures we've enjoyed in the frontier, a U-shaped stretch of desert—with the Cortés between its two narrow legs—so dramatically created ...**OF SEA & SAND.**

CHAPTER FIVE
Conclusion

Whereas this is this book's final chapter, there is no way I could end this adventure without the following wildlife story. I was troubled as to where to place it until I realized it, like the four preceding chapters, is a tale involving turbulence. A true story, albeit of the type that happens but once in a lifetime, its drama reminds us the highway is as much a part of the desert as any other.

Highway Robbery

I'm not sure I could believe this story if I was you. As for me I've spent enough time in the wilds to know we humans are not the only ones who can think, plan, and understand cause-and-effect relationships. This event occurred on the outskirts of San Felipe. Freda and I departed our home at 5:30 a.m. for an appointment we had in California. A few minutes later, heading north along

Highway 5, I noticed something on the road ahead. At first it was but a patch of black in the distance. As the seconds ticked by—and we advanced on the patch—it became birds: Ravens and red headed turkey vultures. Something had been killed and a detachment from Natures cleaning crew was enjoying an early morning repast.

It is not surprising to see two types of birds dining together, nor is it surprising to find two (or more) different animal species enjoying the same food. Recently, for example, we came upon a squirrel and a raven enjoying parts of the same sandwich someone had dropped; each apparently secure in the belief the other was no threat to its life.

Conversely, I remember watching an interesting show play itself out (in nearby mountains) when a gray squirrel tried to rob acorns a woodpecker had stashed in the bark of a tree. Starting from a distance the furtive squirrel inched its way to the tree only to be dive-bombed by the alert woodpecker as it came within a meter of its goal. Over and over the drama continued until the squirrel gave up (with sore spots on its head?) and went away.

Because this story of highway robbery involves a coyote, I should mention Freda and I once chanced upon a coyote searching for shrimp in a river-like salt-water streambed. What's more, crossing the Laguna Salada one morning, we encountered two Mexican wolves returning from the shore where we knew they'd been for breakfast. In fact, one of the most surprising discoveries of my life was to watch a coyote fishing for crab with its tail. With extreme patience the coyote allowed its tail to float on incoming tidal water until a crab, searching for a breakfast morsel, grabbed the tail with a pincer. Reacting with the speed of light the coyote yanked its tail to the side tossing the startled crab on the shore where, seconds later, it became the canine's commission.

This has to be learned activity. Can you imagine a mother coyote teaching her pups to fish? This activity involves an understanding of the incoming tide, the seasonal (and daily) return of crab, the use of the tail as a tool and of a cause-and-effect relationship:

Waiting, that is, until the crab has a secure grip on its tail. But now, returning to Highway 5...

As we approached the birds feasting on an early morning road kill—I was driving at the rate of 65 miles per hour (95 feet per second)—the most timid of the birds lifted off first followed, seconds later, by the others. Suddenly, with the scavengers but a few feet overhead and our car close enough to be concerned, a coyote darted from the side of the road where it laid in wait to grab the fresh-killed carcass and retreat to the brush from whence it came.

This was a case of an experienced and wily coyote giving the birds the bird. Following an early morning trek to the shore it was returning to its daytime den when it chanced upon the birds enjoying a feast that could be his (or hers). Thinking there would be automobile traffic it hunkered down in the brush from where it also knew it had but a handful of seconds—once the birds lifted off—before it, too, could become road kill.

Analyzing the coyote's actions, it planned and perpetrated this early morning heist in the space of so few seconds we had no time to react with a camera. There were the birds, the car, liftoff, pure highway robbery and the thrill of witnessing an act of survival of the fittest ...but one of the many reasons we love the desert so dearly.

A Turbulent Past

Prior to writing this book, I wrote and published, over a span of fifteen years, 168 articles describing the living drama of Mexico's western frontier. In preparation for the writing of this book I reread several of those articles but realized I had newer information as a result of having retraced so many of my steps through the places described therein. Consequently, this book contains the latest information I'm capable of providing about these many sites, their treasures, and the beauty to be found throughout the Altar and San Felipe desert regions.

There will always be a question about the true location of Melchior Díaz's grave. When Cal and I began our search in earnest, word was sent throughout the publishing industry that I wanted to discuss her articles with Ms Pepper. Similarly, when I began this project I sent word to her via a publisher that I wanted to discuss my explorations with her. For whatever reason she ignored my request.

Whether her silence was due to a final illness is a fact I chose not to pursue. As far as I know, her former husband Jack Pepper preceded her in death as did a friend of hers named Earl Stanley Gardner. So the mystery of Melchior Díaz must remain as it is. The fact that Herbert Bolton found sufficient evidence in historic recordings to take Melchior and his party five or six days beyond the geothermal site is enough for me to believe his remains are (or were) to be found in the Pinta/Tinaja region.

My critics will ask why I failed to expound upon the canyons of the Sierra de Juarez. My response is to repeat my earlier claim: There are so few visitors to those canyons that I felt it best to concentrate on places my readers are more likely to visit and enjoy. Admittedly, there is a degree of selfishness here based on a demonstrated reluctance for the many to drive "so far." But the west flank of the Laguna Salada is and, as far as I've been able to ascertain, always has been a most difficult place to penetrate. Prevailing winds, I presume, created an extraordinarily deep sand bench fronting most of the canyons. Passage over that bench by rubber tired vehicles ranges between difficult and impossible (except for the best equipped and most determined teams).

I am thrilled to have seen what I did while I was in the Juarez because I am left with the knowledge that I walked many of the same paths indigenous man used. This is not to say that my exploration compares with that of Glen and Betty Conklin. On the contrary, we were in two different leagues. My interest was as deep as his but I chose to limit my exploration of the frontier to the regions covered by this text. For that I am both happy and proud.

Yes, we ventured beyond the frontier into such places as El Marmol, Santa Catarina and the turquoise region of west-central Baja. We also investigated a substantial part of the region south of Puertecitos.

Campo Bufeo is my favorite of all the southern campsites. Freda and I had the pleasure to meet and chat with Señor "Papa" Fernandez when he was reputed to be 102, 103 and 104 years of age. We met his wife and saw him again after she passed. We explored the desert west of these campsites and found onyx that I presumed was an extension of the intrusion at El Marmol.

We searched the gold mining region a few miles south of Gonzaga Bay. We explored Las Arastras, the Calamajué, Bahia de Los Angeles and the road to Misión San Borja. In my humble opinion there's not a place we could go that isn't as rewarding, in its own particular way, as the places described herein. On the road to San Borja, for example, there is a Y with the left fork leading to a rocky structure in which there are Indian drawings. At San Borja we learned the mission was still in use. And, less than a day's ride from there we bought, cooked and enjoyed fresh lobsters at Laguna Manuela.

I once published fourteen articles in a series I entitled "The Beauty of Baja" and feel as keenly about that beauty today as I did then. What's more, I will never forget the day I was stopped in my tracks by fear and still feel I was under the watchful eye of a cougar that made a conscious decision not to attack me.

Veni, vidi, vici:(I came, I saw, I conquered) …but in my case, I came, I saw, I was overwhelmed: By sea and sand …by history and present day reality …and by the men, women and animals of a truly magnificent land.

PART SIX

BACKMATTER

EPILOGUE

One year after his arrival in Mexico, Viceroy Mendoza returned to Spain to make a personal report to the King of his findings, accomplishments and views of New Spain's future. When asked what the new territory was like the Viceroy crumpled a sheet of paper and laid it on the king's desk saying, "It is like that (pointing to the crumpled paper), a kingdom of mountains."

A seventeenth century Spanish cavalry commander serving in Baja California once wrote, "This land is worse than any I have imagined. Even the Indians are impoverished by its intolerable climate, cactus and sand."

When, in 1825, Royal Navy Lieutenant Hardy's ship grounded in the Colorado River he cursed the mud-covered Indians that volunteered to tug his ship to freedom. He was outraged by his ship's grounding, the heat and humidity, the mosquitoes and a people who smeared themselves with mud (for protection from the mosquitoes).

Joseph Wood Krutch, a noted naturalist, described the peninsula, "...like a ragged and meaningless appendage precariously attached at the point where California ought to end."

What a shame it is that at least four influential men voiced such opinions of a truly beautiful land. In my opinion...

—Viceroy Mendoza was faced with one of the most difficult tasks imaginable: Bringing order to complete mayhem.

—The cavalry officer, like so many early Spaniards, hated his assignment, hated the Indians, murdered more than a few and departed at the earliest opportunity.

— Hardy was in search of oysters, sailed past millions of them without realizing it and had no idea how to cope with his environment.

—Mr. Krutch is the epitome of all who fail to recognize the beauty of a place indigenous man, and a few million others, refused to leave.

Having opened with a statement involving geologic time I will close with a reminder that dinosaurs enjoyed at least one hundred sixty million years of stable (warm and humid) climate. On the heels of their demise, however, climate seems to have gone on a roller coaster, a fact we may presume to be responsible for the subsequent development of an otherwise unimaginable variety of the animal kingdom.

Whereas the scientific community is only beginning to find how dramatic that variety became, today is today and you and I are here as surely as Neanderthal was in his time and Australopithecus in hers. What does tomorrow hold? Based on what we did yesterday, I believe we'll do as they did: We'll pave our way to oblivion. Along the way, since our focus is on sea and sand, I believe we'll eventually see dramatic changes in the Mexican frontier. Not soon, but some in my children's lifetime with considerably more occurring during the following twenty-five years.

I would love to say the results of this book will bring a wave of men and women interested in exploring everything this book describes. But can I see significant development in this region in my lifetime? Yes and no. You see, we have described a particular land (or two) but not its people: Those of us who live in these lands know better than to meddle in Mexican politics; what the future holds is almost entirely dependent upon them.

There are political battles to be fought, between allies and enemies, over the land now seen as a gold mine: the greater San Felipe region. Suddenly, it seems, previously closed eyes are opening to see a land presently being likened to Baja California's "Gold Coast" (between Tijuana and Ensenada). This land, spanning the distance from the south flank of the Sierra Pinta to Puertecitos (approximately 100 miles in length) is suddenly being considered Mexico's next major source of tourist dollars. Would you believe billions of them?

Picture Cancún, for example, and try to envision San Felipe dressed in tomorrow's finery. Today, in this distant desert community, you cannot buy a decent bottle of cologne. Tomorrow, in the center of the new wonderland, the new San Felipe will be a virtual copy of Cancún. That is, the finest clothing, perfumes, jewelry and world-renowned chefs will be commonplace (and there will be professional tours into the desert). There will be uncountable houses in modern housing developments including a few 6-, 7-, and 8,000 square footers. There will be bona fide shopping centers, at least one additional marina and a casino. (How long do you think Mexico will tolerate its money going to Laughlin and Las Vegas?)

There will be a divided four-lane highway with major off-ramps at Chinero, Moreno, San Felipe and Percebú. Surrounding each of these intersections will be townships bearing the same names with shopping centers linking each in a manner not unlike Baja's Gold Coast

Owing to the present-day existence of supermarkets and shopping centers in Mexicali (Sam's Club, WalMart, Costco and Home Depot) I suggest another Anza Borrego not only could be but probably will be established somewhere along the eastern base of the Juarez. The drawing card? Pure air, for openers, but let's not forget tourism and men like Salvador León and Los Rurales. Where there's a will there's a way and there is untapped wealth in the Juarez (including minerals, potable water and undiscovered Indian artifacts).

Think of America's western towns where mock gunfights are staged at 10, 2 and 4 o'clock daily and tourists flock to them each and every season. Apply that thought to this new community, add essential actors and you have a multi-cultural setting to draw upon with 1910's Indians, 1930s' Mexicali and today's tourists. Bring in water, electricity telephones, sewage disposal and pavement and you have another (desert) Garden of Eden. In fact, if you can't see what I see read "How To Retire Cheaply—And Well," in the July 29, 2002 edition of TIME magazine. "…more and more Americans are retiring south of the border…."

On the one hand, America turned its back on Baja California many years ago. On the other, this is the Mexican frontier: Two remote desert regions that can wait while the remainder of the country struggles to catch up with the modern world. Earlier in this text I mentioned how the nobility of New Spain treated common men and women. Whereas times have changed, to date Mexico has endured a little over three hundred fifty years of abuse by its ruling class(es).

That thought reminded me of my chance encounter with diva Lily Pons, my love for the color orange (renewal), Homer's Odyssey and the Trojan horse.

Three hundred years is a huge chunk of history to overcome although change appears to be in the wind. Besides, let us not forget Mexico is the leader of Latin American countries. One day in the not too distant future it will proudly take its place on the world stage as a shining example of what can be done with education, planning, investment and a stalwart willingness to overcome the past.

San Felipe will continue to grow as it has over the past eight years. At the center of this action, El Dorado Ranch will peak as competition (the Trojan horse?) captures a significant part of future action and, little by little, a new Cancún is created. Think of fine hotels and restaurants, world-renowned chefs, expensive clothing, perfumes, colognes, Bally and Florsheim shoes, Southern California's yachting crowd and a swarm of curious men and women suddenly wanting to experience the Matomí or tan somewhere along that 100 miles of tranquil sandy beach.

I can imagine daily tours to pumpkin rock as easily as I can imagine ladies and gentlemen telling stories of these adventures to family and friends in northern states and provinces: "…and they served the best filet mignon you can imagine… a thousand miles from nowhere."

The Mexican frontier is a land of living drama although it is not as remote as you may think. Yes, western Sonora will be slower to develop but when professional tours are organized, funded and operated with informed guides, satisfying luncheons (and all the tricks of the trade) the craters will become a part of a huge national park with insufficient parking space.

If that's not enough the region's 600 volcanoes will become the drawing card, tourists will see things they've never seen before and there's something like three hundred million of them to draw upon. Lava will become a focal point, photography the action and satisfaction responsible for tomorrow and tomorrow and tomorrow.

The cougar may suffer, unless steps are taken to protect him, but because he and she are an equal part of this living drama, our sea and sand will survive… at least as long as we do.

'I fear thee, ancient Mariner!
I fear thy skinny hand!
And thou art long, and lank, and brown,
As is the ribbed sea-sand'

Coleridge

BIBLIOGRAPHY

BANDELIER, ADOLPH F., Hemenway Southwestern Archæological Expedition. Contributions to the History of the Southwest Portion of the United States. Papers of the Archæological Institute of America. American Series V. Cambridge University Press. J. Wilson & Son, Cambridge 1890.

————, The Gilded Man. D. Appleton and Company, 1893.

BISHOP, MORRIS, The odyssey of Cabeza de Vaca. Century, New York, 1933.

BOLTON, HERBERT E., Spanish Borderlands. Yale University Press, New Haven, 1921

————, Spanish Explorers in the Southwest. Charles Scribner's Sons, New York, 1916.

————, Coronado, Knight of Pueblos and Plains. University of New Mexico Press, Albuquerque, 1949.

CASTANEDA, PEDRO DE, Narrative of the Expedition of Coronado. In Bureau of American Ethnology, Fourteenth Annual Report. Smithsonian Institute, Washington, D.C., 1892

DAY, ARTHUR G., Coronado's Quest-The Discovery of the Southwestern States. Greenwood Press, Westport, Conn, 1964.

DIAZ DEL CASTILLO, BERNAL, True History of the Conquest of New Spain. R. M. McBride, New York 1927

————, The Discovery and Conquest of Mexico. H. Wolff, New York, 1956.

FARB, PETER, Man's Rise to Civilization. E. P. Dutton & Co. Inc., New York, 1968.

FISKE, JOHN, The Discovery of America. Houghton Mifflin, Boston, 1892

CAGE THOMAS, The English-American, A New Survey of the West Indies. R. Cotes, London, 1648

HALLENBECK, CLEVE, Journey and Route of Cabeza de Vaca. Arthur H. Clark, Glendale, 1940

HAMMOND, GEORGE P. and **ERY, AGAPITO**, Narratives of

the Coronado Expedition 1540-1542. The University of New Mexico Press, Albuquerque, 1940.

HARING, G.H., Spanish Empire in America. Oxford University Press, New York 1947.

HODGE, FREDERICK W., Spanish Explorers in the Southern United States. Charles Scribner's Sons, New York, 1907

HODGE, FREDERICK W., The Narrative of the Expedition of Coronado by Castañeda. Charles Scribner's Sons, New York 1907.

INNES, HAMMOND, The Conquistadors. Alfred A. Knopf, New York, 1969.

KIRKPATRICK, F.A., The Spanish Conquistadores. A. & C. black, London, 1934.

MACLEOD, WILLIAM C., The American Indian Frontier. G. P. Putnam's Sons, New York, 1928.

MARTINEZ, PABLO L. A History of Lower California. Translation from Spanish by **ETHEL DUFFY TURNER.** EDITORIAL BAJA CALIFORNIA "Por la cultura peninsular." Av. Escuela Industrial No 46 (Col Industrial). Mexico D.F. 1960

MCFARLAND, BATES H., "Alvar Núñez Cabeza de Vaca." Texas State Historical Quarterly, Vol. 1.

MOSES, BERNARD, Establishment of Spanish Rule in America. G.P. Putnam's Sons, New York, 1898.

NUNEZ, ALVAR CABEZA DE VACA, Relación. Zamora, 1542.

————, Relación de los naufragios y comentarios. Vallodolid, 1555.

————, Navigazioni et viaggi. Venice, 1556.

————, Purcas, His Pilgrimes. London, 1613.

————, Relación y comentarios. Madrid, 1736.

NUNEZ, ALVAR CABEZA DE VACA, Historiadores primitovos de las Indias Occidentales. Madrid 1749.

————, Voyages. Paris, 1837.

————, Historiadores, primitivos de las Indias. Madrid, 1852.

————, Colección de libros y documentos referentes a la historia de America. Madrid, 1906.

OVIEDO Y VALDES, G. FERNANDEA DE, Historia general y natural de las Indias. Academy of History, Madrid, 1852

PHINNEY, A.H., "Narvaez and de Soto: Their Landing Places." Florida Historical Quarterly, 1925.

PONTON, BROWNIE, "Alvar Nuñez Cabeza de Vaca." Texas State Historical Quarterly, Vol. 1.

PRIESTLY, H.I., The Coming of the White Man. Macmillan, New York, 1930.

————, The Mexican Nation, Macmillan, New York, 1923.

RICHMAN, I.B., The Spanish Conquerors. Yale University Press, New Haven, 1919.

SIMPSON, J.H., Coronado's March in Search of the Seven Cities of Cíbola. From Manuscripts by Jesuit Missionaries

SIMPSON, L.B., The Encomienda in New Spain. University of California Press, Berkeley, 1929.

WELLS, JOSEPH K., "First Europeans in Texas." Southwestern Historical Quarterly, Vol. 22.

WINSHIP, GEORGE PARKER, The Journey of Coronado. A.S. Barnes, New York, 1904.

GLOSSARY

Abrasion: The grinding away of rock by friction and impact during transportation.

Accretion Stage: Stage in the evolution of major mountain belts characterized by accumulation of great thicknesses (several kilometers) of sedimentary or volcanic rocks.

Aftershock: Small earthquake that follows a main shock.

Alluvial Fan: A large, fan-shaped pile of sediment that usually forms where a stream's velocity decreases as it emerges from a narrow canyon onto a flat plain at the foot of a mountain range.

Alluvium: Unconsolidated gravel, sand, silt and clay deposited by streams.

Anticline: An arched fold, usually in the shape of an inverted U.

Arid Region: A region with less than 25 cm of rain per year.

Arroyo: A dry desert gully.

Bajada: A broad, sloping depositional deposit caused by the coalescing of alluvial fans.

Batholith: A large discordant pluton with an outcropping area greater than 100 square kilometers.

Beach: Strip of sediment, usually sand but sometimes pebbles, boulders or mud, that extends from a low-water line inland to a cliff or zone of permanent vegetation.

Blowout: A depression in the land surface caused by wind erosion.

Breakwater: An offshore structure built to absorb the force of large breaking waves and provide quiet water near shore.

Butte: A narrow flat-topped hill of resistant rock with very steep sides.

Caldera: A volcanic depression much larger than the original crater.

Cement: The solid material that precipitates in the pore space of sediments binding the grains together to form solid rock.

Cenozoic Era: 0 to 65 million years before present. (The Cenozoic Era includes the Quaternary and Tertiary Periods.)

Cinder Cone: A volcano constructed of loose rock fragments ejected from a central vent.

Delta: A body of sediment deposited at the mouth of a river when the river velocity decreases as it flows into a standing body of water.

Desert: A surface region that receives less than 25 centimeters (10 inches) of annual precipitation.

Desert Pavement: A thin surface layer of closely packed pebbles.

Desert Varnish: A hard, daily darkening polymer coating on rocks caused by chemical action in the presence of direct sunlight.

Detritus: Boulders, rocks, gravel, sand, soil that has eroded from mountains over time.

Glossary

Dunes: Mounds of loose sand grains shaped up by the wind.

Fiord: A coastal inlet that is a glacially carved valley, the base of which is submerged.

Formation: A body of rock of considerable thickness that has a recognizable unity or similarity making it distinguishable from adjacent rock units.

Geyser: A type of hot spring that periodically erupts hot water and steam.

Glacier: A large long-lasting mass of ice formed on land by the compaction and recrystallization of snow, which moves because of its own weight.

Hogback: An eroded, steeply tilted ridge of resistant rocks with equal slopes on the sides.

Horizon, A: The top layer of soil characterized by the downward movement of water; also called zone of leaching.

Hoodoo: A column or pillar of bizarre shapes caused by differential erosion on rocks of different hardness.

Isostacy: A theory that continents and ocean basins float in approximately hydrostatic balance with one another: continents and mountains are high because the curst beneath them is light while ocean basins are low because their crust is dense.

Jurassic Period: The age in which dinosaurs flourished, 144 to 288 million years ago.

Loess: A deposit of windblown sand and clay weakly cemented by calcite.

Mesa: A broad, flat-topped hill usually surrounded by cliffs and capped with a resistant rock layer.

Playa: A flat dry lakebed of hard, mud-cracked clay.

Mesozoic Era: 66 to 245 million years ago, includes the Cretaceous, Jurassic and Triassic Periods.

Monocline: An open, step-like fold in rock over a large area.

Paleozoic Era: 245 to 570 million years ago.

Pangea: The most recent in a series of super continents broken apart 200 million years ago to form the present continents.

Pediment: A gently sloping surface, usually covered with gravel, the result of erosion.

Plate Tectonics: A theory describing the earth's surface as an assemblage of individual "plates" (containing both continents and ocean basins) that are driven by convection currents rising from the heated mass of Earth's interior.

Precambrian Era: The all-encompassing era prior to 570 millions of years before present (The Precambrian ended with the beginning of the Paleozoic Era.)

Semiarid: Receiving between 10 and 20 inches of annual precipitation.

Syncline: An arched fold in the shape of a U.

Theory: An explanation for observed phenomena that has a high possibility of being true.

Theory of Glacial Ages: At times in the past, colder climates prevailed during which significantly more of the Earth's land surface was glaciated than at present.

Topographic Map: A map on which elevations are shown by means of contour lines.

Triassic Period: 208 to 245 million years ago when large predatory reptiles (dinosaurs) evolved.

Vent: The opening in the earth's surface through which a volcanic eruption takes place.

Viscosity: Resistance to flow.

Volcanic Dome: Steep-sided dome or spine-shaped mass of volcanic rock formed from viscous lava that solidifies in or immediately above a volcanic vent.

Volcano: A hill or mountain constructed by the extrusion of lava or rock fragments from a vent.

Weathering: The group of processes that change rock at or near the earth's surface

Wegener, Alfred L: The man accredited with the first bona fide hypothesis of continental drift, which he presented in a book entitled "The Origin of Continents and Oceans."